Medieval England

Medieval England

A social history and archaeology
from the Conquest to A.D. 1600

Colin Platt

Routledge & Kegan Paul
London and Henley

First published in 1978
by Routledge & Kegan Paul Ltd
39 Store Street,
London WC1E 7DD,
Broadway House,
Newtown Road,
Henley-on-Thames,
Oxon RG9 1EN
Set in Monophoto Plantin
Filmset and printed by
BAS Printers Ltd, Over Wallop, Hampshire
Colour plates originated by
City Engraving Ltd, Hull
and printed by
Ebenezer Baylis Ltd, Worcester

British Library Cataloguing in Publication Data

Platt, Colin

Medieval England.
1. England – Social conditions   2. England –
Antiquities
I. Title
309.1'42   HN385   78-40115

ISBN 0-7100-8815-9

Contents

Illustrations

Colour Plates

Preface and Acknowledgments

A book of this kind can lend itself to many different treatments, two of which, certainly, I considered. It might have been more immediately useful to some, that is, if I had kept to my original intention of arranging the material thematically, so that the castle and the manor-house, the parish church, monastery and village could each be considered in its turn. Yet to have done so would have been to risk concealing what I consider myself to be the most important guiding principle of medieval archaeology as we now know it, being its essential interrelationship with history. In effect, my purpose throughout this book has been to set one sort of evidence alongside another, so that the two, far from standing out in aggressive contrast, are at all times mutually complementary. To this end, I have found myself favouring the chronological approach, and this is how the book has developed. For those who might have wished it another way, the consolation may lie, as I have found it myself, in the unveiling of unexpected connections.

Medieval archaeology is a young discipline, very much younger than history, and one of the troubles of working within it is that many of its conclusions are still tentative. I have had myself, far too often, to work from exiguous data, available only in interim notes and sometimes the merest jottings from occasional conversations and lectures. I am grateful, of course, for the material I have gathered in this way, and am much obliged to its originators for permission to use it in my book. However, I cannot fail to have missed a good deal that has neither been written nor spoken about in public at all, nor have I always been able to determine whether the first thoughts of the excavators on important and original sites, some of them vital to my argument, are also their final conclusions. Where I have used such unconfirmed conclusions, I have done so only if, on other evidence, they have seemed to me not to have been implausible. I cannot see how I could have done otherwise.

Another disadvantage that will surely occur to those familiar with the present archaeological scene in Britain is that the pace of work has so vastly increased in recent years that whatever is available in print at this time may quickly be swamped by new data. Indeed, this is probably the case. But at least a part of the purpose of the book I have written is to improve the intelligibility of the archaeological sites yet to be excavated, by giving them an historical context. This book itself is by way of being an interim report on on-going work of the very greatest interest and importance. It may have some of the qualities also – or so I would like to believe – of a manual.

These qualities, of course, would be much reduced, especially in a discipline like archaeology, were the written word not strongly backed by illustrations, and it has been a purpose of mine from the very beginning to relate these as closely as possible to the text. For these, I have been as dependent as always on the skill and resource of Alan Burn and his staff, of the Southampton University Cartographic Unit, to whom I am indeed most grateful for the redrawing, especially for this book, of every map and other line-drawing in it. Inevitably, some adjustments have been made, in individual cases, to the composition of drawings, to scales, and to perspectives, nor should the drawings reproduced in this book be preferred, as a basic data source, over the originals from which they have been derived. For permission to work from these originals, generously given sometimes in advance even of publications of their own, I am grateful to David Algar and John Musty for Fig. 71 (*Current Archaeology*, 14 (1969)); to Alan Baker for Fig. 66 (*Economic History Review*, 19 (1966)); to Caroline Barron and Terry Ball for Fig. 128 (*The Medieval Guildhall of London*, 1974); to Guy Beresford for Figs 38, 89 and 131 (*Medieval Archaeology*, 18 (1974); *The Medieval Clay-land Village*, 1975; *Records of Buckinghamshire*, 18 (1966–70)); to Martin Biddle for Figs 3 and 157 (*Antiquaries Journal*, 55 (1975); *Surrey Archaeological Collections*, 58 (1961)); to Dr R. W. Brunskill for Fig. 148 (*Transactions of the Cumberland and Westmorland Antiquarian and Archaeological Society*, 56 (1956)); to Professor L. M. Cantor for Fig. 26 (*Transactions of the Leicestershire Archaeological and Historical Society*, 46 (1970–1)); to Alan Carter for Fig. 130 (*Norfolk Archaeology*, 36 (1974)); to Mr F. W. B. Charles for Fig. 164 (*Transactions of the Worcestershire Archaeological Society*, 3 (1970–2)); to Helen Clarke for Fig. 19 (*Excavations in King's Lynn, 1963–1970*, 1977); to Howard Colvin and the Comptroller of H.M. Stationery Office for Figs 1, 46 and 102 (*History of the King's Works*, 1963 and 1975); to David Crossley and Alan Aberg for Fig. 163 (*Post-Medieval Archaeology*, 6 (1972)), and to David Crossley again for Fig. 165 (*The Bewl Valley Ironworks*, 1975); to Brian Davison for Fig. 2 (*Somerset Archaeology and Natural History*, 116 (1972)); to Gerald Dunning and Lesley Ketteringham for Fig. 36 (*Alsted*, 1976; *Medieval Archaeology*, 10 (1966): Great Easton; *Excavations in Medieval Southampton*, 1975; *Transactions of the Thoroton Society*, 66 (1962):

xvi

Nottingham), and to Gerald Dunning again for Fig. 141 (*Antiquaries Journal, 32* (1952)); to Robin Glasscock for Fig. 70 (*A New Historical Geography of England*, 1973, and *The Lay Subsidy of 1334*, 1975); to Barbara Hanawalt for fig. 72 (*Crime in East Anglia in the Fourteenth Century*, 1976); to Mark Harrison, John Schofield and Tim Tatton-Brown for Fig. 126 (*Current Archaeology*, 49 (1975); *Transactions of the London and Middlesex Archaeological Society*, 25 (1974)); to Bob Hogg and Mr D. J. C. King for Fig. 6 (*Archaeologia Cambrensis*, 119 (1970)); to Brian Hope-Taylor for Fig. 7 (*Archaeological Journal*, 107 (1950)); to Henry Hurst and Arthur Harrison for Fig. 101 (*Antiquaries Journal*, 54 (1974); *Archaeologia Cantiana*, 84 (1969)); to John Hurst and the Medieval Village Research Group, executors for this purpose of the late Mrs E. M. Minter, for Fig. 24 (*Medieval Archaeology*, 8 (1964)), and to the same for Figs 34 and 53 (*Deserted Medieval Villages*, 1971; *Current Archaeology*, 49 (1975)); to Edward Johnson for Fig. 142 (*Medieval Archaeology*, 8 (1964), 9 (1965), and 10 (1966), and personal communication); to Stanley R. Jones for Fig. 108 (*Medieval Archaeology*, 12 (1968), and personal communication); to John Kent for Fig. 8 (*Medieval Archaeology*, 5 (1961), 6–7 (1962–3), and 8 (1964), and personal communication); to David Martin for Fig. 76 (personal communication); to Philip Mayes and Jake Goodband for Fig. 39 (*Current Archaeology*, 9 (1968), and personal communication); to Eric Mercer for Figs. 134 and 150 (*English Vernacular Houses*, 1975); to Dennis Mynard and Chris Mahany for Fig. 106 (*Medieval Archaeology*, 10 (1966), 14 (1970), 15 (1971), and 16 (1972), and personal communication), and to Dennis Mynard again and Paul Woodfield for Fig. 95 (*Milton Keynes Journal*, 3 (1974)); to Helen O'Neil for Fig. 58 (*Transactions of the Bristol and Gloucestershire Archaeological Society*, 75 (1956)); to Adrian Oswald and J. T. Smith for Fig. 37 (*Medieval Archaeology*, 6–7 (1962–3), and 9 (1965); to the executors of the late W. A. Pantin for Fig. 115 (*Oxoniensia*, 35 (1970)); to Brian Philp for Fig. 16 (*Excavations at Faversham, 1965*, 1968); to Jack Ravensdale for Fig. 23 (*Liable to Floods*, 1974); to Brian Roberts and the Moated Sites Research Group for Fig. 73 (personal communication); to Warwick and Kirsty Rodwell for Fig. 17 (*Antiquaries Journal*, 53 (1973)); to John Sheail for Fig. 147 (*Transactions of the Institute of British Geographers*, 55 (1972)); to Peter Smith and Mr J. T. Smith for Fig. 33 (*Houses of the Welsh Countryside*, 1975; *Archaeological Journal*, 115 (1958)), and to Peter Smith again for Fig. 151 (*Houses of the Welsh Countryside*, 1975); to Terence Paul Smith for Fig. 121 (*Archaeological Journal*, 132 (1975)); to Denys Spittle for Figs 102 and 105 (*Archaeological Journal*, 131 (1974), and 124 (1967)); to John Steane for Fig. 80 (*Journal of the Northampton Museums and Art Gallery*, 12 (1975)); to Christopher Taylor for Fig. 22 (*Fieldwork in Medieval*

Archaeology, 1974); to Mr C. F. Tebbutt for Fig. 31 (*Proceedings of the Cambridge Antiquarian Society*, 63 (1971)); to Michael Thompson for Fig. 9 (*Medieval Archaeology*, 4 (1960)); to Mr A. B. Whittingham for Fig. 109 (*Archaeological Journal*, 125 (1968)); and to Charmian and Paul Woodfield for Fig. 49 (*Archaeological Journal*, 128 (1971)).

For the plates published in this book, the copyright of which remains with the photographers, I am grateful to Peter Addyman for Fig. 57; to Aerofilms Ltd for Figs 10, 15, 61, 63, 64, 103, 116, 118, 122, 123, 140, 143, and 153; to Hallam Ashley for Figs 12, 60, 92, 93, 97, 100, 117, 119, 120, 146, and 155; to Evelyn Baker and the Bedfordshire County Council Photographic Unit for Fig. 81; to B. T. Batsford Ltd for Figs 14, 62, 112, and 113; to the British Museum for Figs 40, 41, 56, 79, 124, 159, and 161; to James Brown and David Neal for Fig. 47; to the Committee for Aerial Photography, Cambridge, for Figs 4, 5, and 111; to Patrick Greene for Fig. 65; to John Hurst and the Medieval Village Research Group for Figs 18 and 21; to Mr A. F. Kersting for Figs 28, 48, 96, 110, 137, 144, and 154; to the Lincoln Archaeological Trust for Fig. 20; to Chris Mahany and the South Lincolnshire Archaeological Unit for Fig. 107; to Dr R. Marks for Fig. 98; to David Martin for Fig. 75; to Dr Michael Metcalf and the Ashmolean Museum, Oxford, for Fig. 135; to Pilkington Brothers Ltd for Fig. 77; to Clive Rouse and the Salisbury Photo Press for Fig. 35; to the Royal Commission on Historical Monuments (National Monuments Record) for Figs 11, 13, 25, 27, 29, 30, 32, 42, 43, 44, 45, 50, 51, 52, 54, 55, 59, 74, 88, 90, 91, 94, 99, 104, 105, 114, 125, 129, 132, 133, 139, 145, 149, and 160; to Brian Spencer, Philippa Glanville, and the Museum of London for Figs 68, 78, 82, 83, 84, 86, 87, 127, 138, 152, 156, 158, 162, 166, and 167; to Derek Stirling for Fig. 85; to the Warburg Institute for Fig. 136; to Ray Warner Ltd for Fig. 69; and to the York Archaeological Trust for Fig. 67.

For the colour plates, again copyright of the photographers, I am indebted to Alan Aberg for Plate Z; to Evelyn Baker for Plate Q; to the Bodleian Library, Oxford for Plates D, J, T and X; to the British Museum for Plate V; to Lawrence Butler for Plate M; to Jonathan Coad for Plate A; to Christina Colyer, Michael Jones, and the Lincoln Archaeological Trust for Plate C; to the Dean of York and the National Monuments Record for Plates E and F; to the Department of the Environment for Plates B, G and H; to Mr P. J. Drury for Plate P; to David Hinton and the Ashmolean Museum, Oxford for Plate W; to Elizabeth Lewis and Mr D. J. Rudkin for Plate Y; to Philip Mayes for Plate N; to the Museum of London for Plates O and U; to Breandán Ó Ríordáin and the National Museum of Ireland for Plate K; to Miss M. Pemberton for Plate S; to Philip Rahtz for Plates I and L; and to Derek Stirling for Plate R.

For permission to use material in their unpublished theses, I am obliged to Mr A. D. K. Hawkyard and Mrs Barbara Ross, and to Drs R. H. Britnell, R. K. Morris, J. Sheail, N. P. Tanner, J. A. F. Thomson, and L. S. Woodger. I have gained much from my students of the class of 1976/7, in particular from the criticism, kindly meant, of John Kenyon and Alex Parsons, to whom I am happy to acknowledge my debt.

I dedicate this book with affection and gratitude to my wife, Valerie, and to our children, Emma, Miles, Tabitha, and Theo.

1 The Anglo-Norman Settlement

The Domesday survey of 1086, experimental in form though it might be, had very specific objectives. While designed to untangle at least some of the tenurial complexities which characterized post-Conquest England, an essential purpose was to lay down the terms of a new rating system that would protect and enlarge the king's revenues.[1] This it could achieve only by counting, for it was on the totalling of rateable units that liability to tax must be assessed, and it is the *statistics* of Domesday that give it its importance, to the archaeologist no less than to the historian. In itself, of course, the year 1086 had little significance, for much was still subject to change. Yet here, at one point in time, the historical landscape of late-eleventh-century England stands frozen uniquely, and the picture has many surprises.

Chief among these, at any rate to the newcomer to Domesday, is the extent to which the land of England had already been settled and tilled. A conservative estimate of England's arable acreage in 1086 has placed it as high as 93 per cent of the total area still under the plough as recently as 1914,[2] and this was before the considerable expansion of cultivation into waste and marginal lands that occurred in succeeding centuries. Servicing these fields, there were some 13,000 vills individually named in Domesday, a number not significantly increased, at least by permanent settlements, until very recent times.[3] Of course, village-type settlements were not the norm everywhere in England. In the Domesday survey, many of the vills are very small, and there were areas such as Devonshire where the isolated homestead was as much the usual farming unit some nine centuries ago as it continues to be to this day.[4] Nevertheless, there had been powerful social pressures, starting long before the Conquest, to make England the land of communities which the Normans preserved largely unchanged. For purposes of taxation and for policing, for geld and tithing, all men belonged to a vill.[5] Since the tenth-century edicts of Edmund and Edgar, formally requiring the regular payment of tithes, they had belonged to a parish as well.[6]

In rural settlement, it has often been remarked, the elements of continuity stand out. Yet Domesday preserves, too, a record of accelerating change. We have to be careful now where we place the genuine beginnings of the manor, but there is no doubt that *manorialization*, although always unequal in medieval England, spread appreciably under the Normans.[7] Likewise, extensive royal forests, reflecting Norman enthusiasm for the chase, are another clear mark of the Conquest, as might have been also the quite considerable laying-down of vineyards in England which was to characterize the first two decades of their rule.[8] Yet there is one thing in particular, during these immediately post-Conquest years, that grips the attention of the archaeologist, and this is the evidence for a Norman military presence in the former Anglo-Saxon kingdom, as manifested above all by the castle.

The Anglo-Saxons, nobody could doubt, knew something of the techniques of fortification. Like their contemporaries on the exposed continental seaboard, they had had to learn such skills in the hard school of repeated Viking attacks. However, their 'castles' were fortified boroughs or defended camps, rather in the fashion of the Danes themselves. And although these, of course, had a function of their own in the systematic defence of the realm, there is no convincing evidence in pre-Conquest England of the royal castle, in the Norman manner, conceived as an instrument of government, nor has the Anglo-Saxon private castle been any easier to identify. Important early manorial sites at Goltho, in Lincolnshire, and Sulgrave, in Northamptonshire, have both yielded evidence of substantial pre-Norman enclosure banks. Yet, at both, the major effort at systematic fortification was clearly begun rather later, the defended ring-works that characterize each site being dated not earlier than the late eleventh century.[9] It remains possible, and indeed probable, that more evidence of Saxon defended enclosures will come to light in due course. But unquestionably the major impulse to deliberate fortification, on royal and private estates alike, came with the arrival of the Normans in England, exactly as Goltho and Sulgrave have demonstrated.[10] It was the inevitable product of the violence that followed the Conquest, and of the prolonged uncertainty of tenure which ensued.

It is in the Conqueror's own activity as a castle-builder, recorded in Domesday and elsewhere, that we can see these conditions most clearly. Orderic Vitalis, who described himself as an Englishman but who also knew Normandy well, thought that it was by their castles that the Normans had established themselves in England.[11] And although he was clearly making a case for the English defeat which included such imponderables as moral decline among his countrymen, his point was certainly well made. The Norman king-duke's castles

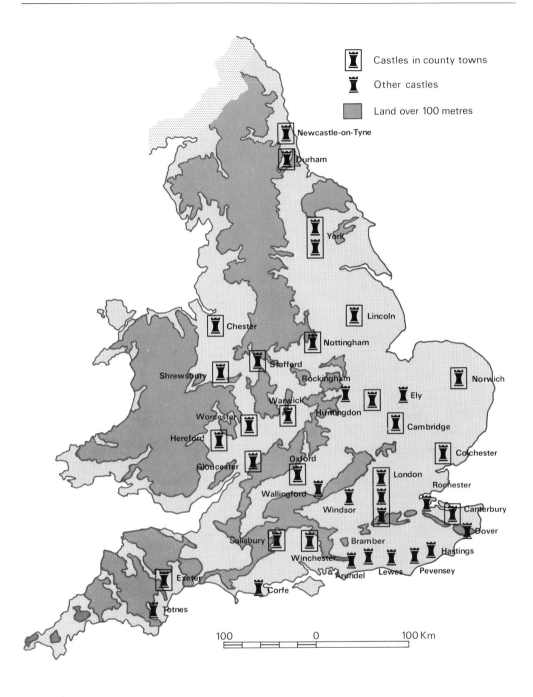

1 The castles of William I and his barons, sited mainly in the county towns or along the threatened south coast (*King's Works*)

in London, made 'against the fickleness of the vast and fierce populace',[12] were only the beginning of a programme of castle-building in the towns, responsive to every fresh crisis and new campaign. Castles at Warwick, Nottingham and York, Lincoln, Huntingdon and Cambridge, marked the military progress of the king up to the north and back again in 1068. Earlier in that same year, William had ordered the building of a castle at Exeter, following the rebellion in the west, while in 1070 he was to raise castles at Chester and at Stafford, in 1071 at Ely, in 1072 at Durham.[13]

Some of the haste of this work, placing great burdens on many local populations and itself a powerful promoter of discontent, can be recognized in what are coming to be called the 'proto-castles' of the immediate post-Conquest years. It seems likely, for example, that the primary ring-work at Castle Neroche, in Somerset, refortifying a smaller area within existing prehistoric earthworks on this naturally defensible promontory site, can be dated to the period of the western rebellions of 1067–9, just when William was building his castle at Exeter. Within a few years, at Castle Neroche, these first campaign defences were converted into the more permanent motte-and-bailey castle still recognizable on the site today.[14] At Launceston, in Cornwall, the primary bailey rampart has been attributed to the same West-Country disturbances,[15] while there has been a suggestion that the earliest defensive earthworks at a similar 'proto-castle' at Ludgershall, in Wiltshire, may be of eleventh-century date,[16] and a case has been made for the first hasty fortification, with rampart and ditch, of the south-east corner of the Roman enclosure of London, where the White Tower would be built not many years later and the castle extensively developed.[17]

These early stages in castle-building, only recently hypothesized, have not been easy to date. Yet there is clear evidence, too, of a comparatively rapid remodelling of the primary post-Conquest defences at such castles as Winchester and Northampton, suggesting haste in the initial stages of the Norman invasion and settlement, followed by a replanning at leisure. At Winchester, the first bank and ditch, at the south-west corner of the walled town, was already strengthened, before 1072, by the addition of a castle mound, or motte. Then, early in the twelfth century, the motte itself was levelled, making way for a stone keep in the new, more durable fashion, and concealing beneath the debris of the fresh construction the remains of an earlier stone chapel.[18] In somewhat different circumstances, Northampton Castle, when it came into the king's hands at just about this time, was extensively rebuilt in a grander manner, the later bailey bank of the king's remodelling crossing and sealing the remains of earlier timber buildings on the site. Northampton's first motte, which may have been raised initially as late as

1084, had been a small ditched mound with adjoining timber buildings, enough for the purposes of its original builder but totally inadequate for the king.[19]

In the towns, already thickly settled, such early defensive works might often be found room only at the expense of existing householders, whose loss of property would later be recorded in Domesday. We know, for example, of the demolition of houses, probably or even specifically for the purpose of castle-building, at Exeter, Lincoln, Canterbury, Shrewsbury, Cambridge, Huntingdon and elsewhere,[20] and there is archaeological evidence to establish a similar pre-Conquest occupation of the land below the castle mound at Oxford, of which Domesday has nothing to say.[21] Meanwhile, in the country, forced appropriations of property on a still grander scale built up the 'castellanies', or military estates, so essential to the strategy of the Conquest. Usually, William's deliberately concentrated military fiefs have received less emphasis than his contrary policy, likewise recorded in Domesday, of rewarding his followers with widely scattered lands. Nevertheless, such fiefs were clearly an important feature of the military settlement of Kent, of the Sussex rapes south of Battle, of Cornwall, the Welsh borderlands, Holderness, and the north.[22] Furthermore, what they represented, in almost every case, was less a strategy of defence than a deliberately conceived and ruthlessly executed colonization, its purpose the permanent endowment of a parvenu aristocracy for which there was no longer adequate living-space at

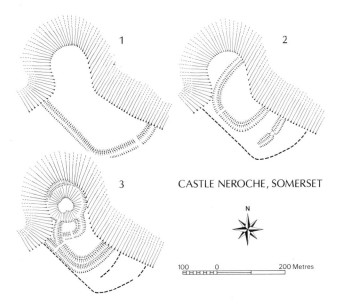

1

2

3

CASTLE NEROCHE, SOMERSET

N

100   0   200 Metres

2   The refortification in two stages by the Normans of the prehistoric defences of Castle Neroche, in Somerset (Davison)

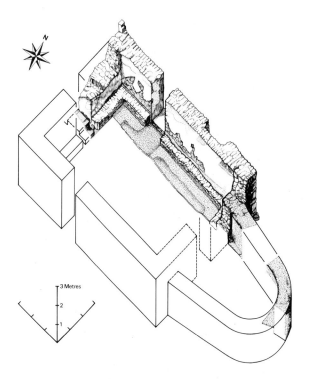

3 Metres
2
1

3 The post-Conquest chapel at Winchester, later concealed below the levelled spoil of the castle mound on the construction of a new stone keep (Winchester Excavation Committee)

home.[23] It was this colonization, cutting across earlier territorial divisions and rendering former estates valueless, which probably accounted for the large areas of so-called 'waste' in Yorkshire, still appearing as such in the Domesday record of 1086, and until recently explained as a consequence of the Conqueror's punitive expeditions to the north.[24] A great two-storied stone hall at Castle Acre, Norfolk, only lightly defended by a palisaded bank, was the centre-piece of one such military fief, entrusted by William to his friend and long-time associate in war, William de Warenne.[25] And the same process of estate-building and subsequent defence may be recognized again in the traces of an Anglo-Saxon field system found buried under the earthworks of Roger de Montgomery's borderland castle at Hen Domen,[26] with the arrogance of the colonization just as surely displayed in the siting of the prominent motte-and-bailey earthworks at Mileham, in Norfolk again, some six miles or so from Castle Acre, boldly astride the main road.[27]

The picture Domesday captures of a countryside still in the process of reorganization should bring home to us those special conditions which promoted castle-building in the immediate post-Conquest years and which would scarcely ease during the next two decades following William's death in 1087, just after the

4   Roger de Montgomery's motte-and-bailey castle at Hen Domen, built to protect the Welsh Marches (Cambridge: Committee for Aerial Photography)

survey had been completed. To the many who held land by conquest rather than by inheritance, titles were blurred and the line of succession far from clear. Moreover, title to castles, as has been pointed out, was 'markedly less secure than title to land'.[28] Just after the Conquest, when the king's interests and those of his barons were identical, this may not have been much of a problem. Nevertheless, it had become so already before the death of William, to grow during the so-called 'tenurial crisis' of the late eleventh century, and to flower, in particular, during the upsets and hardships of the mid-twelfth-century Anarchy, the unhappy reign of Stephen. From an early date, in response to these difficulties, the building of a castle could only be undertaken with the prior consent of the king. Nor might this

5   The great motte-and-bailey castle at Mileham, designed so as to straddle the main road
(Cambridge: Committee for Aerial Photography)

consent be granted if restrictions in size were not agreed, for there is evidence to
suggest that double-ditched enclosures were positively discouraged in the castles
of the baronage, and that this was thought a measure of their size.[29] In such
matters, to ignore the king's regulations was to risk forfeiture; to build too grandly
was to invite, just as surely, royal occupation.

What determined the ultimate scale of baronial castle-building, then, was
only in part the level of resources of the builder. In times of intense political crisis,
the castle had an important military role. But much of this importance depended
on speed of construction, and what went up quickly could equally quickly come
down. The temporary quality of many such defences has made them, of course,
almost impossible to date archaeologically. The tall motte, or castle mound, might
be a characteristic of the late-eleventh-century castle-building style, as the square
motte could be of the twelfth.[30] And there is something to be said for the theory of

8

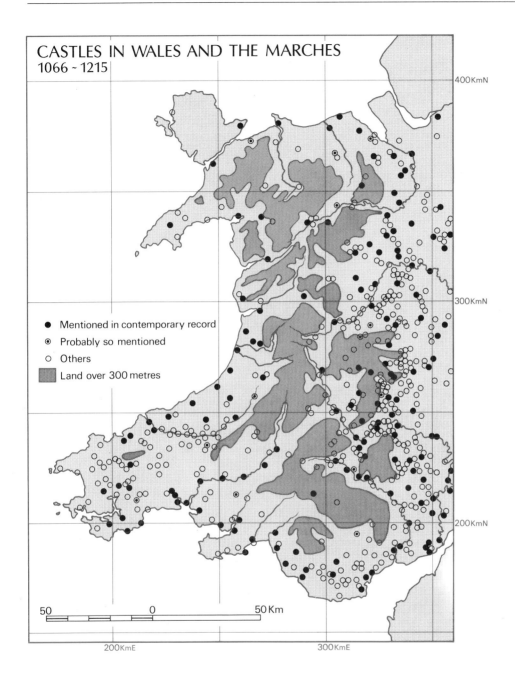

CASTLES IN WALES AND THE MARCHES
1066 ~ 1215

400KmN

● Mentioned in contemporary record
◉ Probably so mentioned
○ Others
▓ Land over 300 metres

300KmN

200KmN

50   0   50 Km

200KmE   300KmE

6   The spread of early castles in Wales and the Marches, showing concentrations on the border with England and in the Norman southern counties (Hogg and King)

the ring-work, or banked and ditched enclosure, as an especially early castle form.[31] However, the Normans were to use castle mounds and ring-works indifferently in the conquest and settlement of South Wales, and although there are North-Country examples at Aldingham, in Lancashire, and Burton-in-Lonsdale, in Yorkshire, of the conversion of ring-works into mottes, neither is sufficiently early in date to persuade us convincingly of the model.[32]

Yet, if we can say little so far of the dating criteria to be used in the assessment of these castles, much more is now known to us of their form. Plainly, the raising of a

7   A conjectural reconstruction from post-hole evidence of the motte at Abinger, in Surrey (Hope-Taylor)

10

mound must present different problems according to the nature of the terrain. Thus Bramber, in Sussex, on a level site, was constructed of the upcast from a quarry-ditch cut in the natural chalk, strengthened with a mixture of alluvial clay and clay-with-flints, giving the mound extra body; while Duffield, in Derbyshire, could be fortified very much more simply by scraping round an existing knoll, afterwards flattened at the top to the bed-rock.[33] And there were to be many understandable variants on these techniques. More interest attaches, however, to the identification and analysis of the buildings set upon these mounds, the classic demonstration of which remains the excavations on the motte at Abinger. On this Surrey site, undisturbed since its twelfth-century abandonment, the summit of the castle mound was cleared down to the sand of its original construction, revealing in the pattern of post-holes thus exposed the line of an encircling timber palisade, strengthened by bracing-posts on the interior. At the centre of the mound, exposed in the same surface, were the post-holes that had held the timber supports of a watch-tower; at the bottom, crossing the shallow moat at the foot of the mound, a causeway had formerly supported the bridge.[34] No less important in the Abinger analysis was the recognition that these buildings were not the first to cap the original castle mound. They had replaced a structure of comparable form, dating to about 1100, which had either collapsed accidentally through faulty building or had been allowed to do so when conditions in the area improved. In point of fact, the value of the excavations at Abinger lies at least as much in the demonstration of the essentially temporary nature of many such fortifications of the civil-war periods, as in the building evidence recovered there.

Indeed, Abinger's refortification before the mid-twelfth century may surely be associated with the Anarchy. In these conditions, the defences of even a great and permanent estate-centre like Castle Acre would undergo yet another remodelling.[35] And elsewhere castles would spring up to meet the needs of the time, to last only as long as they persisted. One of these, at Therfield, in Hertfordshire, which seems never to have been completed, was probably put up specifically to protect the area from the notorious, but short-lived, plunderings of Geoffrey de Mandeville in the war-torn years 1143–4. Attached to it, unusually, was a defensive earthwork which may, at the time, have surrounded the adjoining village and which seems certainly to have been contemporary with the castle. Yet the castle mound itself, like that at Abinger, was diminutive, perhaps never reaching its full height. There were no traces of buildings upon it, nor were the bailey defences, still the most obvious surviving feature of the earthworks at Therfield, completed around their full circuit.[36] Geoffrey de Mandeville, the cause of these works, died at Burwell, in Cambridgeshire, not very far from

Therfield, and here again the removal of the threat brought to an end the programme of castle-construction initiated by Stephen to contain and defeat his forces. At Burwell, the spoil-heaps of the original castle-builders may still be identified on the present-day site, overlying earlier earthworks of peasant houses and garden plots cleared to begin on the construction.[37]

Essentially temporary fortifications like those at Therfield and Burwell could be structurally very uncomplicated. But not all castles, of course, were intended to be short-lived, and even at those that were, problems of subsidence and timber-rot had always to be coped with by their builders. In recent years, some of the most interesting work on the lesser earthwork castles has included the identification of bracing structures, actually within the mounds, which, with the various techniques of layering and reinforcement of the body of the mound itself, were intended to support overlying buildings. Traces of a timber skeleton within the mound, presumably for this purpose, were found at Burgh Castle, in Suffolk.[38] And other examples of work of this kind are sure to be revealed during the excavation of further English mottes, as they have been already on the Continent. But nowhere to date has there been a site to compare in interest with that of South Mimms, in Middlesex, again associated with Geoffrey de Mandeville, although this time as one of his properties. Here a substantial timber-built tower had been set on a flint base, itself founded on the original ground surface. Later, the tower

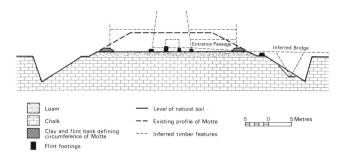

8   Sketch section, showing the inner chamber and entrance passage, of Geoffrey de Mandeville's motte at South Mimms, in Middlesex (Kent)

was concealed beyond basement level by the loose upcast of the motte, through which a passage-way gave access to the buried chamber, now effectively hidden in the mound. Over the whole, the tower that capped it was solidly based on its rigid supporting structure, unlikely to be affected to any serious degree by subsidence.[39]

Mound and tower at the castle at South Mimms were mutually supporting, and it was only a short step from timber constructions of this kind to the substitution of more permanent below-ground structures in stone. At the smaller castles, contemporary or nearly so to South Mimms, buried stone towers are known at Ascot Doilly, in Oxfordshire, and Aldingbourne, in Sussex, both of which have been tentatively dated to the Anarchy. Very probably the Aldingbourne tower was designed first as a free-standing keep, shortly to be partially buried, and then heightened, as marshy conditions on the castle site threatened to bring about a collapse.[40] However, at Ascot Doilly, mound and tower were evidently raised together, the latter being of approximately the same dimensions as its timber equivalent at South Mimms.[41] Significantly, where the same principle of stone-founding through the body of the motte was followed again at Henry of Blois's very much grander castle at Farnham, in Surrey, the builders were clearly adapting techniques which they had practised originally on similar structures of timber. In these, of course, the timber framing could well support an overlying tower larger at its base than the structure hidden in the mound. But at Farnham, the broadening of the keep base to form a stone platform substantially oversailing its substructure on every side and resting on the compacted mound surface, risked precisely that subsidence and collapse which the below-ground structure had been put up at such cost to avoid.[42]

Henry of Blois, the builder of Farnham, stands out as one of the wealthiest men of the Anarchy generation, as he was also one of the most cosmopolitan. Bishop of Winchester, abbot of Glastonbury, and brother of the king, he had access to exceptional resources to fund the building programmes for which he became, during his long life, well known. Yet it was his wealth rather than his passion for building which set him apart from his fellows, for he shared his enthusiasm for leaving his mark on the land with all who could afford it in the Anglo-Norman ruling class, and with none more so than with the king. The Conqueror himself had demonstrated this most obviously in the two outstanding monuments of the Norman settlement, the castles at London and at Colchester – as much residence as fortress, administrative centre, barracks and military store-house all in one. It seems likely that the remote origins of these castle-palaces were Carolingian, and that their immediate prototype was Duke Richard's tenth-century fortress at Rouen.[43] They shared the characteristics of a lavish provision of upper-floor residential accommodation, with great halls and other chambers, and with a massive apsidal-ended chapel projecting in each case from the south-east corner of the keep. But what is especially important about these buildings is that they comprise a class on their own. While a fitting demonstration, essential in their time, of the Norman military presence, they were yet too expensive to repeat.

At Norwich, Henry I's great stone castle, replacing the timber-built castle of

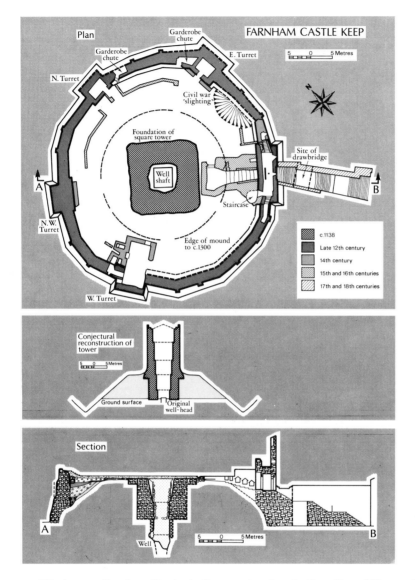

9   The keep at Farnham Castle, in Surrey, showing the founding of Henry of Blois's great tower on the original ground surface (Thompson)

his father, is the closest parallel to the Conqueror's extraordinary works at London and at Colchester. Even so, it introduced what was essentially a new class of square, or rectangular, stone keep which, although often thought of as the archetypal Norman castle, had little to do with the experience of the Conquest and much more with a strictly contemporary military expertise acquired, in particular,

10 William I's fortress-palace at Colchester, Essex, showing the apse of the chapel protruding from the main structure to the right (Aerofilms)

11 The Conqueror's chapel at the Tower of London (R.C.H.M.)

15

12   Henry I's early-twelfth-century keep, later drastically restored, at Norwich: one of the first rectangular stone keeps of the new tradition (Hallam Ashley)

on crusade.[44] Already, at Norwich, the internal military arrangements of the castle are markedly more sophisticated than were those of the Conqueror's original massive palace-keeps, despite their great size and expense. It is these which take us forward, rather, to the period to which most of these so-called 'Norman' keeps, in point of fact, truly belong: to that general conversion from timber to stone that characterized the second half of the twelfth century, and to the renewal of the king's interest in castle-construction in England, as opposed to his French possessions, he being then the wealthiest patron of them all.

The Conqueror, in his day, had encouraged castle-building, and had engaged in it extensively himself. But both he and his sons, where others were concerned, would impose their own limits upon it, and, if these were not always too explicit, they included the daunting possibility of a royal expropriation for crimes against the state whether actual or imagined, a powerful disincentive to investment. No such limits, on the other hand, attached to the building programmes of the clergy. Next to the king, and far in advance of the magnates, the Anglo-Norman Church financed a building renewal in post-Conquest England which was one of the outstanding achievements of the age.

At least in part, this renewal owed its impact to an apparent stagnation in English architectural practice which had lasted a couple of generations or more. Already, it had shown some signs of lifting in the great works of Edward the Confessor, completed at Westminster shortly before his death. Nevertheless, where English prelates remained in office following the Conquest, they took no hand, significantly enough, in building programmes like those their Norman colleagues everywhere were launching. Rather, they preserved the old ways or remained inactive, leaving change in this, as in other things, to the Normans who immediately succeeded them.[45] What this came to mean in practice was that there could be little continuity in English ecclesiastical architecture over the Conquest decades. The Romanesque tradition, introduced from the mid-century, sprang from no local roots. Like the Normans themselves, it was alien, deeply influenced, of course, by what had recently been happening in the immediate Norman homeland, but displaying also the more exotic strains which reflected the varying Continental background and experience of William's freshly imported clergy.[46] One product of these was Robert of Lorraine's two-storeyed, centrally planned chapel at Hereford, built before the end of the eleventh century, which echoed in many essentials of its plan the famous royal chapel of the Emperor Charlemagne at Aachen, certainly known to Robert.[47] Another, a generation later, was the over-ambitious domed nave of the priory church at Leominster, abandoned by its builders for a more conventional northern treatment, but conceived originally in an exotic southern manner with antecedents as distant, perhaps, as Cyprus.[48]

On occasion, the new traditions and the old were to come together uneasily. Edward the Confessor, well before the Conquest, had shown his admiration for Norman work by modelling his church at Westminster on the recently completed abbey at Jumièges. But when the Normans returned the compliment, in their own fashion, by continuing to work within the existing Anglo-Saxon sculptural tradition, as they did at Ely still as late as the 1090s, they helped neither the indigenous tradition nor their own.[49] There are happier examples, of course, of artistic continuity in the lively manuscript drawings of the Canterbury school, influential already in Normandy before the Conquest, and very important there after it.[50] And, on a much humbler level, there was craftsman-continuity also in the practice, for example, of the tin-plating of iron spurs, passed on from one English spurrier to another from the tenth to the seventeenth century.[51]

17

13 Norman cathedral
architecture at its most
impressive: the nave of
Durham Cathedral
(R.C.H.M.)

Nevertheless, what the story of the Canterbury drawings also shows us is the tension
which existed within the Church, as much as within lay society, during the
immediate post-Conquest decades. Of the two great monastic communities at
Canterbury, that at St Augustine's remained the more persistently opposed to
Norman domination, even rising in open rebellion against it. And, not
surprisingly, it was in the writing-house, or *scriptorium*, of St Augustine's Abbey
that the Anglo-Saxon traditions, both of writing and of illumination, were most
sedulously preserved.[52] In contrast, these same traditions at Canterbury
Cathedral Priory, although maintained by Archbishop Lanfranc and his imported
monks of Bec, to become influential back in the Norman homeland, did not prove as

14 Early-twelfth-century arcading at Norwich Cathedral, begun under Bishop Herbert Losinga (1090–1119) (Batsford)

strong. The archbishop, perhaps, had been more tactful in his handling of the community than his contemporary, Abbot Scotland, at St Augustine's, and there were not the same tensions at the cathedral priory as had been evoked at St Augustine's by the prospect of a limitation of its privileges. Nevertheless, what must also have contributed to the archbishop's relative success with his monks would surely have been the completion of the fine new cathedral church at Canterbury as early as 1077.[53] At Canterbury certainly, and probably elsewhere, the Normans found a point of reconciliation with the conquered in church-building, frequently on the most lavish scale, where similar activity in castle-building had merely served to drive the breach still wider.

Between the two, the links continued to be very close. At Winchester, for example, the transformation of the ancient royal city of the Wessex line, although begun in 1067 with the building of the castle, was followed some three years later by the extension of the palace to twice its former area, and was concluded by the complete rebuilding of the Anglo-Saxon minster, on a vastly enlarged scale, begun in 1079.[54] Still more directly, Gundulf, architect of the White Tower at London and 'the most celebrated castle-builder of the eleventh century', was also bishop of Rochester from 1077, where he rebuilt his own cathedral church and started work on the formidable defences of the castle.[55] Obeying the building instinct which was always very powerful with the Normans, Herbert Losinga's campaign of works at Norwich Cathedral began immediately after the transfer of the see from Thetford in 1094/5. Already, by 1100 at latest, the choir of the new cathedral was complete, and something of the bishop's driving energy in the work comes through in the rebuke he delivered to the monks of Norwich who, when others were active, 'meanwhile are asleep with folded hands, numbed as it were, and frostbitten by a winter of negligence, shuffling and failing in your duty through a paltry love of ease'.[56] Not even Herbert Losinga, in such conditions, could work building miracles by himself, and his cathedral remained only partly finished at his death in 1119. But it is notable that one of the reasons why he failed to do so was that others in the area were almost as active as himself. In each case, the magnates of the region were already committed to major works of piety of their own.

Herbert Losinga had bought his bishopric in 1090. At the same time, he had obtained preferment for his father to the vacant abbacy at Hyde in a business transaction which, for the period, was still exceptional only in its scale. Nevertheless, the public outcry provoked by Herbert's deal must have shown very clearly the way that the wind was now blowing.[57] Out of the so-called Gregorian reforming programme of the 1070s, initiated by the papacy and widely disseminated by the scandals of the Investiture Contest it provoked, had come a very general reaction against the practice of lay proprietorship in the Church, against the buying and selling of ecclesiastical office of which Herbert and many of his contemporaries were guilty, and against clerical marriage as the powerful promoter of long-lasting episcopal dynasties by which the interests of the Church were deflected. The righteous anger of the reformers, given much contemporary force by the evident 'miracle' of the First Crusade, contributed also to the makings of a spiritual revival. Laymen, already made reluctant to break God's law by retaining their interest in the Church's patrimony, now eagerly competed to enlarge it: none more so than the Anglo-Norman aristocracy, so recently enriched by the extraordinary windfall of the Conquest.

It was not long, certainly, before the king and his magnates were seeking to attract over the Channel to England churchmen of the high quality they now needed. Naturally, the response was not always immediate. Abbot Hugh of Cluny, when approached to supply monks from his own great house to colonize William de Warenne's new priory at Lewes, professed himself reluctant to do so because of the distance but 'most of all because of the sea'.[58] However, such attitudes became less common as the rewards were raised and the Normans tightened their hold. William de Warenne had been attracted to Cluny, and to the relatively old-fashioned practices of its order, by his personal experience of the life at Cluny itself, which he had come to know while resting there in the course of a pilgrimage to Rome.[59] Others found more to interest them in the new orders which multiplied so startlingly in the monastic revival that characterized the twelfth century: in the Cistercians, perhaps, or in the Augustinians, and sometimes, too, in a lesser order like the Victorines, as we know to have been the case at Wigmore Abbey, in Herefordshire, the foundation narrative of which so closely parallels the much earlier experience of Lewes.[60]

What many of these new foundations had in common, and what distinguished them most often from the older houses either sited in towns or round which a town had grown, was a virgin site and the opportunity for planned expansion in an orderly fashion to meet every requirement of the Rule. In such conditions, the Cistercians in particular, for whom isolation was a principle of life, might indulge their taste for a standardization of their houses, one not uncommonly being copied directly from another.[61] And then when prosperity came upon them, as so often happened later in the twelfth century at the high tide of the order's popularity, they would find themselves free to expand. Such was the case, certainly, at Fountains, in Yorkshire, originally established in the winter of 1132 by a breakaway Benedictine group from the abbey of St Mary's at York, and received into the Cistercian order probably no later than the autumn of the following year.[62] Very likely it was as a direct consequence of this reception that the infant community, which had all-but foundered during the first months of its existence, went on to accumulate its endowment. Within a decade, the monks had laid out and made a substantial beginning on their church and first claustral ranges, setting a scale that was already impressive although very quickly to be enlarged. Then, as the community continued to expand, both the church and the cloister were soon remodelled, with considerable extensions of the existing buildings both to the south and to the east, and with changes also to the drainage system which had preoccupied already the founding fathers of the abbey, drawing them initially to their valley-bottom riverine site.[63]

15   The church and claustral buildings at Fountains Abbey, Yorkshire, completed for the most part before the end of the twelfth century (Aerofilms)

Progress at Fountains was undoubtedly rapid, yet we need not suppose that it was smooth. The major period of expansion of the house, as would be the case with many Cistercian and most Augustinian communities, coincided with the troubles of the Anarchy, into which the monks of Fountains must surely have been dragged by the long-lasting dispute with Stephen over their abbot's election to the

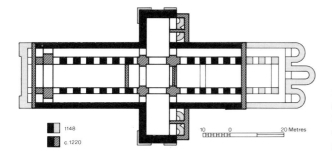

16   Faversham Abbey, Kent, showing the contraction on Stephen's original plan for the church when the king's patronage ceased (Philp)

archbishopric of York. Furthermore, building works on such a scale, with very few precedents in the north, cannot have failed to run into technical difficulties. Indeed, the great aisled nave of the church at Fountains, it has only recently been demonstrated, was built part-by-part, with temporary blocking walls to enable the church to be used, and with evidence of at least one serious error in the placing of the clerestory buttresses.[64] In much the same way, at another Cistercian house at Rufford, in Nottinghamshire, the temporary church of the founding monks had evidently got in the way of those building its permanent replacement, preventing an accurate sighting through the nave arcades and causing a lack of symmetry in the construction of the church, reminiscent, both in cause and effect, of what had already happened many years before during the building of William Rufus's great palace hall at Westminster.[65] Over-ambitious planning, of which Westminster is again an example, could tax building skills beyond the limit or, more often, fail completely for lack of resources. The canons of Lilleshall, in Shropshire, although members of one of the richest of the Augustinian communities founded during Stephen's reign, were never to complete, beyond foundation level, the aisled presbytery they may originally have intended to replace the east end of their church.[66] Nor would the Benedictines of Stephen's own foundation at Faversham, despite the king's intention to provide for them elaborately as the guardians of his 'tomb-house', prove any luckier in the event. After Stephen's death, bringing with it a drying-up of royal grants, work slowed down at Faversham and may even have stopped altogether. And when, early in the next century, a determined effort at last could be made to finish the work on the church, this could only be done on a much reduced scale, while updating what had become, in the interval, an unfashionable architectural conception.[67]

Inevitably, the matching of ambitions against available resources remained a condition of building progress even at those greater churches where the king and his magnates found themselves personally committed to dramatic demonstrations of their piety. But there were, too, a great many monastic establishments less fortunate even than Faversham, and we should keep it in mind that those wealthy new houses of the mid-twelfth century, which had been able themselves to capitalize on monastic reform and the profound recent excitements of the Crusade, had followed what were already two full generations of monastic beginnings in post-Conquest England, characterized rather by diminutive foundations, the alien priories of houses in Normandy to which the new aristocracy, looking back to its homeland, continued to recognize an obligation. It was these priories in particular, considered 'one of the most unfortunate by-products of the Conquest',[68] that produced many of the shipwrecked houses that littered the landscape of late-medieval England. And while some of them, like Gorefields, in Buckinghamshire, and Grafton Regis, in Northamptonshire (below, pp. 158–60), succeeded in attracting sufficient communities from an early stage to warrant buildings that were monastic in plan, the majority differed little, if at all, from the manor-houses of lay estates equivalent to those on which they were originally established.[69] Small communities, at all times, were peculiarly exposed to failure, there being many, especially among the lesser Augustinian foundations, that never succeeded fully in establishing themselves.[70] It must have been this, with other reasons, that turned Wulfric, the recluse of Haselbury Plucknett, against the Austin canons of his day for whom, very evidently, he had less time than for the Cistercians. It was he who, by the mid-twelfth century, was sufficiently concerned at the concentration of monastic interests in his area of Somerset to dissuade his lord, William Fitzwalter, from establishing an Augustinian priory at Haselbury.[71] Wulfric died in 1155, and competition by then was fierce.

Wulfric had a friend and confidant in Brihtric, the parish priest of Haselbury, whose church adjoined his cell. We know that Brihtric, an Englishman like Wulfric himself, was a man of considerable substance and great piety, and the parish, evidently, with two such 'seraphim' at its centre, was exceptionally well served by its priesthood. Nevertheless, Brihtric was married, to be succeeded by his son in the cure of souls at Haselbury. And Brihtric, to his chagrin, spoke no French.[72] Hereditary priesthoods for the one part, socially divisive language barriers for another – these were the circumstances that spurred the reformers into action, to bring about a transformation of religious life at grass-roots level which would leave its mark as surely on the landscape of the day as would the more spectacular works of piety of the king, his barons and his monks.

Of course, the origins of the parochial system itself, in the form we have come to know it, go back much further than the Conquest, and there had been a progressive separation of parish church from minster pre-dating by many years the reforms of the in-coming Norman prelates. In a not uncommon development, the late-tenth-century parishioners of Rivenhall, in Essex, were already sufficiently confident of the dignity of their church to rebuild it substantially in stone,[73] while the parish churches of England carry many recognizably pre-Conquest dedications, and the Domesday clerks of 1086, whenever they felt called upon to do so, recorded a land that was already thickly churched.[74] Nevertheless, the processes of parish formation (and still more often parish definition) were still going on in twelfth-century England, as they had been at Domesday and before. A recent study of church provision in London before 1200 has shown how many of the churches of the city originated in the eleventh and twelfth centuries,[75] and similar county-based studies have demonstrated a doubling of parishes in post-Conquest Lancashire between Domesday and the mid-thirteenth century, with closely comparable developments in Staffordshire and Cheshire, each associated with urban growth and with the Norman manorialization of those counties.[76]

One explanation of parish-church growth, over the face of twelfth-century England, must be mounting population pressure; another, just as certainly, is the contemporary re-ordering of estates. But as important as these was the altering status both of parish church and priest, a change that had begun already in the eleventh century, and was accelerated by the reforms of the twelfth. It would be wrong to conclude that the Anglo-Saxon priesthood, even in the depths of the countryside, was of uniformly low class and status. We have Brihtric, among others, to show that it was not. Nevertheless, the common pre-Conquest view of the church as private property, with its inevitable consequences in a hereditary priesthood and the fractional holding of churches, had degraded, in many cases, the individual church and came to discredit its priest. Hereditary benefices, whether passed from father to son or merely kept within the family for a younger son who might otherwise have had little to inherit, persisted everywhere in England well into the thirteenth century, such recently discussed examples as those of Eye, in Herefordshire, and Letheringsett, in Norfolk, being exceptional only in their documentation.[77] But at least as characteristic of the period was the revulsion against this antique and no longer acceptable custom that led Richard of

Ilchester, then archdeacon of Poitiers and later bishop of Winchester, to transform the long-established hereditary shrine of St Nectan at Hartland, in Devonshire, into a house of Augustinian canons. Hartland Abbey later became one of the wealthier houses of its order, but much of its initial funding came, in a complex deal very characteristic of the times, from the vicarial revenues of the parish church of North Petherwin, in the same county, of which the abbot and convent of Tavistock were patrons.[78]

In the event, something like a quarter of the parish churches of England had come before 1200 into the hands of religious houses like Tavistock, or indeed like Hartland Abbey itself, while many others, too, had fallen to the bishops in each diocese, the alteration in proprietorship encouraging in each case a reform of worship which must frequently have resulted in a rebuilding. In the new conditions, hostile to antique proprietorial customs, lay owners of churches had found it increasingly difficult to make a worth-while profit from their investment, but it was immediately obvious that an ecclesiastical beneficiary, whoever he might be, could expect to do much better.[79] Certainly, the value placed by the monks on a benefaction such as this was high, and they would be prepared to go to great lengths to preserve it. In a celebrated three-cornered dispute, lasting the better part of two reigns, the monks of Reading and Gloucester, with the canons of St Augustine's, Bristol, fought out a settlement on the churches of Berkeley Hernesse, in Gloucestershire, from which all emerged dissatisfied and Reading with no church of its own.[80] And so great was the lure of a parish church like Babraham, in Cambridgeshire, near which they already had some property, that the Cistercians of Sawtry Abbey, in the adjoining county of Huntingdon, disputed its possession with the wealthy Austin canons of Waltham, in Essex, neglecting their Rule and even honesty to do so.[81]

In large part, the value of a church was what could be reserved by the appropriator from its tithes. Typically, a monastic appropriator would take to himself the greater tithes (on cereal crops, hay, and the product of the mill), while assigning the remaining revenues of the parish to a vicar, appointed to the cure in his place. And though such profits were not always considerable (there being cases, particularly in the later Middle Ages, where an appropriation might lead to a net loss), they remained for many houses, especially those of the Augustinian order, an indispensable financial support. For the Austin canons and for others like them, the appropriated parish church was seen first as an investment, to be developed where possible but also, in their own best interests, to be preserved and scrupulously maintained.

Our best record, of course, of this continuing concern is the fabric of the

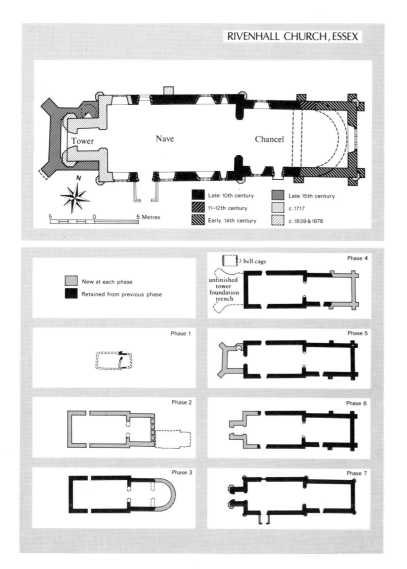

17   The plan-development of Rivenhall Church, in Essex, from the Saxon timber building (phase 1) to final works in the nineteenth century (Rodwell)

parish churches themselves. While not the *only* reason for the very common remodelling of many parish churches in twelfth-century England, appropriation must undoubtedly have been one of them, it being noticeable how often it was the chancel especially (by tradition the charge of the rector) that was the subject of particular embellishment. It was not a monastic appropriator, so far as we know, who rebuilt the chancel of the Essex church at Rivenhall, extending the original very substantial stone structure that had been put up in the late tenth century (above, p. 25). But it is very likely, all the same, that the fine new apse in the twelfth-century manner, replaced once again in the early fourteenth century by the square-ended chancel of today, commemorates a change of ownership at Rivenhall.[82] And, indeed, just such an event may be recalled at the parish church of Wharram Percy, near Malton in Yorkshire, where the masons' marks on the stonework of the late-twelfth-century manor-house have been found to match, in at least one instance, a mark on the demolished apse of the nearby church of St Martin. Plainly, a change of tenure or similar event at Wharram in the late twelfth century could have been the occasion for a major rebuilding, as much at the church as at the manor-house itself.[83]

Characteristically, although not of course exclusively, the apsidal-ended chancel that we have seen adopted both at Rivenhall and Wharram maps the progress of Anglo-Norman ecclesiastical reform. Surviving twelfth-century apses are still plain for all to see, and there are now a number of excavated examples to add to these – at London, Norwich and Winchester, at Thetford (Norfolk), Barpham (Sussex), and Irthlingborough (Northants).[84] With this, too, went the enlargement of the body of the church itself, whether by the addition of aisles, as at Wharram or Thurleigh (Bedfordshire), or by such major extensions of the nave as have been noted at Angmering (Sussex) and St Mary-le-Port (Bristol).[85] To follow these changes through the older study of church dedications, particularly beloved by the Victorians, is to recognize an overwhelming preponderance of dedications to St Mary, known all over the country and reflecting a twelfth-century preoccupation with the cult of the Virgin which coincided with the contemporary multiplication of parishes. Other dedications, as identifiably twelfth-century or later, are those to St Michael and St Stephen, both favourite Norman saints, to St James the Elder, patron saint of pilgrimages, and, before the end of the century, to the martyred St Thomas of Canterbury.[86]

Usefully, what the study of such dedications can remind us is that there were other pressures and fresh ideas, alongside those of the Normans, to transform twelfth-century England. The cult of the Virgin, although certainly continental in origin, had no need of a Norman invasion to introduce it over here. Nor can church reform, any more than the expansion of the economy itself, be seen as the work of the Normans alone, even if it remains true that their arrival assisted it. England, in the late twelfth century, bore the mark of an alien presence in its castles, its monasteries, its manor-houses and even its churches. But much of this, too, was local in inspiration, and it is scarcely in doubt that the English landscape would have acquired these additions whoever had triumphed at Hastings. The most

18   The stone foundations of an earlier Saxon building showing in the excavated floor of
Wharram Percy Church, in Yorkshire (Medieval Village Research Group)

important characteristic of St Thomas of Canterbury, it must be obvious, was not
that he was a Norman. Both Becket himself and the plainly alien St Hugh of
Lincoln, who came to England as a direct consequence of the murdered
archbishop's death, were to be thought of not as foreign intruders but as truly
national saints.

2　Economic Growth

Levels of wealth in a medieval society are at all times difficult to measure, and though Domesday has its value in this, as we have seen, it is made the more important by the fact that there is nothing in any way to take the place of the Domesday record before the lay subsidy returns of 1334, now at last in print,[1] even these telling us less than the earlier document can usually be made to do. However, it is at least clear that the most important characteristic of the English economy, in the thirteenth century through from the twelfth, was growth; not evenly sustained and not equally beneficial at every level of society, but a fact to be lived with all the same. It was swelling marketable surpluses on the land which financed the stone castles of the king and his magnates, which built the new monastic houses, and which found permanent and visible expression locally in the transformation of the parish church. It was to dispose of these surpluses, and in turn to encourage and create them, that the towns of England flourished and then multiplied.

Undoubtedly, the Normans played their part both in the foundation of new towns and in the enlargement of the old, using them, as they had done the castle and the monastery, very deliberately as instruments of colonization. But the great period of borough foundation, unconnected with the Normans, occurred rather later, in the century 1150 to 1250. And it was then, too, that urban communities in England most commonly acquired their precious identity in the law, further promoting their growth. Of urban institutions, it is enough here to say that they had achieved, within this period, substantial independence from the countryside, with valuable freedoms and specially tailored exemptions which helped develop the professionalization of trade.[2] Alongside this, the physical evidence, though less subtle, is considerably more dramatic. It shows us first the proliferation of trading communities, at just this time, with a claim to be described as 'towns'. And then, as excavations continue on urban sites throughout the country, it is beginning to establish for us, in a number of ways, the lines along which such growth may actually have occurred.

Few counties, perhaps, are likely to illustrate this proliferation of boroughs more vividly than Staffordshire, where the Domesday total of only three in 1086 can be shown to have climbed before 1300 to no fewer than twenty-two.[3] Yet in Devonshire, also, the five Domesday boroughs had already been joined by thirteen others by 1238,[4] and both counties clearly shared the experience of the rest of the kingdom in an urban expansion concentrated, for the most part, in the century before 1250. Indeed, market grants, although admittedly no certain guide, whether to borough status or to the precise date of growth, very obviously tell the same story. Of course, the king recognized market rights at a wide variety of communities, some of them very small. Nevertheless, the multiplication of market grants and their clear bunching within the first three-quarters of the thirteenth century remains highly significant.[5] It was then, on other evidence, that the established towns can be shown to have been at their most vigorous, and it was then, naturally enough, that commercial optimism was at its peak among their imitators. Significantly, although the network of markets through the Warwick-shire countryside showed few gaps by the end of the thirteenth century, the primary determinant of market foundation was less local need than the supposed economic interest and actual political muscle of ambitious individual landowners in the county.[6] In neighbouring Staffordshire, where the pressure towards new foundations was the same, the abbot of Burton found himself both willing and able, early in the century, to push his right to establish markets and fairs at Burton and Abbots Bromley, overriding the combined objections of the men of Tamworth, Stafford, Tutbury and Lichfield, who had privileges of their own to protect. The sole provision upheld in the court against him was that he should hold his markets and fairs on different days from those already reserved by his neighbours.[7]

This phenomenon of the newly founded town in twelfth- and thirteenth-century England has now been very thoroughly explored.[8] However, the oft-debated issue as to whether or not such towns were deliberately planned from the beginning, as many of them undoubtedly were, has claimed attention frequently for the wrong reasons, as if town-planning in medieval England were the drawing-board exercise of today.[9] Where evidence of town planning may indeed be important is not in aesthetics but in precisely those issues that principally concern us here. It can serve, that is, as a measure both locally and through time of the degree of contemporary commercial optimism; it may suggest the emergence of a will in the community to get together in the determination of its future development; more frequently, as with the markets of the abbot of Burton, it may demonstrate the initiative and the drive of the lord. In surviving records, seigneurial initiatives are plain to see in the six 'planted' towns of the bishops of

Winchester, each of them founded within the first half of the thirteenth century and not all of them ultimately successful.[10] There are the five boroughs, four 'organic' and one 'planted', of the bishops of Hereford, each promoted by the interest of the bishops,[11] with Stratford-upon-Avon, that notably successful late-twelfth-century enterprise of John of Coutances, bishop of Worcester.[12] Each of these, it might be said, would have been known to us without the benefit of archaeology, while in many there is evidence of medieval planning preserved still in the street layout of today, which is repeated in other towns as yet to be archaeologically explored. However, it is to the details, rather than to the overall pattern, of urban expansion in medieval England that archaeology is beginning to contribute new evidence, and this is important as much for what it tells us by implication of the quality of urban living as for what it shows us more directly in town plans.

It is of interest, for example, in the context of urban development, that adjoining house plots in thirteenth-century Chelmsford, originally laid out to a standard width and separated by a dividing gully, can be shown not to have been taken up immediately by the builders, having to wait as much as two decades before, in a new campaign of building, the plots were joined together for the single building that was eventually erected upon them.[13] And this element of speculation, clearly present at Chelmsford, can be demonstrated too in the many town foundations which, occurring after 1250, never effectively took root. It may be this at Cestersover, in Warwickshire, granted rights of market in 1257, which explains, as a failed extension of the vill, the planned layout of a number of crofts, south of the manor-house, that seem never to have been fully settled.[14] Almost certainly, the plots within the so-called Battle Ditches at Saffron Walden, in Essex, another probably late-thirteenth-century speculative extension of the town, were never taken up.[15] And it was doubtless the much earlier date of a similar extension of Wimborne, in Dorset, southward onto the Leaze, which was the principal guarantee of its success. Even here, though, the life of this development was to be limited in practice, for when, with the return of hard times, the community at Wimborne contracted again in the fourteenth century, the streets and the house plots on the Leaze were abandoned, the site reverting to its original pasture.[16]

Extensions, as on the Leaze at Wimborne, might be one answer to the problem of intense urban development at the turn of the twelfth and thirteenth centuries. Another, on less adaptable sites, would be such deliberate transformations of the existing urban environment as seem to have occurred at contemporary Bristol in the reconstruction of Mary-le-Port Street,[17] at St Neots, in Huntingdonshire, when the present-day street pattern was laid down in the early thirteenth century,[18] and perhaps most obviously at Southampton, in the archaeologically demonstrable clearance and replanning of a part of the ancient parish of Holy Rood, subsequently to become, over many years, the wealthiest quarter of the town.[19] In early-thirteenth-century Southampton, too, the marking-out and development of the new house plots in Holy Rood was accompanied by other manifestations of a fresh style of urban living, matching-up with the constitutional and economic freedoms which the borough had lately secured. There is less evidence, for example, in thirteenth-century Southampton, as would be the case contemporaneously in the very much more rural community at Wimborne, of stock-keeping and other farming activity on house plots within the town boundaries. And where, at Wimborne, terraced shops of craftsmen replaced the peasant smallholdings that had characterized the earliest stages of development on the Leaze, at Southampton even these craftsmen were banished to the less valuable properties at the north end of the town, away from the rich waterfront and its quays. At just this time, as has been demonstrated archaeologically, there was a marked improvement in the quality of diet at Southampton, with many indications of specialized trading, both in the meats and the fruits now available. A flourishing overseas trade brought wine from Bordeaux, silks, spices and vessel glass from the Mediterranean, oil and iron from Spain, cloth from Flanders, and decorative clay pots from each one of these places, of a quality unobtainable at home. From the late twelfth century, Southampton merchants engaged in this trade lived in fine stone houses, as large and as expensively equipped as anything to be found in their day.[20]

Indeed, the Southampton stone houses of the late twelfth and early thirteenth centuries were particularly impressive, being the cause of remark by contemporaries. And no doubt the choice of building material, at Southampton as elsewhere, was dictated at least in part by the fear of fire, a hazard known already to have been provided against in the municipal building regulations of London and of which we have good evidence archaeologically, although only of a much later date, at Northampton and Norwich, where fires swallowing one house after another may be shown to have devastated whole streets.[21] However, it is perhaps better to see stone-building in the towns, with its contemporary parallels in the countryside, less as the adoption of fire precautions than as evidence everywhere of wealth. Accompanying this growing prosperity, merchant houses entirely of stone, with roofs of tile and slate, begin to appear at many towns at just the period they are first seen at Southampton. They are known, for example, at Lincoln and Norwich, Bury St Edmunds and Canterbury, at each of which they are usually associated, if only now by legend, with particularly wealthy men.[22] And where similar conversions from timber-building to stone occurred elsewhere, as they did in thirteenth-century King's Lynn, they were frequently accompanied by other clear evidence of a considerable, and a growing, prosperity. It was, that is, over the century 1250 to 1350 that the systematic development took place of the waterfront at Lynn, taking the form of a progressive pushing-forward of the quays of the borough as the river itself changed its course.[23] At contemporary Shrewsbury, one

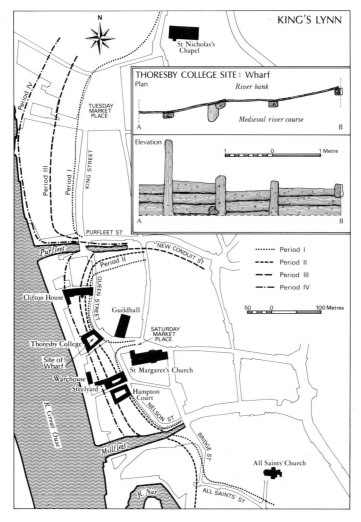

19   Reclamation on the medieval waterfront of King's Lynn, Norfolk (Clarke)

20 Fine-quality stonework at the base of the Lucy Tower, Lincoln, dating to the mid-thirteenth century (Lincoln Archaeological Trust)

of the purposes of the reclamation and consolidation of the low-lying land, enclosed within a loop of the Severn, was to provide a firmer foundation for stone houses.[24]

Just as certain an indicator of wealth in the towns, coinciding very exactly with their rebuilding, was the provision, or redesign, of defences. To be sure, there is little evidence in medieval England of population pressure forcing a continual enlargement of the defended circuits of the towns, such as is known to have occurred on the Continent. Nevertheless, there were many towns in thirteenth-century England which found the resources, in labour and capital, for the digging of rampart and ditch defences, while others embarked con- temporaneously on the costly process of building their walls in stone.[25] Motives for wall-building, no doubt, were mixed, and if a wall were put up primarily for reasons of prestige, the workmanship might frequently be shoddy. While we know of fine work on the city wall at Lincoln, datable to the mid-thirteenth century,[26] and there is similar evidence of considerable care and expensive workmanship on the contemporary bastion recently excavated on the line of the Marsh Wall at Bristol,[27] the common practice of most other towns was undoubtedly rather

35

different. At Newark, a town wall less than three feet in width, although it might have served as a barrier for tolls, could not have kept out a determined intruder, nor were the massive Roman walls of medieval Winchester maintained at their original width, being progressively narrowed in the rebuildings attributable to the thirteenth and fourteenth centuries.[28] Indeed, as borough economies, for one reason and another, foundered in the fourteenth century, earlier ambitions everywhere were modified. The gang-building of walls by separate stages, each gang taking up the work where its predecessor had recently left off, has left enough traces to show up very clearly a steady decline in standards. At Nottingham, when one gang followed another on the building of the town wall by Park Row, the second has been shown to have skimped on the foundations and to have economized very obviously in stone.[29] Likewise, as the years advanced in medieval Lynn, the over-ambitious stone wall, never to be fully completed, deteriorated in quality, section by section, so long as the authorities continued to push the work forward.[30] Coventry's town wall, begun in the fourteenth century, unusually late in the day, as a demonstration of municipal self-confidence and pride, was not to be joined round the full circuit of the brough for over two hundred years. Exactly as at Nottingham, recent excavations at a junction between successive sections of the wall have shown the second to be markedly inferior.[31]

The wealth that had tempted so many towns to begin over-ambitious wall-building programmes in the thirteenth century, being still present at Coventry in the fourteenth, was rooted, inevitably, in the countryside. A recent study of Colchester and its region in the fourteenth century has stressed usefully the interdependence of the two economies at that date. But, of course, the links between the two must go back much further than that, and the same economic forces that were bringing expansion to Colchester itself in the thirteenth century, promoted also the growth of lesser communities in the Essex countryside, some of these even within the market region of an existing centre like Colchester.[32] One of the reasons why deliberately 'planted' towns did not characterize thirteenth-century Cambridgeshire, it has been argued, was that a process of quasi-urbanization, affecting many villages in the county, had made such plantations unnecessary. Thus the characteristic grid plan of many thirteenth-century planted towns is still to be seen in the earthworks of Landbeach, a Cambridgeshire village which had expanded to its maximum in the thirteenth and early fourteenth centuries and has since very considerably contracted,[33] while at Clopton, in the same county, a large rectangular cobbled area, just north of the church and adjoining the main street of the village, has been plausibly interpreted as a marketplace. Repeatedly relaid and repaired over the course of two centuries, it is likely to have been one of many such market-places, scattering the Cambridgeshire countryside at the peak of the thirteenth-century expansion.[34]

It would be hard to determine on whose initiatives a market had been established at Clopton, whether that of the community or the lord. However, there is other intriguing archaeological evidence of a community voice, given expression at Clopton in the orderly layout and systematic re-use of grave plots in the churchyard,[35] and inviting comparison with those other more usual indications of contemporary community consent – regulated cultivation of the common field, assent in the operation of the village bye-laws commonly agreed, and the planning or replanning of the villages themselves, with the systematic apportionment of their territories. Community consent can rarely have been expressed, in this earlier period, as clearly as it was at Harlestone, in Northamptonshire, in 1410, in the agreement that an elected standing committee of nine good men was to lay out

21 Medieval graves laid out in orderly rows at Wharram Percy churchyard (Medieval Village Research Group)

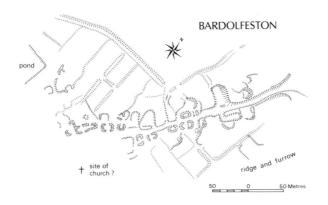

BARDOLFESTON

pond

† site of
  church ?

ridge and furrow

50   0   50 Metres

22 Superimposed settlement plans
at the deserted village of
Bardolfeston, Dorset (R.C.H.M.)

and manage a new field near the settlement for the benefit of 'the whole of the
villagers'.[36] Nevertheless, as we have been shown on the estates of the abbots of
Ramsey, the dynamic element in village society was more often the community
than the lord.[37] And while it might be that it was primarily the economic enterprise
of the prior of Durham, another prominent ecclesiastic, that drove forward,
during the twelfth and thirteenth centuries, the colonization of new lands in his
lordship, there are surely other explanations than this enterprise alone for the
'repetitious regularity' of the plans still characteristic of the villages he is known to
have developed.[38]

Clearly, what determined the planning of villages, as was the case in
contemporary planted towns, was the need to arrive at some equitable
apportionment within the community both of rights to the land and of tax charges
payable upon it. In Durham, as in the neighbouring county of Yorkshire, recent
work on such villages of regular plan has suggested a link between house-plot
measurements and geld, or tax, assessments closely paralleling the calculations
already proposed for the sub-divided territories of these settlements.[39] Such
arrangements seem already to have been old by the thirteenth century, and
although there is no way of determining the date by which they were actually
arrived at, the most probable solution is that the villages were planned, and the
fields more equitably divided, no earlier than the eleventh century nor later than
the twelfth, as population pressures mounted in the countryside, as manorialization extended, and as the lord tightened his grip. Already, that is, in the twelfth
century and before, the circumstances had arisen for a physical transformation of
the English countryside at least as dramatic as the contemporary transformation of
the towns; not always dominant, as in those regions of Devonshire where
continuing land surpluses rendered common-field apportionments unnecessary,[40]

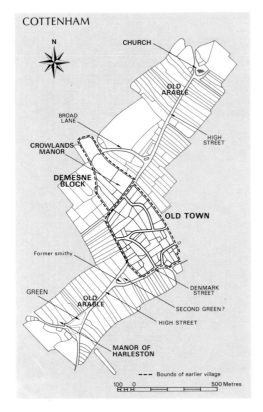

23 The growth of Cottenham,
Cambridgeshire, outwards from its Anglo-
Saxon core (Ravensdale)

and frequently responsive as much to social practice (for example, habits of inheritance) as to economic pressure,[41] but bringing great changes all the same. It was in the twelfth century, continuing well into the thirteenth, that common-field systems were to be devised and adopted in those areas, especially in central England, where population growth forced on the villagers an urgent rationalization of their assets.[42] And contemporaneously, as was only to be expected, change would come to the villages themselves. The early plan of a settlement at Bardolfeston, in Dorset, preserved below the earthworks of a village later to be abandoned in its turn, may recall in outline the pre-expansion community on that site.[43] But even if it does not, there are plentiful examples, everywhere in England, of a twelfth- and thirteenth-century extension of village streets to accommodate a growing population, and it was by extension rather than by an overall replanning that such development must more usually have occurred. It was in the second half of the twelfth century, for example, that the Oxfordshire village of Seacourt began its further development both to the north and to the west, taking in new house

39

plots of approximately standard dimensions which probably reflected their taxable value in each case and which have since given to the earthworks of the abandoned settlement a deceptively one-period appearance.[44] At Cottenham, in Cambridgeshire, in an equally characteristic development that continued over many years, the village expanded from its original rectangular late-Saxon core northwards along the roadside to the post-Conquest church and southwards to the manor-house, next to the green, newly built for the bishops of Ely.[45]

Of course, the expansion of settlements like Seacourt and Cottenham is no proof of increasing peasant wealth, and similar evidence of overcrowding in these villages by the later thirteenth century may be used to establish their poverty. Nevertheless, there was land still to spare in many areas before this date which was ripe for conversion to arable, and there are indications too, in the archaeological record, of improving standards of living. In particular, this was evident in housing, for at least one good reason for the poverty of our survivals of pre-thirteenth-century peasant houses in England is that there was nothing much in them to be preserved. Such houses at Goltho, in Lincolnshire, identified in fragmentary remains, have been conjecturally reconstructed as simple cob-walled buildings on a light frame of straight ash poles, cut in the local woodlands.[46] And scarcely more substantial were the earliest structures, perhaps turf-walled, at those West Country sites like Hound Tor and Hutholes, in Devonshire, or Boscastle and Tresmorn, in Cornwall, where it has been possible to establish unusually long sequences of settlement.[47] In the thirteenth century, at each of these sites, stone replaced the earlier, less durable and cheaper materials, while general rebuildings, everywhere characterized by the use of stone or by relatively sophisticated timber-framing where stone was in short supply, became familiar all over the country at just about this time. They occurred, for example, at Goltho, replacing the earlier light-framed buildings of the twelfth-century peasant community,[48] and have been identified also at Faxton and Wythemail, in Northamptonshire,[49] at Seacourt, in Oxfordshire,[50] Hangleton, in Sussex,[51] Upton, in Gloucestershire,[52] West Whelpington, in Northumberland,[53] as well as at many closely comparable deserted village sites, the number of which increases with new excavations every year.[54] At Barrow Mead, in Somerset, and Barton Blount, in Derbyshire, the rebuildings, although known to have occurred in the fourteenth century, seem not have been begun much before it.[55]

Even on this scale, rebuilding can be claimed to be of limited value as a guide to the accumulation of real wealth, in much the same way as the expansion of settlement has already been regarded as suspect for such a purpose. The use of stone, it has plausibly been suggested, might have resulted from a shortage of good

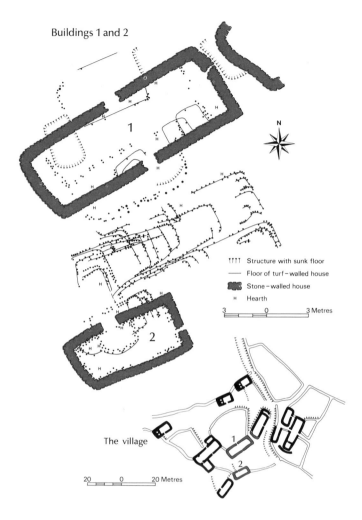

Buildings 1 and 2

Structure with sunk floor
Floor of turf-walled house
Stone-walled house
H   Hearth

3   0   3 Metres

The village

20   0   20 Metres

24   Thirteenth-century stone houses at Hound Tor, Devonshire, overlying earlier timber structures (Minter and the Medieval Village Research Group)

timber,[56] and the peasant long-house, in any event, is likely to have been confined in use to the better-off families, even in those areas where it most commonly occurred and from which the bulk of our evidence derives. Yet it is true also that the long-house, with its characteristic two-chamber division and central opposing entrances, was not the only house-type familiar to the richer peasantry, nor was the thirteenth-century rebuilding of peasant housing at sites like Seacourt, in Oxfordshire,[57] and Goltho, in Lincolnshire,[58] where the long-house occurs only rarely if at all, confined to the better-quality dwellings. In other ways, and on other sites, there is little to establish, at least in this century, extremes of rural poverty. Remote village communities, as recent excavations have shown, not uncommonly made use of richly decorated pottery, some of which was certainly imported, while one of the more characteristic finds on village excavations of this period is the Eifel lava quernstone, the ultimate source of which, however it came to be transported, can only have been the Rhineland.[59] At Seacourt, a fragment of blue glass, recovered there by the excavators, may have originated as far afield as the distant Mediterranean;[60] at Goltho, the metal-work in common use by the villagers of this small arable community included buckles and decorated belt-chapes, a finger-ring, spurs, and harness pendants that were decoratively gilded and enamelled.[61]

One of the explanations for this evident prosperity, uneven though its incidence always was, was an assarting movement, enclosing and cultivating common lands and waste on a very considerable scale. At Domesday, settlement had already been thick in the prime arable regions, and it was these old 'fielden' communities which would remain in the thirteenth century, as they were to do again during the next period of major population expansion under the Tudors, relatively unaffected by new settlement.[62] Elsewhere, in the unexploited forests, the moorlands and the fens, the common experience was very different. In Warwickshire, for example, an instructive contrast can be made within the county between the old-established manorial economy of the richer lands in its southern and south-eastern areas, and what grew up alongside this economy on the poorer soils of the Forest of Arden and its fringes in the north. In the former, population growth was slow, the manorial institutions still holding their grip and the incidence of free tenures, outside the traditional system, remaining relatively low. In the latter, however, settlements multiplied quickly as population grew: four times as fast in Arden, in the north, as they would do south of the Foss. Both free settler and enclosing landlord, sharing out the uncultivated lands between them, had room in these areas and to spare.[63]

This drive to clear, to cultivate and to reclaim waste lands was powerful all over the country. It was in the thirteenth century, most particularly, that the vast royal forests, which had been so much a feature of the Norman settlement, were steadily eroded as peasant and landowner both competed for expensive licences to disafforest.[64] In the Sussex Weald, where the larger freeholders and customary tenants had led in the twelfth century, smaller men were to follow in the thirteenth, pushing back the remaining woodlands with the active encouragement of the great landowners.[65] Peasant assarters, in just this way, were to follow the monks of Peterborough in a long campaign of recovery from the waste which had begun already in the mid-twelfth century near Peterborough Abbey itself, but which extended ever further afield in later years into the Forest of Rockingham.[66] Peasant and seigneurial initiatives together explain the contemporary cutting-back of woodland and extension of arable in the Blackmoor parishes of Stalbridge and Pulham, in Dorset, while the cultivated boundary of Whiteparish, in Wiltshire, gradually moved during this period, into the royal forest of Melchet.[67]

All of these – the Weald, Rockingham, and the forests of Blackmoor and Melchet – offered one sort of opportunity, in the clearance of woodland, for progressive colonization and new settlement. The fens offered another. Of course, there were to be marked differences in the rate of growth on the relatively infertile peat fens of Cambridgeshire on the one hand and the rich silt fens of Lincolnshire on the other. Nevertheless, in the latter, the increase in tenants on the Spalding Priory estates has been shown to have been anything from 5-fold to 11-fold in the two centuries after Domesday, while at Fleet, in the same period, an increase of 62-fold would be difficult to parallel anywhere else in England.[68] Much of this growth was promoted by deliberate seigneurial investment in the reclamation of waterlogged lands. However, what chiefly attracted new settlement on the Spalding granges and still more, of course, outside them, was the weakness of lordship on the reclaimed fenlands and the broad unmanorialized acres.[69] In a society which, despite its textbook image, was still strikingly mobile, there were men in the thirteenth century continually deserting the older manorialized settlements to establish themselves on the moving frontiers of cultivation – on the moorlands, in the forests and on the fens. Indeed, the drive towards colonization in Arden, shaking out settlement into a fresh pattern of isolated woodland homesteads, led to some of the first village shrinkages in medieval England, as the more ambitious of the peasant community moved out of the original settlement nuclei to populate the former waste.[70] Yet there were usually men enough to take the place of those who, for whatever reason, had left, and the outstanding characteristic of population movements in the thirteenth century remains the spreading outwards of the unencumbered and the increasingly desperate, away from a self-replenishing stock in the richer areas of long-established settlement, ever further into the more remote and the marginal lands. It is a process still easy to recognize on the ground.

Plainly, movements outward on this scale could be supported only by a considerable extension of the arable acreage, well beyond that total which, at Domesday, had already been strikingly high. Some of the cultivation of the inhospitable uplands had begun under the Anglo-Saxons or before, and one of the most interesting revelations of a moorland site like Hound Tor, in Devonshire, has been the extent of pre-Conquest settlement.[71] Nevertheless, the thirteenth century, even at Hound Tor, constituted the period of maximum expansion, and this was the shared experience of many moorland hamlets in Devonshire and Cornwall, as in every upland region in the country. The wastes of Dartmoor, as a recent study has shown, were thickly studded with homesteads and hamlets, deserted now but attributable, in the main, to this period.[72] And the lifetime of a farmstead like the one on Dean Moor, towards the southern edge of Dartmoor, coming into being not earlier than the mid-thirteenth century to be abandoned again after less than a century of use, can scarcely have been exceptional.[73] Closely comparable dates of occupation have been suggested, for example, at the diminutive upland settlements of Wroughton Copse, on Fyfield Down in Wiltshire,[74] of Braggington, in Shropshire,[75] and of Millhouse, in Westmorland,[76] although Wroughton Copse may have begun rather earlier and Braggington was a later survival. Meanwhile, down on sea-level, there are similar indications in the archaeological record of a pushing-out of settlement, this time in the drainage and subsequent occupation of the marshes. On the Pevensey Levels, in Sussex, where the monks of Battle had interests to promote, the thirteenth-century reclamation of the marshes is recalled still by the lines of successive sea-walls, strengthened but not otherwise significantly altered by the early-modern enclosers.[77] And, in less favoured areas, the austerity such settlement must frequently have meant is demonstrated by the scanty remains of a shepherd community, found at Red Hill, on Canvey Island, close to the mouth of the Thames. Here, although three hearths were identified, no traces of any permanent structures were recognized by the site's excavators. Furthermore, over a long period of occupation extending from the twelfth to the fifteenth century, the diet of the Canvey Island shepherds, as evidenced by the contents of their middens, showed little variety and no change. What they ate, for the most part, was mutton, with whatever shellfish they could gather on the shore.[78]

As investors, the monks of Battle had been attracted to Pevensey by the promise of rich yields on the reclaimed lands, which they were to use both as arable and as pasture for their sheep. However, they could not have found the resources for such extended campaigns of agricultural improvement had they not been prospering as landowners already. Marshland reclamation is, indeed, only one example of such long-term capital investment, in which the activity of the monks of Battle on the Pevensey Levels was to be matched, in their own areas, by that of Canterbury Cathedral Priory in Kent, of Spalding Priory in Lincolnshire, and of Meaux Abbey on the southern coast of Yorkshire.[79] Another example is the elaborate terracing of hillsides, once thought to have been prehistoric in origin but now recognized, at least in parishes like Worth Matravers, in Dorset, and Mere, in Wiltshire, as one further manifestation of population growth in medieval England and of the drive to cultivate new lands.[80] Both were very expensive.

There have been many explanations of this high level of agricultural enterprise on the part of thirteenth-century landowners, not all of them easy to accept. However, it is at least clear that a high proportion of the greater landowners, both ecclesiastical and lay, was engaged in direct, or demesne, farming from the early thirteenth century, and that the reasons for the very general abandonment of the leasing policies which had characterized the previous century were social as well as economic. There can be little doubt, that is, that the notorious inflation of John's reign (1199–1216), itself very probably resulting

25   Medieval terracing (lynchets) at Mere, in Wiltshire, probably dating to the period of maximum population growth in the late twelfth and thirteenth centuries (R.C.H.M.)

from an influx of silver brought to England as the price of her wool, encouraged the conversion to demesne farming.[81] More money in circulation resulted in higher prices for agricultural products, the consequence being new pressures on landowners both to raise rents (and thereby lose tenants) and to take up the more profitable farming for themselves.[82] Yet the movement towards demesne farming, although certainly hurried by inflation, had not been created by it. Some decades before, the evils of long-term leases had been recognized. Converted insensibly into hereditary tenures, they had diverted the real profits of an expanding economy from the landowner to his irremovable lessee. Thus, on the Canterbury manors, hurried on by papal urging, the recall of lands into demesne had begun already in the late 1170s, and was virtually complete before the death of Archbishop Hubert Walter in 1205.[83] And although the process was not everywhere as rapid, being far from general even at the end of John's reign and in places never undertaken at all,[84] what demesne farming plainly offered to many landowners, attracting them inevitably towards it, was direct access to the profits on their lands just when those profits were burgeoning. One of the things that the archaeology of the period is best able to show us is how these landowners were then moved to dispose of their surpluses.

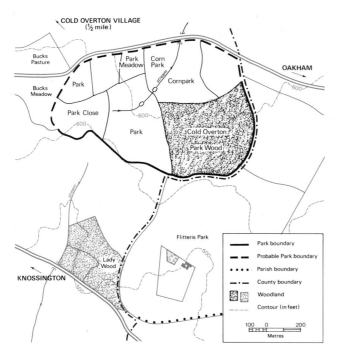

26   A thirteenth-century enclosed deer-park at Cold Overton, Leicestershire (Cantor)

An obvious manifestation of this new wealth, for example, frequently indulged in by the greater thirteenth-century landowners, was the practice of emparking: not the creation of those 'amenity' parks which would come to surround the great houses of the fifteenth century and later, but the setting up of expensively enclosed deer-parks specifically for hunting, usually between 150 and 300 acres in extent and sited at some remove from the manor-house.[85] Obviously, the banks and ditches of such parks as these, if they were to prevent the deer escaping, had always to be very considerable. Where they survive, as they do in large part at Cold Overton, in Leicestershire, a 200-acre deer-park first mentioned in 1269, the banks alone may be as much as 30 feet in width,[86] and it is their sheer scale, of course, which has left them today as much a diagnostic feature of the thirteenth-century landscape as the earthwork castle may be of the twelfth. Certainly, between 1200 and the beginnings of the retreat from demesne farming not more than a century later, deer-parks proliferated on all those estates of which the lord himself might have expected to make personal use, each of the eight known castles of north Staffordshire, for example, having its associated deer-park.[87] Yet the yield on such parks, even taking into account their other uses as a source of timber, for the pannage of pigs and for the occasional pasture of cattle, was always comparatively small. They were obvious luxuries: a manifestation of conspicuous consumption in a period which could clearly afford it. In the later Middle Ages, with less to support them, widespread disparking, at least on the Duchy of Cornwall estates, might be seen as a 'sensible economy'.[88]

Greater use of a manor had been the principal reason for a lord to establish a deer-park there, and such parks were recognized as a needless extravagance only when demesne farming itself had retreated. Similarly, profitable demesne farming, carrying with it, even if only occasionally, the actual physical presence of the lord, was the cause of the considerable programmes of new building on the manors which came to characterize the thirteenth century. Most obviously still, such programmes can be measured in the great stone-built barns supplied, probably within the first half of the thirteenth century, at the granges of a wealthy Cistercian abbey like Beaulieu, the personal foundation of King John. Here, the barn at St Leonard's, not far from the abbey, can bear comparison with any of its kind in the west, while the still intact barn of the same abbey at Great Coxwell, in Berkshire, on one of Beaulieu's more remote estates, while not as large as the roofless St Leonard's, is yet a most remarkable survival.[89] Less spectacularly, there is similar evidence throughout England at just this time of a very general remodelling of the buildings, both agricultural and domestic, at many of the larger manors, getting under way in the late twelfth century and still in progress in the

27   Beaulieu Abbey's thirteenth-century stone barn at Great Coxwell, Berkshire (R.C.H.M.)

28 The Shaftesbury Abbey
barn at Bradford-on-Avon,
Wiltshire, dating to the early
fourteenth century (Kersting)

29 The interior of the
Bradford-on-Avon barn
(R.C.H.M.)

earlier decades of the fourteenth. Such rebuildings, usually accompanied by a substantial increase in scale, have been identified, for example, during recent excavations at Faccombe, in Hampshire,[90] at Tewkesbury, in Gloucestershire,[91] Wintringham, in Huntingdonshire,[92] Weaverthorpe and Low Caythorpe, in East Yorkshire,[93] and Thrislington, County Durham.[94] They were characterized by the greater use of more expensive building materials like stone, by the introduction of individual improvements, among them tiled floors in the chambers and better cobbling in the yards, and by advances in structural carpentry to make more effective use of space.

Leaving aside the barn, the most important of the new buildings at most manorial establishments was the hall, doubling as court and residence of the lord and constituting an obvious nucleus for the estate. On such a building, the reasons for lavish expenditure were not always entirely practical, having to do with a way of life which now, of course, has long since disappeared. When, in the early 1240s, Bishop Grosseteste took it upon himself to advise the countess of Lincoln not to permit the members of her household to eat anywhere but the hall, he reasoned not just that waste would result from such a practice but that it would bring 'no honour to lord or lady'.[95] As the focal point of the 'family' of the manor, the hall was the natural candidate for particular attention, as such being repeatedly rebuilt.

Undoubtedly the earliest hall plan, as it would long remain the most characteristic, was for a single- or double-aisled structure, rarely equipped with

30 A late-twelfth-century stone-built aisled hall at Oakham Castle, Rutland (R.C.H.M.)

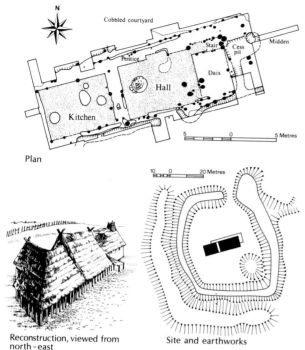

Plan

Reconstruction, viewed from north-east

Site and earthworks

31 A plan and conjectural reconstruction of the mid-twelfth-century manorial buildings at Ellington, in Huntingdonshire (Tebbutt and Rigold)

internal divisions, at any rate in the earlier versions. Aisled buildings, of course, go back into prehistory, and the type was to survive in England at least into the fifteenth century in a series of remarkable aisled-hall houses only recently recognized in the north-east (below, pp. 202–3). Nevertheless, it is only from the late twelfth century that we have our earliest survival of the baronial aisled hall, handsomely finished in stone, at Oakham Castle, in Rutland, while it has been mainly to this period, or even a little later, that our excavated examples have usually proved to belong.[96] One likely mid-twelfth-century specimen, although a date in the third quarter of the century is also considered possible, is the aisled hall, traces of which have been found sealed under the upcast of the moat at Ellington, in Huntingdonshire. The exact dating of the successive phases of the buildings at Ellington is obscure, but the hall seems in its final stages to have been a single-aisled structure, with an aisle, or outshot, on its northern side, and with a terminal outshot at the eastern end, furthest away from the kitchen.[97] Contemporary single-aisled halls, perhaps representing the most common type at lesser manorial establishments in the twelfth century, have been recognized also at Goltho, in Lincolnshire, and Faccombe, in Hampshire. Both show some evidence

51

32   The first-floor hall at Boothby Pagnell, Lincolnshire, built about 1200 (R.C.H.M.)

of the internal divisions which became usual in domestic ranges from the thirteenth century onwards, and both were replaced within a comparatively short space of time by new and better buildings – at Goltho, by a larger and more sophisticated aisled hall dating, probably, to the late twelfth century, and at Faccombe, by a hall rather smaller than the earlier building but reconstructed more expensively in stone.[98]

In a different tradition which may, indeed, have owed something to monastic precedents, the stone-built first-floor hall, relatively exclusive and of which Boothby Pagnell, in Lincolnshire, is the best-known surviving example,[99] was contemporaneously making its appearance. Characteristically supplied with a hall and private chamber, the whole set over a vaulted undercroft and approached by an external stair, such first-floor-hall houses continued to be built throughout the thirteenth century, providing domestic accommodation of a sophisticated standard on many of the more important manors, whether ecclesiastical or lay.[100] But although there is some evidence, to judge from the survivals, that such halls would be preferred by the higher aristocracy over halls of the older ground-floor plan, there is nothing to establish that they ever replaced, in common esteem, the very much larger aisled hall or its more sophisticated successors. In south-west Wales, where the nobility chose to live in first-floor halls, their preference probably originated in the individual circumstances of the twelfth-century conquest and settlement of Pembrokeshire. Elsewhere in Wales, where ground-floor halls predominated, there were no such class distinctions in the choice of building style.[101] Significantly, the first-floor hall of the manor-house at Alsted, in Surrey, built shortly before 1250, was replaced within a generation by a more commodious aisled hall, timber-built on stone foundations, with an annexed stone-built solar block and with a kitchen which, although initially detached, was later joined to the hall itself in a way that further enlarged it.[102] Evidently, what was sought at Alsted, and what the first-floor hall could rarely offer except at considerable expense, was space.

Indeed, it was just this demand for more usable space that brought about the development, from the mid-thirteenth century, of new roof structures of increasing elaboration, their principal purpose being to span wider areas without the interruption of aisles. Undoubtedly, the pace of such developments was forced by the building boom which characterized the thirteenth century, nor has the association of 'base-cruck' halls with the lords of demesne manors, in effect the principal building class of the period, passed unnoticed by recent commentators on this particular building technique.[103] In practice, what was sought was a method of preserving both the width and the strength of the original aisled building, at the same time lifting the whole structure away from the floor, whether on naturally curved principal trusses (the base-cruck) or by the use of tie-beams and hammer-beams to support a roof which, from the late thirteenth century, was often of crown-post form.[104] As techniques improved, the simpler roofing methods found their way down through the social classes, so that cruck-built houses, for example, were erected quite commonly in the fifteenth century by peasants of the more prosperous kind.[105] However, the importance of these developments lies arguably less in the detail of timber-frame construction, absorbing though many have found this study to be,[106] than in the evidence they can yield us of a growing concern, at least among those who felt they could afford it, for an improved standard of domestic accommodation, almost regardless of cost.

A dramatic illustration of this willingness to invest, dating to the early thirteenth century, is the abandonment of the very substantial stone-built manor-house at Wharram Percy, in Yorkshire, put up for the lords of the manor as late as the 1180s and yet deserted for a fresh site away from the village within less than a

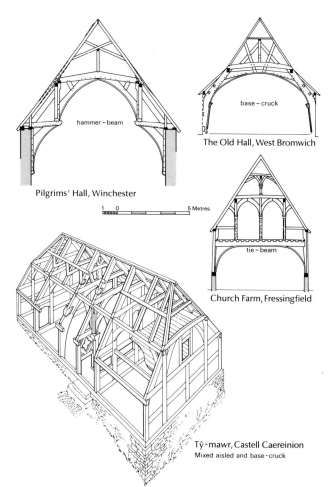

hammer – beam

Pilgrims' Hall, Winchester

base – cruck

The Old Hall, West Bromwich

1 0   5 Metres

tie – beam

Church Farm, Fressingfield

Tŷ-mawr, Castell Caereinion
Mixed aisled and base-cruck

33 Techniques of roof
construction, as used in larger
buildings from the mid-thirteenth
century to clear the floor of aisles
(J. T. Smith and R.C.H.M.)

generation of its construction.[107] Similar desires for more living-space and privacy
may have been behind the approximately contemporary move of the manor-house
at Goltho away from the centre of settlement,[108] while the clearance of houses and
insertion of moats, a century later, at Milton (Hampshire), Ashwell (Hertfordshire), and Northolt (Middlesex) could scarcely have been achieved without
considerable disruption and expense.[109] No doubt, such moves as these must
always have remained exceptional, yet there is evidence everywhere at just this
time of steadily improving domestic standards throughout rural England, and it is
certainly true that, by the fourteenth century, the good-quality tiled floors, the
painted window glass, the fine yard cobbling and well-drained latrines of a

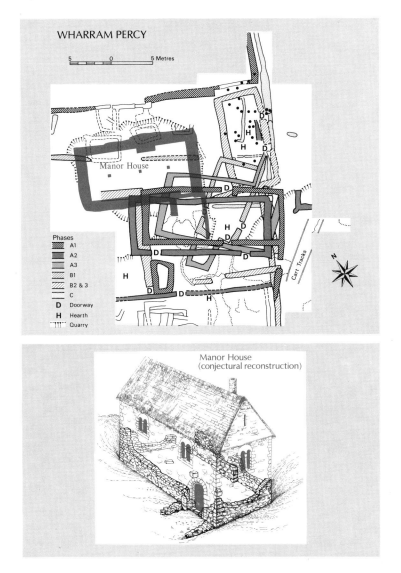

34 A late-twelfth-century manor-house at Wharram Percy, Yorkshire, abandoned shortly after building to be succeeded by peasant long-houses re-using the area over the filled-in basement (Medieval Village Research Group)

manorial site like Kent's Moat, near Birmingham, would have ceased to be the cause of remark.[110] While it would be difficult to parallel elsewhere the very remarkable early-fourteenth-century wall-paintings at Longthorpe Tower, near Peterborough, commissioned by a lay patron of surely unusual sensitivity, the

35 Early-fourteenth-century wall-paintings at Longthorpe Tower, near Peterborough (Salisbury Photo Press)

practice of wall decoration in buildings of this kind, otherwise lacking in distinction, was undoubtedly more common than its survivals.[111] One area, in particular, for which archaeology is yielding increasing evidence of extravagant tastes in both patrons and building in thirteenth-century England, is in the study of tiles and other roof-furniture – those elaborate ridge-tiles, finials and pottery louvers everywhere found on the wealthier sites of the period. Among the more expensive embellishments, for example, of the new domestic range of the Surrey manor-house at Alsted (above, p. 53) was a ventilator finial, perhaps one of several, of a very characteristic elaboration.[112] Like the similarly magnificent pottery louver found in the kitchen area of the contemporary manorial site at Great Easton, in Essex,[113] it belongs to a class of roof ornament that attracted special care in the late thirteenth and early fourteenth centuries, matching the improvements in construction and adornment which we have already seen to have been a characteristic of the roofs themselves. Furthermore, the use of such ornament would scarcely itself have been conceivable had there not been a widespread change in the cladding of roofs, from thatch to tiles and slate. In part a response to fashion, this was also undertaken as deliberate fire-proofing, more worth the thought and expenditure that such precautions would demand now that there was something of high quality to protect. And here was the context, too, for another contemporary innovation, the pottery chimney-pot, unknown before the late thirteenth century.[114]

One of the causes of increased fire-risk, and hence of measures designed to prevent it, was a growing tendency for manorial buildings to be grouped in courtyard complexes, perhaps owing something in this to the force of contemporary monastic example in what had become, over the whole face of Europe, the standard claustral plan. Of course, detached kitchens, through most of the Middle Ages, were built that way as a sensible precaution against fire. There are good excavated examples of these at Goldsborough, in Yorkshire,[115] and at

POTTERY ROOF FURNITURE

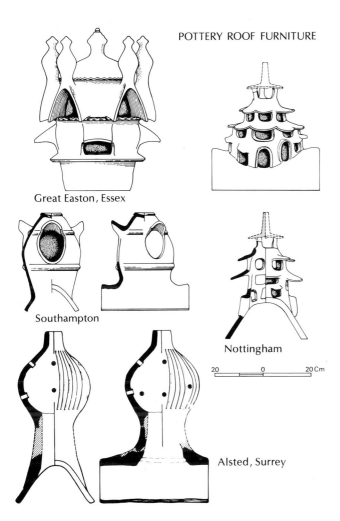

Great Easton, Essex

Southampton

Nottingham

Alsted, Surrey

36 A ventilator finial (bottom left) and pottery louvers from sites at Alsted, Great Easton, Southampton and Nottingham (Dunning)

Wintringham, in Huntingdonshire,[116] with the remarkable survival of a large part of such a building at Weoley, near Birmingham, preserved under the upcast of the late-thirteenth-century moat.[117] But at Weoley, the almost random scatter of the earlier buildings on the site, with their linking pentices or covered corridors, was not repeated in their modernized successors. Such a scatter, seen again at a thirteenth-century Kentish site like Joyden's Wood,[118] was already becoming less usual than the more orderly distribution, on three sides of a courtyard, of the chapel, chamber, hall, kitchen and gatehouse of another contemporary building complex, the royal hunting-lodge at Writtle.[119] One particularly striking

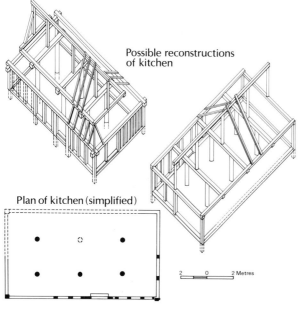

Possible reconstructions of kitchen

Plan of kitchen (simplified)

2   0   2 Metres

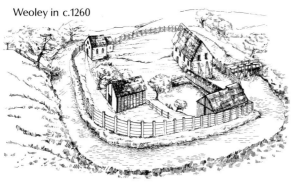

Weoley in c.1260

37 The dispersed scatter of the thirteenth-century buildings at Weoley, near Birmingham, with suggested alternative reconstructions of the contemporary timber kitchen (Oswald and J. T. Smith)

58

demonstration of the form such buildings, during the thirteenth century, were ever more likely to take, is the manor-house at Jacobstow, in Cornwall, formerly the manor of Penhallam and held in succession by the Cardinhams and the Champernownes, two of the county's wealthiest families. At Jacobstow, the late-twelfth-century stone-built chamber block, a sophisticated two-storey building similar in plan to the more common first-floor hall, was retained through the later rebuildings of the thirteenth century, to be incorporated in a range of domestic apartments which would eventually fill the whole interior of the original twelfth-century moat, surrounding a central courtyard. Abandoned before the mid-fourteenth century and untampered-with after that date, the buildings at Jacobstow were preserved, at foundation level, as an unusually complete example

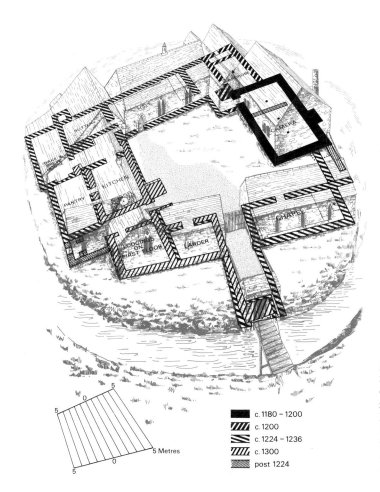

■	c. 1180 – 1200
▨	c. 1200
▤	c. 1224 – 1236
▨	c. 1300
▨	post 1224

5 Metres

38 A conjectural reconstruction from the excavated evidence of the manorial buildings of Penhallam at Jacobstow, in Cornwall, mainly of the thirteenth century and exhibiting a compact courtyard plan (Beresford)

of the standard of accommodation a pre-plague gentry family could reasonably have come to expect.[120]

A restricted site, penned in by the moat at Jacobstow, would have been one of the reasons, in addition to fashion, why the buildings should have taken that form. However, where there were less constraints on building, the domestic court in a manorial complex might be one element alone in a very much more generous courtyard plan which took in additionally the full range of stables, barns and workshops. A fine example of just such a plan has been excavated recently at South Witham, a Templar estate and later preceptory which would have served as an administrative centre for all the order's possessions within its area, including parts of Lincolnshire, Leicestershire and Rutland. In 1308, the Templar estates in England were sequestered by the Crown, to be followed four years later by the brutal suppression of the order. But South Witham had already suffered a prolonged decay of profits, and it was probably for this reason that the Hospitallers did nothing to revive it when, after 1312, the estate centre and its buildings came permanently into their hands. Just as at Jacobstow, it was this early abandonment of the buildings at South Witham that has kept them unusually complete. Set about a great court, they had included a gatehouse on the north, a fine range of barns on the west, a domestic complex with hall, chambers, chapel and kitchen on the south-east, and a workshop area, with its ovens and kilns, on the east. Beyond the great court, towards the river, the former preceptory had had a water-mill and fish-ponds of its own.[121]

South Witham, with its many agricultural enterprises, would have required a large permanent staff. We know, for example, that comparable Cistercian farm centres in the mid-thirteenth century were carrying staffs of anything between ten and twenty servants in addition to the supervisory lay brethren charged with the running of these granges, and we may suppose that a proportion, at least, of the labour force on such establishments must have been found accommodation in the court.[122] Certainly, on the Merton College manor at Cuxham, in Oxfordshire, so long as it remained in demesne, the members of the household, or *familia*, of the manor were expected to reside within its court, for they might be fined if discovered to have slept anywhere else.[123] At Witham it is hard to see where such labourers and their families might have been accommodated, and it is possible that they lived at the village near by. However, the concentration of the Templars' domestic range at Witham, with its own small court tucked into a corner of the great preceptory enclosure, echoes once again the common monastic practice, the cloistered monk turning his back on the noise and activity of the farmyard by which he was sustained. Thus the home farm of the Augustinian canons of

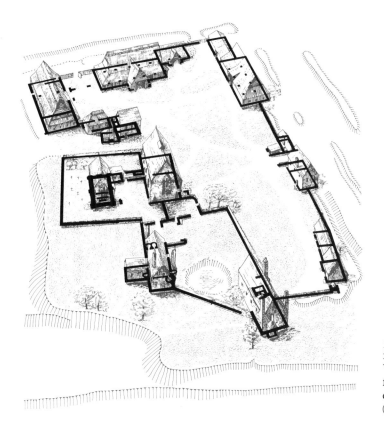

39   The domestic and
farm buildings at South
Witham, in Lincolnshire,
from the evidence of
excavated foundations
(Mayes and Goodband)

Waltham, just to the north of the abbey church and cloister, was grouped away
from the monastery, concentrated in a close of its own,[124] while Cistercian
granges, not uncommonly, were equipped both with an inner and an outer court,
the former preserving its privacy.[125] Presumably, it was in the outer court that the
farm servants, or *famuli*, usually lived, this being as true of a lay manor-house like
Cuxham, in Oxfordshire, as it must have been of Merthyrgeryn, a grange of
Tintern, or Ropsley, a grange of Vaudey, both noted for the size of their
enclosures.[126]

Such coincidence of lay and monastic practice, perhaps especially on something
like the ground-plan of a manor, might seem a little less surprising were we to
recall how much of England, by the mid-thirteenth century, had come into
monastic hands. It is true that the great flood of pious donations to the Church, so
much a characteristic of the previous century, was now over. However, almost
every landowner in thirteenth-century England would have had a man of religion

40 The building of the Tower of Babel; English, *c.* 1300 (B.M., Egerton 1894, f.5v)

41 Masons building a wall to the direction of their patron, the king; French, fourteenth-century (B.M., Cotton Nero E2 (pt. i), f.73)

as his neighbour, nor were the religious houses of the period, with their many financial advantages, inactive in the market for land. Battle Abbey, by the purchase and resumption of lands in the period 1240 to 1305, achieved during this time an almost six-fold increase in rents at its own borough of Battle, with comparable gains, this time at the expense of the Sussex gentry, in its surrounding region, or *banlieu*.[127] And while it was precisely to protect the interests of the lay landowner, by forbidding further gifts of land to the Church, that the Statute of Mortmain was enacted in 1279, there is little to establish that Edward I's legislation achieved its desired effect.[128] In every manner of property transaction, the great advantage of the religious community lay in the perspectives its estate managers enjoyed. When Westminster Abbey, after the fire of 1298, embarked on the appropriation of the parish church of Longdon, in Worcestershire, as a means of recouping its losses, its initial expenses, including the cost of a licence obtained from the king, were very high. Yet in the long run the investment, as the abbot and his obedientiaries must have known, was sure to be a profitable one. By the early 1340s and continually thereafter, the receipts from Longdon Church, bringing in annually between £30 and £40, provided the basis for a permanent repair fund at the Abbey.[129]

If the abbot of Westminster could bide his time, it was because he was sure of the succession at his abbey. And it was this large view of a secure future, common to the monks especially, that everywhere promoted a scale of building at the monastic houses which few laymen of the time could equal. Many communities, it is true, whether through over-ambitious building programmes or more simply through their own financial ineptitude, ran themselves seriously into debt.[130] But such were the resources of the monastic houses, and so steady was the interest of their patrons, that few went under absolutely in the thirteenth century while, for many, the level of capital investment in their buildings would never again be as high. The great decagonal chapter-house of the Cluniac monks of Pontefract, for example, was a work of the thirteenth century. With other major rebuildings of the east cloister range, it probably accounted for a large part of the debt of over £2000 which the priory had built up for itself by 1267. Yet by 1279 already the debt had been reduced to no more than £233, and one of the other things noted that year by the official Visitors from the mother church at Cluny was the fine state of the buildings at Pontefract Priory, some of which were certainly new.[131]

Undoubtedly, one of the more important contributions of archaeology to the study of the monasteries of this period has been the demonstration of works like these continually in progress at houses up and down the land. As at Pontefract, rebuilding of the chapter-houses at Newminster, in Northumberland, Elstow, in

Bedfordshire, and Norton, in Cheshire, was undertaken within the thirteenth century. It was in the late thirteenth century that the chapter-house at Newminster was modified, following the completion of the main conventual ranges earlier in the century and after major programmes of work in the late twelfth.[132] At Norton, while the priory church itself was progressively enlarged, the size of the chapter-house was doubled, seen there, as it was at Elstow too, as one element alone of a continuing campaign of improvements to the cloister which might persist well into the fourteenth century.[133]

42   The fourteenth-century cloister of Gloucester Abbey, now incorporated in the cathedral (R.C.H.M.)

64

43   John of Wisbech's Lady Chapel at Ely, noted particularly for the quality of its fourteenth-century stone-carving (R.C.H.M.)

Elstow was a house of Benedictine nuns, and many communities of its kind suffered, round about 1300, the severe overcrowding that was one of the causes of the financial difficulties which few entirely escaped.[134] Nevertheless, overcrowding was not the only reason for the enlargement of the conventual buildings even at such relatively impoverished nunneries; at the wealthier communities, in the great possessioner houses, we may doubt that it could ever have been the most important. A perfectly natural ambition of every great abbot, and of many of his obedientiaries too, was to leave a memorial in stone. Thus the names of John of Wisbech and Alan of Walsingham are still associated with major works at the cathedral priory at Ely, completed in the first half of the fourteenth century, while their contemporary, John of Wigmore, and his successors, Adam of Stanton and Thomas of Horton, are as well known for their work on the choir and then the cloister of the abbey church at Gloucester.[135] At Ely, John of Wisbech's great work was the Lady Chapel, remarkable for its stone-carving and for its unusual situation almost detached from the church, but yet a building very much of its time. Lady chapels, reflecting the contemporary cult of the Virgin, were a very common addition to both cathedral and monastic churches of the thirteenth and fourteenth centuries, being building projects of wide appeal for which funds were readily obtainable. Dated 1315, the text of the agreement for the building of such a chapel has survived for Lacock Abbey, in Wiltshire, a house of Augustinian canonesses which, although not the poorest of its order, was not over-wealthy either. In point of fact, the building of the chapel was financed not by the canonesses themselves but by John Bluet, lord of Lackham, their nearest wealthy neighbour. It was to measure 59 feet by 25½ feet, and would cost at least two hundred marks, which seems to have been the amount advanced. To be completed within twelve years, the work was to include the knocking-out of arches between the church and the new chapel, taking care not to endanger the church vaulting. There was to be an appropriately lavish roof structure, leaded on the outside 'bien e covenablement', and panelled and painted within.[136]

Clearly, lay patronage would always remain important to the monastic houses, and the scale of the works at many communities continued to depend, in the final resort, on the number and the wealth of their friends. Abbot Thokey, who had been John of Wigmore's immediate predecessor at Gloucester, had had the foresight to collect the remains of the murdered Edward II from Berkeley and to bury them, with great ceremony, at his abbey. Within a few years, the pilgrims, attracted in great numbers to Edward's miracle-working shrine, financed the rebuilding of the choir at Gloucester, largely determining its new form.[137] In just the same way, it had been the cult of Thomas Becket, the murdered archbishop, that had provided funds for the reconstruction, many years before, of Canterbury Cathedral, while other great houses, all over the country, found martyrs of their own to build up a profitable tourist industry, commemorated still in the many pilgrim souvenirs found on medieval sites.[138] However, of more immediate effect in the funding of works, compressing activity, for obvious reasons, within the lifetime of an individual donor, was the personal involvement of a single patron, in particular if he should happen to be the king. John, for example, was to be a great patron of Beaulieu Abbey, in Hampshire, as Richard of Cornwall, his son, was of another Cistercian house at Hailes, in Gloucestershire, and neither community would have accumulated the wealth that it did without the continuing concern and benevolence of its founder. Yet there would be no royal patron, with the possible exception of Henry VI in the mid-fifteenth century, to equal John's eldest son, Henry III, whose excessive expenditure on Westminster Abbey became, in his own time, notorious. From 1245, when he began the work, till his death in 1272,

44 The shrine of Edward the Confessor at Westminster Abbey, formerly decorated, by order of Henry III, with marble inlays in the Italian manner (R.C.H.M.)

Henry III spent well over £40,000 on Westminster, the approximate equivalent of the state's annual income through two full years of his reign.[139] It was very much a personal enterprise, both a fitting shrine for Edward the Confessor and a lavish masterpiece of the new Gothic architecture which, in contemporary France, was inspiring such remarkable achievements. And there were to be many personal touches in its building. With other things, Henry had seen the lectern in the chapter-house of the rich Benedictines at St Albans, and on 23 September 1249, while staying at Windsor, he ordered the making of a 'lectern to be placed in the new chapter-house at Westminster similar to the one in the chapter-house at St Albans, and if possible even more handsome and beautiful'.[140] Three years later, hurrying the work on his favourite project, Henry directed the master of his works at Westminster to 'have all the marble work raised this winter that can be done without danger', being anxious then, as he would remain until his death, 'that the works of the church of Westminster should be greatly speeded up'.[141]

In the event, the completion of the nave at Westminster, halted by Henry's death, was to take another quarter-millennium. And what could happen when the son of a founder took no interest in the works of his father is illustrated almost as well by the sad fate of Edward I's own pious foundation at Vale Royal Abbey, in Cheshire, construction beginning there in 1277, almost at the start of his reign. Characteristically, Edward's plans for this new Cistercian community were ambitious, and the finance he provided there was generous. It was his intention that the church at Vale Royal should be more magnificent than that at his grandfather's foundation at Beaulieu and considerably larger than his uncle's

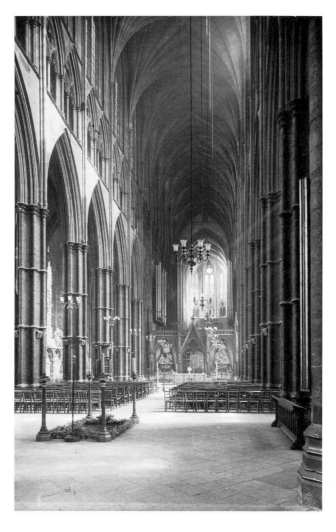

45   The nave at Westminster Abbey, to a design carefully considered by Henry III (R.C.H.M.)

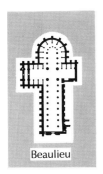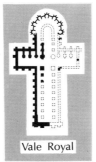

Beaulieu   Hailes   Vale Royal

46 Ambitious competitive planning at the royal abbey churches of Beaulieu (John), Hailes (Richard of Cornwall), and Vale Royal (Edward I) (*King's Works*)

church at Hailes. With a community of a hundred monks, Edward's monastery was to be the greatest of its order in his own kingdom and one of the largest in Europe. But the Welsh wars intervened. In just the year that work at Vale Royal began, Edward simultaneously launched the great programme of royal castle-building in Wales which was to rob the new abbey of both its masons and finance, eventually helping to exclude it from the king's attention altogether. In 1290, although we do not know the precise circumstances of the decision, the king's agent at Vale Royal was informed that Edward had 'ceased to concern himself with the works of that church, and henceforth will have nothing more to do with them'.[142]

Edward II, very briefly, took up his father's patronage of the works 'so nobly and royally begun'. However, his own interest had settled elsewhere in the building of the friary church at Kings Langley, next to a cherished manor, and the works at Vale Royal languished, to be resumed in due course by Edward, the Black Prince, but never to be fully completed. Indeed, that well-known lament of the abbot of Vale Royal, declaring the assets of his house to the then abbot of Morimond, brings home the sad lesson of over-reliance on the continuing generosity of one benefactor. The abbot noted in 1336:

We have a very large church commenced by the King of England at our first foundation, but by no means finished. For at the beginning he built the stone walls, but the vaults remain to be erected together with the roof and the glass and other ornaments. Moreover the cloister, chapter-house, dormitory, refectory, and other monastic offices still remain to be built in proportion to the church; and for the accomplishment of this the revenues of our house are insufficient.[143]

69

47 The recently excavated wine-cellar at Kings Langley, a favourite manor-house of Edward II (Neal and Brown)

In the great gale of 19 October 1360, the successive royal patrons of Vale Royal paid the inevitable penalty for their dilatoriness. The nave collapsed, its columns falling 'like trees uprooted by the wind'.[144]

Edward II had chosen Dominican friars to tend the mausoleum of his favourite, Piers Gaveston, which was how he conceived Kings Langley, and Edward again became well known as the most generous patron of the Austin friars, otherwise the Hermit Friars of St Augustine.[145] Similarly Henry III, his grandfather, had joined readily with other noble patrons in welcoming the first Austin friars to England over half a century before,[146] and had done much already to smooth the initial settlement of the Friars Preacher and Minor, the Dominicans and the Franciscans, for whom he personally had financed the building of houses at Canterbury and Reading.[147] Yet, over the country as a whole, the style of the friars was very different from this. Essentially, they were to direct their preaching mission at the under-served communities of the greater boroughs, and it was there, among the wealthier burgesses, that they usually found their patrons. Over the centuries, this special relationship, established on arrival with the burgesses, continued to serve them well.

Practices differed between the orders, and it was no part, certainly, of the Franciscans' intention to set themselves up in such handsome buildings as were pressed upon them, for example, by their royal patron, Henry III, at Reading, or by the burgesses at contemporary Southampton.[148] Nevertheless, those cottages of mud-plaster and of wood which St Francis had urged upon his first followers were suited only to the migrant life, temporary even with the Friars Minor and rejected by the Friars Preacher from their very beginnings. In friary buildings of the later Middle Ages, one survival being at the Kentish, formerly Carmelite, house at Aylesford,[149] the distinctive feature of the so-called 'undershot' cloister, with a dormitory or individual chambers extending over the top of it, goes back as far as the original Dominican establishment at Toulouse. Here, when Dominic had acquired for his followers in 1216 the church of St Romain, a 'cloister was immediately built, with cells adequate for study and sleeping above it',[150] and certainly the work in which the Dominicans were then engaged, being the seeking-out and combating of heresy, required such facilities for private devotions and study. Equally characteristic of friary buildings, proceeding directly from the

48   The fifteenth-century 'undershot' cloister at the Carmelite friary at Aylesford, in Kent (Kersting)

particular quality of their work, was the enlarged 'preaching' nave to be noticed at many of their churches. At Coventry, the great church of the Carmelites, or Whitefriars, built in the second half of the fourteenth century when the borough's prosperity was still growing, resembled nothing so much as a cathedral. With its impressive aisled preaching nave, it had the slender central tower and narrow choir familiar also in many lesser friary churches, while under the choir stalls, cut into the floor, it possessed the additional refinement of resonance passages, a metre square in section, to develop the quality of the singing.[151] An exact reversal of the Coventry plan, at Edward II's Dominican friary at Kings Langley, usefully emphasizes the more ordinary purpose of friary churches in the boroughs. Kings Langley, unusually, was a rural friary, with little in the way of a permanent congregation and no need for a preaching nave. As the training school of the Dominican province in England, the requirements of the community at Kings Langley, supported by the king's generosity, were for a spacious choir, twice as long and half again as wide as the unusually stunted nave.[152]

This popularity of the friars among lay patrons, continuing in the boroughs as long as the friars remained there, promoted a multiplication of orders during the thirteenth century which was brought to a halt only in 1274 by the prohibitions of the Council of Lyons. By this time, however, the Franciscans, the Dominicans, and the Austin friars had already been joined in England by the Carmelites, the Crutched Friars (Friars of the Holy Cross), the Trinitarians (Red Friars), and the short-lived orders of Pied Friars (Friars of the Blessed Mary) and Friars of the

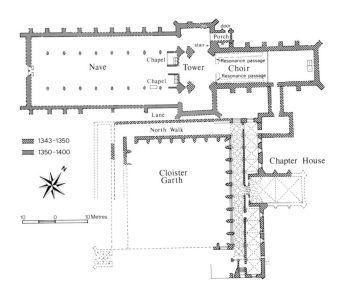

49   The great church and cloister of the Carmelites, or Whitefriars, of Coventry, with its impressive preaching nave and characteristic central tower (Woodfield)

Sack (Friars of the Penance of Jesus Christ).[153] With few exceptions, and with widespread popular support, the friaries enjoyed a building boom which, while concentrating particularly in the last three decades of the thirteenth century, stretched into the fourteenth century as well, and was over by about 1320.[154] Yet, clearly, they could not have achieved this without arousing the enmity of their rivals both in the secular church and in the monastic, and they quarrelled fiercely even amongst themselves. It was only on Bishop Grosseteste's reassurance that alms-giving, in the common experience, had proved a 'living spring which pours forth waters all the more abundantly the more they are drawn' that the Dominicans of Chester agreed to the settling there, not very long after, of Franciscans.[155] And although the bishop was right in the event, both houses surviving without difficulty, there was to come a time, too, when the friars' critics everywhere would discover a 'fly and a friar falling in every dish', and the reasons for hostility were plentiful. High on the list of such causes of discontent, in particular in the secular church, was the growing popularity of the friaries, almost from their inception, as places of burial for the dead, thus unfairly attracting to themselves the donations of relatives and friends, with the legacies of the faithful departed. On friary sites as excavated today, closely packed burials, both within the churches and in the graveyards immediately outside them, have proved an invariable discovery. They have been found, for example, at the Franciscan houses at Northampton and Bristol, with similar evidence at Newcastle and Chelmsford, this time at Dominican friaries.[156] Just a few years ago, massed skeletons were revealed in the foundation trenches of a new office block now erected to the west of Southampton's friary, between the former church and the main street of the town. It was there precisely that the friary cemetery, so much in demand, had had to be extended in 1382, to include a new street-front plot rather more than a hundred feet square.[157]

In the secular Church, both the initial encouragement given to the friars and, in the longer term, the effectiveness of the opposition to them, may best be seen in the context of what has been described as a 'managerial revolution', taking place in the Church during the early thirteenth century and to some extent already in the late twelfth.[158] This managerial shake-up commonly took the form of a thorough-going reorganization of the bishop's household, his estates and his courts-of-law. But it spread down also through the ranks of the clerical hierarchy, taking effect, in due course, in the parishes. Inevitably, surviving records of the period tend to bring out either the faults of the clergy, as corrected in the episcopal courts, or their quality as administrators, whether serving those courts or carrying out other more general business of the diocese. However, there can be no reasonable doubt that, over the clergy as a whole, standards were rising appreciably. One of the principal concerns of the Fourth Lateran Council of 1215, in a general programme of reform, was an insistence on an improvement in the quality of the parish clergy, to be achieved both by the setting of higher educational standards and by measures to guarantee individual incomes. And although, of course, God's vineyard would always have its weeds, the labours there of a man like William Melton, archbishop of York from 1318 and later treasurer of England, constituted yet impressive testimony of what the Church might still, at her best, achieve.[159] In the same province, a century earlier, Archbishop Walter de Gray had had many of the qualities of William Melton, being likewise remembered locally as an effective administrator while holding national office also as chancellor and regent of England. He had shared, too, Archbishop Melton's high sense of the dignity of his rank and office, and it was in keeping with this that he should have made handsome provision for his burial below a fine sculptured monument in that part of the cathedral for the building of which he had probably himself been responsible, the south transept. Archbishop de Gray died, ripe in years, in 1255, and was buried with great pomp in the vestments of his office, with ring and staff, chalice and paten, under a coffin-lid finely painted with an elaborate representation of himself. The opening and restoration, a decade ago, of Walter de Gray's tomb, together with that of Archbishop Godfrey de Ludham, his next-successor-but-one, stands out as perhaps the most spectacular and rewarding archaeological enterprise published in recent years.[160]

Less dramatically, certainly, but on a very much wider scale, monumental sculpture in thirteenth-century England became an important industry, testifying to the strength of the faith. From the twelfth century and even before, the stone-carvers of the Barnack school, working on the fine oolitic limestone of their local quarries, had been supplying decorated cross-slabs to parish churches throughout East Anglia and the East Midlands.[161] And their efforts were paralleled elsewhere by similar stone-carving industries, reaching a peak in productivity during the late thirteenth century, while population remained high and before the brasses and alabaster effigies of the later Middle Ages could begin to dent and take over their markets.[162] Just as surely, the wealth displayed in the commissioning of funerary monuments of an ever-increasing sophistication was reflected, too, in the extension of many parish churches. Barnack itself lay in the very heart of one of the most thickly populated concentrations of good agricultural land, known for its 'rich galaxy' of churches.[163] Both here and, almost equally, across the face of England as a whole, the parish churches which had already been

50 The tomb and monument of Walter de Gray, archbishop of York (1216–55), in the south transept of York Minster (R.C.H.M.)

51 The partly embalmed body of Godfrey de Ludham, archbishop of York (1258–65), as buried at York Minster with his pastoral staff, chalice, paten, and ring (R.C.H.M.)

75

rebuilt in the later twelfth century (above, p. 28) grew still further in the thirteenth. The church of All Saints at Wigston Magna, the religious centre of a prospering and populous Leicestershire village, was reconstructed very extensively in the decades round about 1300, sharing in this the common experience, at just that date, of a great many of the churches of the county.[164] And the same was the case, too, at Thurleigh, in Bedfordshire, rebuilt almost entirely in the late thirteenth century; at Wharram Percy (Yorkshire) and Angmering (Sussex), sprouting north and south aisles respectively in that century; or at St Mary-le-Port, in Bristol, with mid-century aisles both on the north and the south, and with a second extension to the chancel. At each of these churches, significantly enough, there had been some earlier expansion in the twelfth century.[165]

Inevitably, such improvements and extensions to the fabric were accompanied at many churches by new internal decorative schemes. On the floors, that is, the glazed and painted floor-tiles first coming into use at the greater churches and cathedrals earlier in the thirteenth century had reached the parish church before the end of it.[166] Although rarely surviving the burials, heating-schemes and general refloorings of later years, such a pavement, dating to the early fourteenth century, has been preserved in part at the parish church of Northill, in

52 Wharram Percy Church, Yorkshire, showing the blocked arcading of the thirteenth-century north aisle, demolished in the later Middle Ages (R.C.H.M.)

76

Bedfordshire, relaid now in the vestry.[167] At Meesden, in Hertfordshire, the remarkable contemporary tile-mosaic pavement, now before the altar, may well be the best such survival in the country.[168] Scarcely more intact are the wall-paintings with which an individual monied benefactor might beautify his church,

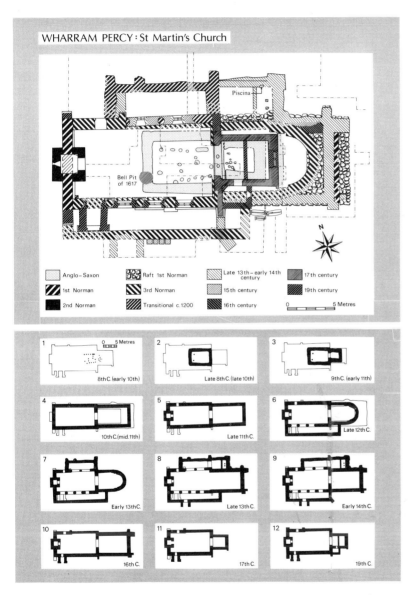

53   The plan-development of Wharram Percy Church, showing maximum expansion in the central Middle Ages before the onset of plague (Medieval Village Research Group)

while doing honour, too, to an especially favoured saint. Belonging to a very much older tradition than the tiled pavement, such paintings have suffered almost as badly over the years. Yet, at a number of parish churches still, there are surviving depictions of St Catherine of Alexandria, as martyred on her wheel, recalling a popular cult which had reached its peak in the early fourteenth century.[169] And more familiar even than St Catherine was St Christopher, patron saint of travellers, whose traditional placing on the wall immediately opposite the church's principal door was so important to departing parishioners that his figure might be allowed, as it was for example at Peakirk, in Northamptonshire, to interrupt an elaborate early-fourteenth-century cyclical representation of the Passion.[170]

At Peakirk, the figure of St Christopher is accompanied, as was not infrequently the case, by a portrait of the painting's donor, kneeling by his side. And it was probably just such another individual benefactor, lately returned from a pilgrimage in Spain, who financed the unusually complete St James Cycle still to

54 A fourteenth-century wall-painting of St Christopher, over a seventeenth-century text, at Brook Church, in Kent (R.C.H.M.)

55 Part of the unusually
complete early-thirteenth-
century St James Cycle of wall-
paintings at Stoke Orchard
Church, Gloucestershire
(R.C.H.M.)

be seen at the church of Stoke Orchard, in Gloucestershire.[171] There is nothing
remarkable about the structure of the church at Stoke Orchard, being work of the
late twelfth century on an altogether unimpressive scale. Yet this first complete
decorative scheme, conceived and executed in a remote Gloucestershire village and
dedicated to a saint popular throughout Europe, can tell us much of the success of
the Church in transcending cultural frontiers. Stoke Orchard, early in the
thirteenth century and whatever the accident that brought it there, found itself in
the mainstream of European religious experience. In contrast, Peakirk Church
retains its original dedication to the obscure St Pega, entirely unknown elsewhere,
who is thought to have been the sister of that other very *English* saint, the eighth-
century St Guthlac of Crowland. It belongs, of course, to an earlier tradition, but
also one which is very much more insular.

One of the qualities of the Stoke Orchard paintings is a distinct Byzantine influence, having parallels with contemporary work, similarly influenced, at the Palace of Westminster, commissioned by Henry III. And it is broadly true that many of the architectural innovations of thirteenth-century England were direct borrowings, if not usually from as far afield as Constantinople, at least from central France. Exceptionally, such a borrowing might be virtually complete, as at the house at Everswell, by Woodstock, built in the Sicilian manner with cloistered courts and pools for Rosamund Clifford, mistress of Henry II.[172] More commonly, the exoticism of 'Rosamund's Bower' was little more than echoed in those imported techniques, quickly copied in this country, which everywhere came to influence the pattern of English building. It is very probable, for example, that the skills that eventually yielded such local products as the tile-mosaic pavement at Meesden (above, p. 77) had been learnt originally from Italian mosaicists, brought to England for work of particular importance like that on the shrine of St Thomas at Canterbury, erected as far back as 1220.[173] And it is certain that the king, especially, was never reluctant to make use of the services of foreign craftsmen in his own building projects, which would then have their influence outside. That lectern, for example, at Westminster Abbey, which was to be 'even more handsome and beautiful' than its original model at St Albans (above, p. 67), was entrusted to the skills of a Flemish carver, Master John of St Omer.[174] Similarly outdoing the monks of Canterbury on what they had provided for St Thomas, Henry III commissioned in 1269 a Roman marbler to decorate the base of the shrine of St Edward, which was to be the centre-piece of the abbey church at Westminster, itself conceived on such a scale as to rival all contemporary royal works in France.[175]

Westminster Abbey, in its own day, was an immensely influential building. And so also were the king's other works, wherever his interest was directly involved and his expenditure proportionately great. It is probable that the great circular tiled pavement which was such a feature of Henry's personal chapel at Clarendon Palace, near Salisbury, was modelled on the similar pavement, slightly earlier in date, at the French abbey at Cunault. However, it is significant that the tiles of the Clarendon pavement were made locally on the site of the palace itself, as were the other tiles from Clarendon's luxuriously appointed chambers, and there is no doubt that the skills perfected in the king's works at Clarendon lay behind the spread of the tile-making industry for which Wiltshire, within the thirteenth century, became a centre.[176] Among the tiles since found at Clarendon have been individual specimens carrying scenes of the duel between Richard and Saladin, and it is evident that Henry himself became particularly interested in crusading

56 Floor-tiles from the queen's chamber at Clarendon Palace, near Salisbury, dating to the mid-thirteenth century (B.M.)

57 A large excavated building at Ludgershall Castle, in Wiltshire, probably one end of Henry III's great hall (Addyman)

themes after he had taken the Cross, being the vow to crusade, early in 1250. Later in that year, the work on the so-called 'Antioch Chamber', below the chapel at Clarendon, was commissioned to include mural paintings of the siege of Antioch and of the Richard and Saladin duel; under these, gilded metal stars and crescents were pinned to the wainscot, brilliant on a field of green.[177]

The wide scatter of the buildings at Clarendon, with their linking covered passage-ways, made it a palace rather in the older fashion than the new. However, the comfort of its brightly painted, well-heated and lavishly paved interiors was something still exceptional in northern Europe, and it helped to set new standards. At the king's neighbouring castle of Ludgershall, the works of this period were to

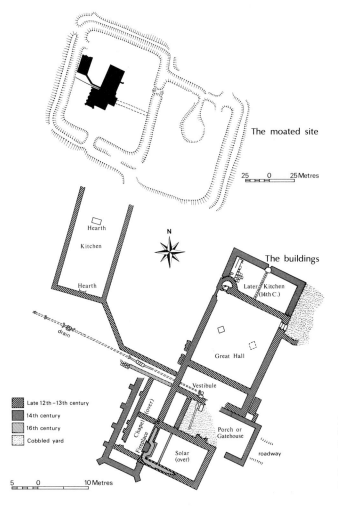

58 The bishop of Hereford's manor-house at Prestbury, Gloucestershire, with its detached kitchen linked to the main buildings by a pentice (O'Neil)

transform it radically from the original fortress of the post-Conquest kings into the comfortable manor-house and royal hunting-lodge which recent excavations have laid bare.[178] And the effect of rising standards and expectations on the domestic architecture of the contemporary magnate class is as well illustrated by the contrast between two episcopal manors: Prestbury, in Gloucestershire, a long-established demesne manor of the bishops of Hereford, and Acton Burnell, in Shropshire, the country house of Robert Burnell, bishop of Bath and Wells. Of course, there was nothing especially cheerless or uncomfortable about Prestbury, which was the favourite country retreat, after Ledbury, of its bishops. Indeed, we know from the surviving domestic accounts of a Christmas spent there in 1289 by Richard de Swinfield, then bishop of Hereford, that the style of life at such an establishment could have been, even by our own standards, very lavish.[179] Nevertheless, the buildings excavated within the main moat at Prestbury, with their great hall and adjoining solar, and with a remote detached kitchen linked to the main living quarters, after the style of Clarendon, by a long covered passage-way, or pentice, appear distinctly old-fashioned.[180] In contrast, Acton Burnell, much of which survives, was a very advanced, centrally planned building, entirely different from Prestbury in the evidence it gives that the bishop's convenience had been closely considered in the adoption of unconventional internal arrangements, specifically to protect his privacy. Robert Burnell, in addition to his episcopal office, was chancellor of England and the long-time associate of Edward I since well before his accession. An outstandingly gifted administrator, he was accustomed to do much of his business at the manor-house which, in the form in which it was rebuilt in the mid-1280s, kept him well clear of his suitors. Whereas at Prestbury the bishop's private apartments had been placed, as usual, in a block at the end of the hall, they were set at Acton Burnell on the third floor, protected from the turmoil of the ground-floor offices by the first-floor hall, chapel and antechamber of the bishop's immediate household. From this antechamber, a circular stair in the south-west tower led up another floor to Burnell's great chamber, with his bedchamber off it, and with a private closet, or latrine. Anybody seeking a private audience with the chancellor would have had to approach him through at least two filters, and probably through many more.[181]

Acton Burnell, for many years, has been loosely described as a 'castle', and although defence, clearly, was never its principal purpose, its characteristics nevertheless were those of the private fortress, at least as such fortresses in contemporary England had by this stage very commonly become. For some decades, in the second half of the twelfth century and in the opening years of the

59 Acton Burnell Castle, Shropshire, built for Robert Burnell, bishop of Bath and Wells
(1275–92) and chancellor of England (R.C.H.M.)

thirteenth, castle-building had continued to make important technical advances.
With increasing use of stone, it had adapted designs to English conditions that had
originally been perfected in the Holy Land, and it had been pushed forward in this
by the drive of energetic castle-builders like Henry II and John. But John, too, was
to become known in his time as a castle-*breaker*. And it was just this combination
of royal initiatives in the remodelling of existing strongholds with the
development of the military resources and skills to prevent such practices in
others, that brought about the decline of the lesser baronial castle, too expensive to
improve up to the standard now required for defence. Already in the 1160s, the
new position had been shown very exactly in the direct confrontation occurring
then between Henry II and Hugh Bigod, earl of Norfolk, shortly afterwards a
leader of the baronial rebellion of 1173–4. The only completely new castle, that is,
to be built in England by Henry II was Orford Castle, in Suffolk, put up by the
king at great expense during the years 1166 to 1172, specifically to counter the
influence of Bigod in Suffolk and to confront his family fortress at Framlingham.

60　Henry II's polygonal keep at Orford Castle, Suffolk, built in the late 1160s as a counter to the Bigod fortress at Framlingham (Hallam Ashley)

61   The late-twelfth-century shell keep built by Roger Bigod at Framlingham to replace the earthwork castle slighted by Henry II (Aerofilms)

On the failure of the rebellion and the earl's submission, Framlingham was demolished, only to be rebuilt again, after the death of Henry, by Roger, Hugh Bigod's son. Caught up once more in the baronial discontents of which the Bigods, traditionally, were leaders, Framlingham was one of the remaining private castles surrendered, after no more than a token resistance, to John in 1216. John's reputation as an artist of siege warfare, established the previous November in the capture of Rochester Castle, had already alarmingly preceded him.[182]

At Orford, the great polygonal keep, despite its unique design, belongs to a whole class of broadly similar tower-keeps for which both Henry II and John were responsible in their time, and of which Conisborough Castle, in Yorkshire, preserves the best baronial example.[183] Yet already, as John's own success at Rochester was to show, improvements in siege weapons were beginning to make the keep obsolete, altering the emphasis in castle warfare so that its purpose might be as much to get the garrison out of the castle at a time of its choosing, as to prevent an enemy getting in. Framlingham Castle, as rebuilt at the end of the

86

twelfth century for Roger Bigod, had been a large, irregularly shaped shell-keep in the new manner, reoccupying the original castle mound and further defended by moats. And the multiplication of such essentially external lines of defence is seen again most impressively at the contemporary royal fortress at Dover, perhaps the greatest of them all, being the setting also of the largest of Henry II's now anachronistic tower-keeps, 'like a conventional battleship in the atomic age . . . obsolete almost as soon as it was built'.[184] Dover had been held successfully against Prince Louis in the siege of 1216–17, but the Dauphin's miners had brought down one of the gate towers at the castle, and it became subsequently a major purpose of royal-castle expenditure, over the succeeding decades, to make Dover truly impregnable. During these years, Dover's already formidable defences were multiplied, new importance being placed on the systematic defence of the resited main gate to the castle, which was now to incorporate in its upper stages the lodgings of the constable himself.[185] An early example of the keep-gatehouse principle, where the most vulnerable point in the castle was also its most strongly fortified nucleus, the Constable's Tower at Dover Castle set an important precedent for the lesser baronial castles of later generations where the keep, as a place of last resort, had all but disappeared.

62   The Constable's Tower at Dover Castle: a strongly-fortified gatehouse, being the key to Henry III's reorganized defences (Batsford)

87

In the meantime, however, royal castle-policy had united with improvements in siege techniques to put the private castle out of the reach of all but the greater lords, and it is significant that there was to be no return to private castle-building in the baronial wars of the 1260s to compare with what, a century before, had happened under Stephen.[186] Yet it would be less true to say that castle-building, at this level, ceased altogether, than that it totally changed in character. When Eynsford Castle, in Kent, was rebuilt following a fire, its originally austere military keep was converted, in the second quarter of the thirteenth century, into a hall and chamber block of considerable comfort and sophistication.[187] And there would have been many castles in thirteenth-century England to share the experience of the important Marcher fortress at Chepstow, in Monmouth, transformed during that century into a fitting residence for the two great baronial families that held it in succession – the Marshal earls of Pembroke and the Bigod earls of Norfolk.[188] It was a Marshal widow, Eleanor, the youngest daughter of King John, whose marriage in 1238 to Simon de Montfort brought him the custody of Kenilworth in 1244, shortly followed by the grant of the castle for life.

63 Kenilworth Castle, in Warwickshire, with the now dried-out water defences developed by Simon de Montfort (Aerofilms)

Already, before 1244, Henry III had done much to make the principal apartments at Kenilworth more habitable, just as he would do again at Clarendon Palace and elsewhere, while John, his father, had spent over £1000 on improvements to the defences, to include an outer curtain wall in the expensive modern style with certain additions to the keep. However, it is to Simon de Montfort himself that the exceptionally elaborate water defences of Kenilworth are usually attributed, making of the castle one of the greatest lake-fortresses of its day. It was these, undoubtedly, which chiefly enabled Earl Simon's followers to hold the castle against the king for a full year after his death at the battle of Evesham in 1265, their submission being brought about by starvation.[189]

Works to rival those at Kenilworth, already as much a royal as a baronial castle, could be financed only by the king, nor is it surprising that the next great programme of castle-building, which accompanied the conquest and final settlement of Wales, should have been the responsibility of Edward I alone, bringing him close to bankruptcy. Edward's castle-building in Wales has been the subject of much excellent work since Sir Goronwy Edward's initial brilliant

64   The last and most perfect of Edward I's Welsh castles: Beaumaris Castle, in Anglesey (Aerofilms)

exposition of 1944.[190] Yet magnificent though the king's total achievement proved to be, it demonstrated also, once and for always, that only *he* might mobilize the labour and find the finance for work of such calibre and scale, and that even Edward had difficulty in matching up to the standards of his sophisticated engineer-architect, the Savoyard Master James of St George. The latest and the most perfect of the Welsh castles, begun in 1295 to designs of James of St George, was Beaumaris, on the Isle of Anglesey. Planned concentrically, with multiple defensive circuits and a strongly fortified gatehouse both on the north and the south, Beaumaris stood at the peak of castle development for its day. Yet Beaumaris, despite mounting expenditure eventually equivalent to the whole cost of the only slightly earlier castle and walls of Conway, remained unfinished. A record still of the king's unattainable military ambitions, it had reached the end of a long and demonstrably impossible road.[191]

3   Set-back

In the tangled argument that centres now on the condition of England at the turn of the thirteenth and the fourteenth century, there is one point, at least, on which there is general agreement. In relation to its natural resources and to the quality of its technology, England at that time was seriously overpopulated. It was ripe for the original Malthusian checks of war, famine and pestilence, and ill-equipped too (as societies tend to be) for the moral restraint that Malthus later agreed might hold back population without them. In effect, the population growth which had developed the wealth of England over the two centuries following the Conquest, had continued to a point at which it now began to threaten that wealth with the dangers of overcrowding. For a generation or so, an individual landowner might profit from abundant labour and an intensifying demand for land which continually pushed up his rents. And there is evidence, for example, late in the thirteenth century, of sophisticated accountancy at Norwich Priory, assessing the real profitability of demesne farming, as then practised, against the probable yield of the identical lands in rents.[1] Nor, indeed, would the down-turn in demesne farming, certainly beginning before the end of the century on estates both ecclesiastical and lay, result necessarily in any net loss at that time. Nevertheless, where there is no appreciable rise in productivity and where population continues to grow, the advance, or even the stability, of the holders of capital can be achieved, if at all, only at the expense of the work-force. There are many pointers in early-fourteenth-century England to what this must have meant before the plague.

Most obvious of these was the peasant land-hunger which pushed out arable farming into ever less suitable soils, while simultaneously breaking down the existing land units into fragments which were steadily less viable on their own.[2] In the old 'fielden' communities, subject to manorial control, population growth had frequently been relatively moderate, and existing interests had been given valuable protection by long-established usage and by the accustomed co-operation of peasant families brought up to cultivation in common. Yet where overpopulation might begin to take effect most cruelly would be, rather, on the exposed frontiers of settlement: on those marginal lands of forest, moorland and fen which had mopped up the surplus of previous generations to a point beyond which nobody else could be absorbed. Of course, on many of these lands there were valuable further resources, whether in grazing or in the exploitation of the subsidiary products of forest, turbary or fen. And nowhere was this more obviously the case than on the rich Lincolnshire fenland estates of the Benedictine monks of Spalding. Nevertheless, large-scale reclamation of the fens ceased even in this part of Lincolnshire before the mid-thirteenth century, while the population of England, however unevenly, continued everywhere to grow. By 1300, that is, the Lincolnshire fenlands were as thickly populated and densely settled as they would be in the much more highly urbanized 1950s, thus reducing the available acreage of arable, meadow and pasture to little more than $1-1\frac{1}{2}$ acres per head.[3] In Lincolnshire, too, the prevailing practice of partible inheritance, dividing holdings equally amongst surviving heirs, had further contributed to the scaling-down, over the years, of the average peasant holding, so that with a household size working out, on the Spalding census evidence, at as many as 4·68 persons, it was not at all uncommon for a south Lincolnshire sokeman of the early fourteenth century to be working a holding of only 5 acres to support a family as large as that in number.[4]

This crowding of the richer fenlands was certainly exceptional, for in other conditions, without the further resources in fishing and wild-fowling of the fens, such a population would have stood no chance of survival. Nevertheless, the population over the country as a whole is thought to have risen between two-and-a-half and four times from Domesday to about 1300, and the amount of England under arable in 1086 (above, p. 1) had already been very large. Clearly, wherever there might be comparatively little new land to be brought into cultivation, the only possible response to population increase must have been the further partition of the old. By the 1250s, on the Huntingdonshire manor of Holywell-cum-Needingworth, some 70 per cent of the families in the village are known to have farmed 10 acres or less, while on at least one contemporary Winchester manor that percentage climbed to nearer 90.[5] And what was happening outside in the fields was matched in the villages themselves. The villagers of Upton, in Gloucestershire, it has recently been shown, brought cultivation almost to their doorsteps.[6] At Upton, too, there is evidence, round about 1300, of two families sharing the single peasant holding which one family unit had lived on and worked before,[7] nor are two generations, living side-by-side and farming the same original holding, likely to have been uncommon by that

A   Excavations in 1976 on the hall/keep at Castle Acre, Norfolk (Coad)

B *above*   Farnham Castle, Surrey, with the foundations of the twelfth-century central tower showing as a light square in the middle of the castle mound (Department of the Environment)

C *below*   St Mark's Church, Lincoln, under excavation in 1976 (Lincoln Archaeological Trust)

D *right*   Gilbert de Clare to Thomas le Despencer, patrons of Tewkesbury Abbey, being part of a fifteenth-century memorial roll of benefactors (Bodleian, Lat. misc. b.2(R))

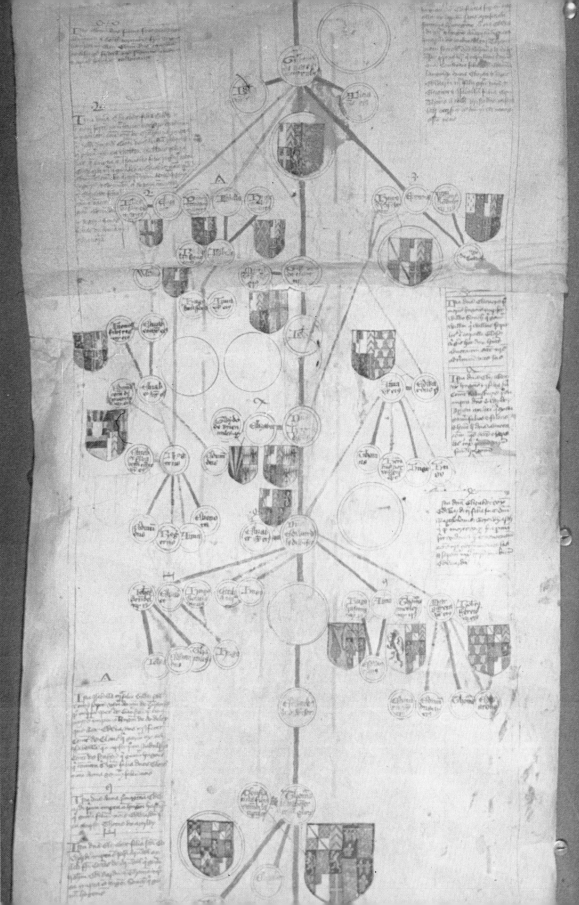

E   The head, on its embroidered
cushion, of Walter de Gray,
archbishop of York (1216-55),
buried at York Minster (R.C.H.M.)

F   Archbishop Walter de Gray's
pastoral staff, chalice and paten
(R.C.H.M.)

date. Such was to be the experience, for example, of the Burton Abbey estates towards the end of the thirteenth century.[8] On the Ely and Peterborough estates, at exactly this time, there were peasant entrepreneurs building cottages to rent on newly partitioned tenement plots, finding room for the 'undersetles' – the servants and occasional labourers – whose role in each village was becoming more obvious as the land grew progressively more crowded.[9]

Inevitably, as population figures rose and as pasture receded before the arable, village livestock declined in number, being restricted, even then, to the richer villagers who were beginning to distinguish themselves from the throng.[10] Once again, the consequences were serious. The growing shortage of good pasture could do nothing but force up its price, meadowland beginning to fetch premiums in the late thirteenth century that put it, increasingly, beyond the reach of the poor. Without the meat they would normally have got from their animals, the poorer villagers suffered from protein deficiencies; without manure, already low levels of productivity on the land fell, inevitably, still further. No doubt, progressive soil-exhaustion was especially serious on the smaller holdings, there being nowhere else to turn. But declining productivity, even on the greater manors, was to raise such problems that those changes in agricultural regime clearly recognizable after the Black Death might very well have happened on many estates even without such a catastrophe.[11] On the Winchester manors, this deterioration in crop yields was noticeable especially in the final decades of the thirteenth century, there being some recovery early in the fourteenth century following on a contraction of the arable.[12] But at Cuxham, in Oxfordshire, the deterioration from the high point reached in the 1290s continued through a full half-century. Wheat, which had yielded in 1288–99 the exceptionally high average of 8·3 quarters for every quarter sown, had declined to barely half as much between fifty and sixty years later. On dredge, the yield fell to nearer a third.[13]

Descending crop yields are an obvious consequence of progressive soil exhaustion. But another factor influential here was a long-term deterioration in the climate. On the Winchester manors, a correlation clearly existed between poor yields and land that had been extensively colonized at a relatively recent date, the older and smaller manors escaping the most savage declines.[14] And it was just this newly cultivated land, pushed out into the inhospitable margins, that could least endure any adverse alteration in the existing climatic balance, whether by a short-term catastrophe like a drought, a flood, a tempest or a frost, or in the longer secular trend.

On its own, climatic deterioration is unlikely to have been the cause of a retreat in settlement, nor can the evidence of the Winchester yields be used to support its occurrence.[15] Nevertheless, there can be little doubt now that the relatively warm period of the eleventh and twelfth centuries – the so-called 'Little Optimum' – was coming to an end in the thirteenth, while one of the characteristics of this period of change was unusual climatic instability, bringing droughts, floods and tempests through much of the thirteenth and the fourteenth centuries, with winters which could be notably mild or, just as often, exceptionally severe.[16] Ice-core evidence, recovered recently in Greenland, has suggested a particular descent, or minimum, towards the end of the thirteenth century, and although this was short-term, being followed almost immediately by a recovery particularly noticeable after about 1350, there are other indications of a downward secular trend, with another much longer-lasting minimum persisting through the course of the fifteenth century and not lifting before the second quarter of the sixteenth.[17] One of the casualties in English agriculture before 1400, constituting in itself some of our best evidence of the deterioration, proved to be the cultivation of the vine. At Norton Priory, in Cheshire, the craftsman's idea for a grape-treading scene, represented on a floor-tile manufactured in about 1300, might not have been of local inspiration, this being traditionally one of a series depicting the passage of the seasons.[18] Yet it is certain, all the same, that the canons of Norton would have understood better the legend of their floor when it was first installed than they could have done a century later. In the interval, viniculture in their part of Europe had all but disappeared.[19]

65 A fragment of floor-tile of
c. 1300, found at Norton Priory,
Cheshire, bearing an incised design of
a man (torso and one leg only)
treading grapes in a barrel (Greene)

The drop in average temperatures of just those few degrees sufficient to discourage the vine might not have had much impact on agriculture as a whole had it not been accompanied simultaneously by what must have been an appreciable rise in rainfall, with sea-level changes bringing coastal inundations that were repeatedly aggravated by storms. A rise in the water-table at Oakington, on the edge of the Cambridgeshire fens, has been seen as the reason for the desertion, early on in the fourteenth century, of the lower part of the village.[20] And it is becoming increasingly obvious now that new drainage ditches, cobbled floors and stone-paved paths were to be the shared characteristic of many villages in the thirteenth century which had not found them necessary before, particularly those on the heavier clay soils.[21] Everywhere, the raised house-platforms and regularly cleaned-out ditches of the late-thirteenth-century village may suggest a preoccupation with water disposal which, at the Dorset site of Holworth, near the coast, remained a problem through the fourteenth century and perhaps into the fifteenth as well.[22] In response, presumably, to the same flooding dangers, the church floors at Bordesley Abbey, in Worcestershire, as at the village church at Broadfield, in Hertfordshire, have been found in each case to have been built-up contemporaneously to a new and a more secure level.[23]

Heavy rainfall at any time may not be the same disaster to everybody, the notoriously wet summers of 1315 and 1316 being known to have produced average, or even above-average, crops on such manors as were especially well-drained.[24] Yet those at risk most certainly in over-wet conditions were the settlers of newly reclaimed lands, and among these losses were heavy. In coastal areas especially, many of the gains of the early thirteenth century were swept away by the gales of a century later, some 4,000 acres of prime agricultural land being lost, for example, in just this way along the length of the Sussex coast.[25] There were similar losses on the Kentish manors of Christ Church Priory, Canterbury,[26] while by 1341, in the Cambridgeshire fenlands, over 1,400 acres of former arable lands were found to lie inundated and waste.[27] In many coastal regions, throughout the fourteenth century, a permanent war (which was usually unsuccessful) came to be waged with the sea. Over this period, in the East Riding of Yorkshire, the monks of Meaux watched the loss by flooding of much of their land at Salthaugh Grange, with the whole of their former grange at Tharlesthorpe.[28] Nor would the next century necessarily bring much relief. It was the return of the floods to Barnhorne, on the Pevensey Levels, as late as the 1420s, that persuaded the monks of Battle, after more than a century of heavy expenditure repeatedly wasted by the sea, to abandon arable farming on this once-favourite manor, to cut down the acreage in demesne, and turn over what was left to cattle.[29]

Opinions still differ as to the real long-term effect of the so-called 'agrarian crisis' of 1315–22, the elements of which were the harvest failures of 1315, 1316 and 1321, the great sheep murrain of 1313–17, and the equally devastating cattle murrain which followed, almost immediately, in 1319–21.[30] However, it has been described, surely with justice, as the 'worst agrarian crisis faced by England as a whole since the aftermath of the Norman invasion',[31] and it was precisely the nationwide spread of each successive catastrophe that must put them, collectively, into a league of their own. Beyond question, the crisis was to have permanent results in the decision forced upon a number of landowners to abandon cultivation in demesne, while it is certainly true that, during these years, transactions in the peasant land-market speeded up appreciably, as the poor sold out what remained of their heritage and the relatively well-off built up their stakes in the land. Yet, outside these crisis years and beyond them, the inevitably regional bias of much of our evidence has led to many contradictory positions being taken on what permanent consequences they may have had. And although the balance of advantage is most probably now with those who see the first half of the fourteenth century as a period of stagnation, both in production and in population growth, the debate is likely to continue.

It is not easy, unfortunately, to arrive with any certainty at a population figure for the period, nor has the attempt to use other evidence to suggest overall population trends been received with general enthusiasm.[32] Nevertheless, mortality undoubtedly rose with the declining life expectations of the later thirteenth century, and most historians would now agree that the upward population trend that had characterized so many generations from the Conquest and before, had at last levelled out into what was nearer stability, or what, in places, could be more like a retreat. Certainly, many of the characteristics of the post-plague era, as these have come to be recognized and defined, were already plainly visible in the English agrarian economy before the great epidemic of 1348–9, and not all of these, by any means, may be directly attributed to the crisis of 1315–22. In individual areas, with special conditions to support it, land demand might keep up well through the period, as it did, for example, in the duchy of Cornwall, with its unique system of conventionary tenure and the many opportunities, locally offered, for income supplementation by mining, in particular, or by fishing.[33] Just such supplementary income resources had kept population steady on the Lincolnshire fenlands, despite the overcrowding,[34] while on the Titchfield estates, on the Hampshire coastal belt, it has been claimed of the period 1325 to 1345 that 'these were fortunate years of favourable weather and good harvests', where 'the prospective ghost of Malthus stalked only in 1348–9'.[35]

Yet on the Bec estates, similarly studied, those changes usually associated with recession after the Black Death were all present, in some measure, before it. They included a decline in population at least sufficient to put certain lands permanently out of cultivation, with peasant rebellions, rising wage bills, and the decline of customary services wherever these were already weak.[36]

Certainly, the common record of land uncultivated and houses derelict, true of many parts of the country through the first decades of the fourteenth century, while it need not mean that population itself had taken a sharp downward plunge, nevertheless must indicate an overpricing of arable in relation to the ability of the peasant to pay for it which, in the long run, would come to very much the same. On the estates of the bishops of Ely at this time, rents were to remain artificially high at the levels they had reached at the end of the previous century, effectively excluding the poorer peasantry from the land, yet simultaneously capital investment declined on the manors and many went out of demesne.[37] Overall, the fall in agricultural profits which had brought about this collapse of investment on the poorer manors had yet to touch the richer and less vulnerable estates, and the retreat from the demesne as a general phenomenon would have to wait, on many of these, for another hundred years. Yet the squeezing of profits on the marginal lands was to have very much more immediate effects. At Ibstone, for example, on the Chiltern uplands, the warden and fellows of Merton College, Oxford, had invested quite heavily, in the optimistic 1290s, in the building and fitting-out of a windmill. Thirty years later, it was derelict.[38]

At Ibstone, the principal reason for the failure of the mill had been the growing inability of the college, well before the plague, to attract new tenants to the vacant lands, at least at the prices still asked for them. And the mill itself, even after its rebuilding in 1339–40, was often without a tenant. Contemporaneously, on the Dorset estates of Glastonbury, the same failure in the demand for land resulted in a decline in the acreage sown with wheat and in the beginning of that movement from arable-farming to pasture which would everywhere characterize post-plague England and which was already, in the former forest assarts, taking shape at that time in the East Midlands.[39] Indeed, the extent of this movement before the plague, showing it to have been very considerable, has been demonstrated only comparatively recently in a study of the so-called *Nonarum Inquisitiones* of 1341/2, being the record of an enquiry into the value of local agricultural production preparatory to a levy in kind. Inevitably, by this date, the reversion of arable to pasture or waste had occurred more generally on the 'half-wanted' soils of the exposed uplands than on the richer lowland manors. And here certainly, on the marginal lands, it was to be accompanied by the abandonment of

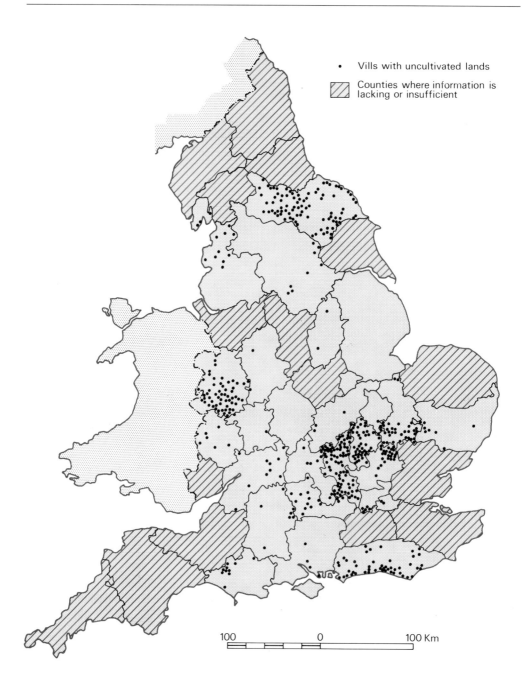

Vills with uncultivated lands

Counties where information is
lacking or insufficient

100   0   100 Km

66   Settlements with waste and uncultivated lands, as recorded in the Inquisitions of the Ninth
of 1341/2 (Baker)

tenements and by other evidence of a population shrinking under the combined oppressions of soil exhaustion and a consistently unfavourable climate. Thus the distribution of uncultivated lands through Yorkshire, Shropshire, and both coastal and Wealden Sussex corresponds very closely to those areas known for their inhospitable soils or for constant exposure to flooding, while, significantly, another very marked concentration of waste in the counties north and west of London, to include areas like the Chilterns where Merton College had built its mill, was explained by the jurors of 1341/2 less in terms of the poverty of the soil than as a result of a failure of tenants.[40] In all these lands and in others too, desertion of the less favourably situated settlements had already begun some decades before the Black Death. Very probably, that is, it was not the plague which permanently emptied such small moorland settlements as Wroughton Copse, up on Fyfield Down in Wiltshire, but the agrarian crisis of 1315–22 with its longer-term consequences in a general retreat from the margins.[41]

The Inquisitions of the Ninth of 1341/2 preserve a record, at parochial level, of complaints of depopulation, of soil exhaustion, and of the persisting hostility of the weather. But they are important, too, as a contemporary comment on the unlooked-for consequences of royal policy over the years and on the oppressive burden of the king's taxation at just that point at which its weight was becoming unacceptable. In reality, these troubles can be seen to have gone back a very long way. War, as the king had found in Wales, had become exceptionally expensive. To pay for it, new expedients would have to be adopted both in taxation and through the manipulation of the currency which, being untried, could have unexpected effects, bringing distress to many local communities quite as great, in all probability, as famine and pestilence, the more obvious Malthusian checks.[42]

One of the disadvantages, for example, of Edward's great recoinage of 1279–80, which had had its purpose also in the funding of the Welsh campaigns, was that it proved to be altogether too successful. English coins of the new minting came to be in such high demand on the Continent that their out-flow created a shortage of coin in England itself, where the king, as early as 1283, found himself forced to prohibit the export of English money. And yet good coins continued in short supply. Foreign princes, unable to obtain English money, manufactured imitations of lesser quality of their own, the 'crockards' and 'pollards' of this continental coinage, flooding England during the 1290s, being often of less weight than their English equivalents though usually of sterling fineness.[43] Other imitative coinages, increasing the confusion, included low-value jettons and those still unusual pewter tokens of the period of which satisfactory evidence is only now emerging in such chance finds as the stone mould from the Bedern site at York, the single token from the Dominican friary at Boston, in Lincolnshire, and the hoard, datable to just this period, from the productive Anglo-Irish site at Winetavern Street in Dublin.[44]

Edward I's monetary policy had the virtue of consistency, and he did his best to continue the discouragement of unwanted foreign moneys by the imposition of controls at the ports. In the late 1290s, probably to avoid such controls, a hoard of coins was concealed at Dover, made up in large part of Irish, Scottish and continental coins, none of which would have been welcome additions to the English coinage stock of the time.[45] Nevertheless, the attitudes hardening in the recoinage of 1299–1302 and in the successful demonetization of the crockards and pollards in 1300, in particular towards the absolute prohibition of English silver exports, prevented any effective response to the great influx of foreign silver which, starting in 1304, was a major factor in the very serious inflation of the immediately following years. With continuing restrictions on the export of silver, much of the foreign coinage brought into England at the time for reminting could not have left the country, thus swelling the number of the coins in circulation and encouraging a sharp rise in prices.[46] And although this, of course, was not the only explanation of the inflation of 1305–10, which coincided, among other things, with a steep ascent in England's export trade in wool, it was yet probably the chief reason for a general price rise all over the country during these years, touching foodstuffs and manufactured products equally. In this short period, as recent work has demonstrated, both grain and livestock prices almost doubled, to be held at a

0 _____ 5 Cm

67 Moulds for a pewter token (left) and a pilgrim badge (right), recently recovered from sites in York and dating to the late thirteenth century (York Archaeological Trust)

68 Pewter tokens, probably late-thirteenth-century in date, from a site near London Wall (Museum of London)

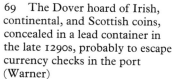

69 The Dover hoard of Irish, continental, and Scottish coins, concealed in a lead container in the late 1290s, probably to escape currency checks in the port (Warner)

high level by the agricultural disasters of the succeeding decade, and to seem all the more oppressive for following a century of general price stability, characterized by increases that were usually moderate if occurring even at all.[47]

Just as surely as an increase in the volume of money and in the velocity of its circulation will push prices up, a shortage will bring them spiralling down again. And this happened, not so very much later, in the two decades after 1322.[48] By the mid-fourteenth century, as a result of the growing shortage of European silver, England too had been forced to adopt its own policy of lighter money, bringing an effective depreciation of the currency as a whole of almost 20 per cent.[49] However, the new financial realism of the royal government in the 1340s, reflected also in a more responsible attitude to the assessment and collection of national taxes, had arrived too late to make up for those losses to which a 'calamity-sensitive' population, in Professor Postan's phrase, had already long been prone. Particularly during that final decade before 1340/1, the major burden of royal taxation had begun to fall most heavily on the peasantry, depriving the poorest sector of the population of the exemption it had previously enjoyed.[50] And already, over more than half a century, the high cost of the king's campaigns, lately stepped up to oppressive new levels by the first exchanges of the Hundred Years War, had been met by levies on movables that were becoming increasingly numerous, by arbitrary 'purveyance', being the compulsory sale to royal officers of foodstuffs and military supplies, and by the requirements of forced service, whether in the recruitment of craftsmen for labour on the king's works or in the raising of troops by local commissions of array. In all of these, a prime cause of popular discontent was at least as much the unequal incidence of royal taxation as the absolute burdens it imposed. There was nothing, that is, to ensure that the king should draw his supplies – in kind, in money, or in men – from those regions, or even those classes, best equipped to match up to his demands. And yet, in society as it stood, there were already profound inequalities, many of which, over the previous century or more, had shown every sign of getting worse.

In regional terms, the most obvious inequality in the wealth of early-fourteenth-century England had come to lie between the wealthy counties of the south and the east and the poorer areas to the west and to the north. Broadly, this reflected the profound arable bias of the agricultural economy of the time, the product of over-extended ploughing. And just as, in each individual county, the wealthiest areas would tend to be those of the richest arable lands,[51] over the country as a whole wealth concentrated in a broad band stretching across the centre of lowland England, from Somerset in the west to Lincolnshire, Norfolk and south-east

Yorkshire in the east, corresponding very exactly with those old-established corn-growing lands where productivity was highest and where the surpluses were such as to show up in the assessments on which the king's taxation was based.[52] Of these assessments, the records of the lay subsidy of 1334 give us what is certainly our widest coverage, and these identify individual pockets of wealth located, for example, in the densely populated south Lincolnshire fenlands, around Spalding, or along the north Kent coast. In 1334, the greatest concentrations of wealth clustered, as might have been expected, in the immediate market regions of the principal cities and other major towns, the greater part of these being either cloth-manufacturing centres or ports and almost all being sited to the south of the

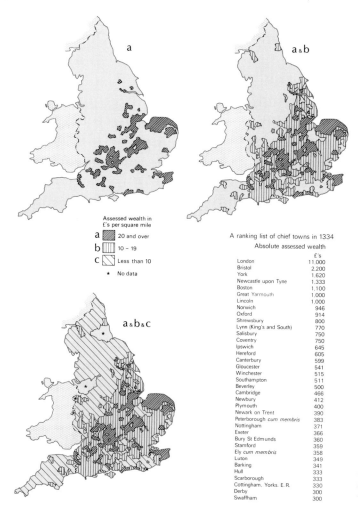

Assessed wealth in
£'s per square mile

a — 20 and over
b — 10 – 19
c — Less than 10
★ — No data

A ranking list of chief towns in 1334
Absolute assessed wealth

	£'s
London	11.000
Bristol	2.200
York	1.620
Newcastle upon Tyne	1.333
Boston	1.100
Great Yarmouth	1.000
Lincoln	1.000
Norwich	946
Oxford	914
Shrewsbury	800
Lynn (King's and South)	770
Salisbury	750
Coventry	750
Ipswich	645
Hereford	605
Canterbury	599
Gloucester	541
Winchester	515
Southampton	511
Beverley	500
Cambridge	466
Newbury	412
Plymouth	400
Newark on Trent	390
Peterborough cum membris	383
Nottingham	371
Exeter	366
Bury St Edmunds	360
Stamford	359
Ely cum membris	358
Luton	349
Barking	341
Hull	333
Scarborough	333
Cottingham. Yorks. E. R.	330
Derby	300
Swaffham	300

70   The wealth of England in 1334, as measured in the lay subsidy of that year, with a ranking list, in order of absolute wealth, of the chief towns (Glasscock)

103

Severn and the Trent. Among them, London evidently had long since established its dominance, being five times as wealthy as Bristol, its nearest competitor in riches. York, creating its own island of wealth in the otherwise impoverished north-east, was next in the list after Bristol. And Southampton, although well down the list of the chief towns of England as ranked in the 1334 assessments, was yet the nodal point of a concentration of wealth conspicuous in southern Hampshire.[53]

In 1334, for the first time, each taxable community had agreed the total sum payable by itself towards the subsidy, and while the system was undoubtedly more efficient than the individual assessments of earlier years, thus contributing to the coverage of the record, its effect was to deprive the rolls of the data on social stratification within communities for which, in general, we must turn to the previous subsidies. Uniquely, the individual assessments of the earlier levies were preserved in Kent, both in 1334 and afterwards, to show us an increase in Kentish taxpayers of almost half as much again by 1338, and to demonstrate in this way the rapid extension downwards of the burden of taxation just as soon as the crown, in reorganizing the levy, had ceased to concern itself with the clear stipulation of a lowest taxable limit.[54] What these records also show, continuing after 1334, are the social divisions which the earlier subsidies had revealed all over the country, keeping wealth and high office consistently in the hands of what was never more than a very small group. One of the characteristics, that is, of the London nominal lists, compiled for the purpose of the immediately previous lay subsidy of 1332, had been the concentration of office-holders within the two highest-rated taxpaying classes in the capital.[55] And five years earlier, to give just one other example, only 56 of the 800 taxpayers of York, listed for the subsidy of 1327, had been rated on assessable goods worth £5 or over, the vast majority clustering well below that point, with many at the bottom of the scale.[56] Regrettably, we have no means of judging, with any precision, the exact proportion of the population assessed in 1327 or 1332, although it may have been as little as a quarter of the total and, in places, could have worked out at very much less. However, of that quarter in Southampton in 1327, no less than 80 per cent of the recorded taxpayers were grouped in the lowest taxation bracket, assessed at under £5, while of the five wealthiest men in the borough of that year, each was a leading merchant of the early-fourteenth-century community and not one failed to hold high public office in the port with additional responsibilities to the crown.[57]

In the countryside, we can hardly doubt, the traditional obligations of the manorial economy, with the strong community sense which these had had their share in creating, held men back from the extremes. Yet even here, at the 'classic' manor of Cuxham, situated almost at the centre of that broad band of arable wealth which cut a swathe through fourteenth-century England, the condition of the servile tenantry was less uniform than it might on the surface have appeared, there remaining 'some scope, however restricted, for the exercise of enterprise and good fortune'.[58] Just as, in 1327, the subsidy list of Wigston Magna, a Leicestershire community, shows the Swan family outstanding in a small class of comparatively well-off peasants, themselves clearly distinguished from the great mass of taxpayers grouping at the bottom of the scale,[59] no more than three villein tenements stand out at Cuxham, well above the rest, and two of these, significantly enough, were the tenements of manorial reeves.[60] On the Ramsey estates, as Professor Raftis has shown us more than once, it was precisely these 'main families' which, in every village, would provide the manorial officials; it was they who made the village bye-laws and then, not infrequently, got together co-operatively to undo them; in their hands lay the responsibility for joint action with any neighbouring settlement, while they themselves, in their own communities, were the principal employers of servants and other hired labour, dismissed when the bad times came.[61]

We have no means of knowing, for every community, when it was that the separation of the principal families began. However, there have been a number of pointers recently to suggest that this was a process advanced by overpopulation in the late thirteenth century, by the unchecked activity of the peasant land-market at just this date, and by the inflationary conditions of the early fourteenth century which favoured those already the holders of some land. Certainly, on Boroughbury, a manor of Peterborough Abbey, no more than eight families engrossed between them all the free land on the manor, achieving this within two generations of 1300, before which the market had been very much more open.[62] Contemporaneously, the practice of gavelkind tenure, while encouraging the partition of many Kentish family holdings, was also making possible the accumulation of land by the ambitious.[63] And on the Durham estates, right at the other end of the country though again at just about this time, there was evidence of certain of the prior's wealthier free tenants actively encouraging his villeins to escape, so as to be able to engross their former holdings.[64]

No doubt, for many families the long process of land accumulation had gone back far into the thirteenth century, this being the case, for example, on the Ely estates where the bishop's reluctance to keep land in demesne opened opportunities for land acquisition to free tenants and villeins alike. Yet at Ely, as elsewhere, by far the best-documented examples of the struggle of the individual peasant up into the ranks of the yeomanry belong, rather, to the end of the thirteenth and the beginning of the fourteenth century, it being then that Stephen Puttock, a villein on the prior's manor at Sutton, was making his land purchases, in the company of others of his kind, with no fewer than seven recorded transactions, some of them quite large, in the space of only ten years.[65] Outside the Ely estates, Stephen found very precise equivalents in such men as Robert ate Grene and John, his son, free tenants of Merton College at Cuxham,[66] in John Brockhall at Weedon, a manor of Bec,[67] in Walter of Coln Rogers and the other Gloucester Abbey villeins who were taking out long leases of the abbot's lands before the end of the thirteenth century,[68] and in those 'tenacious, resilient and enterprising' peasant families on the Ramsey Abbey manor of Holywell-cum-Needingworth: the Hunnes, Lawemans and Lanes, the Riptons, the Scots and the Godfreys.[69]

Mutual support within these family groups is, of course, the chief explanation of their conspicuous longevity and strength. The Holywell-cum-Needingworth families who were still appearing in the mid-fourteenth-century manorial records, had been there at least since the 1250s. And it was the stability and industry of families like themselves which began, back in the late thirteenth century or before, that process of transition from dependent villein to free yeoman farmer which is seen, so often, as such a very much later development. One of the more interesting indicators of the timing of their emergence has begun to be the growing bulk of the archaeological evidence for the replacement of the original village long-houses at many communities by more substantial and elaborate farmsteads, rarely dating before the late thirteenth century. In some cases, as at Upton in Gloucestershire, these farmsteads held two families where one had been before. But although this, in one sense, may be taken as evidence of overcrowding, there is little to establish, in the grouping of village clans, that these clans themselves were the ones economically at risk. Indeed, one of the more obvious characteristics of the final phases at Upton was the high quality not just of the farmstead buildings but also of the material associated with them. Among such finds, there were clothing accessories and other decorative items of gilded metal alloys, with much ironwork and finely ornamented pottery, only a small proportion of which is likely to have been locally made.[70]

The relative sophistication of the last buildings at Upton, abandoned by the late fourteenth century, can be seen again at contemporary farmstead refashionings at Thuxton, in Norfolk, as at Faxton and Wythemail, in Northamptonshire.[71] But the most remarkable sequence from long-house to farmstead of all those yet identified and published is still the one recovered at Gomeldon, in Wiltshire, where farmsteads of the new courtyard plan are known to have replaced the earlier peasant long-houses on at least two village tenement plots, and where the succession of buildings on one of these plots may be traced back into the twelfth century.[72] At Gomeldon, one of these farmsteads has been dated by its excavators to the late thirteenth century, with the other only a few decades later. Like the contemporary farmsteads excavated elsewhere in the country, with which they share the common characteristics of a courtyard plan and of a distinction, clearly made, between living-quarters and byre, these Gomeldon houses are likely to have belonged to the dominant 'main' families of the village. In a material way, they illustrate the emergence of a new class of yeoman farmer within the village as much

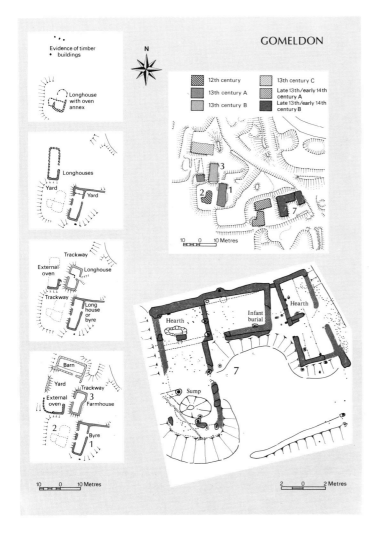

71 The long-house to farmstead sequence at Gomeldon, in Wiltshire, as excavated in 1963–5 (left), with another farmstead excavated at the same site in 1966–7 (Algar and Musty)

as on the assarted lands beyond it, standing at the beginning of a fresh building tradition which reached full development in the substantial two-storey farmhouses of early-modern England, but which still had a long way to go.[73]

The relative prosperity of the principal families in at least some villages in the decades round about 1300 would scarcely have been possible had they been unable to accumulate land. And it was the coincidence of peasant land-hunger with economic adversity and with the seigneurial oppressions such adversity provoked, that led in its turn to peasant discontents and to popular rebellions on an altogether more dangerous scale. Just as soon, that is, as the major landowners began to take the initiative in the quashing of illegal land transfers on their estates, becoming active in this way from the early fourteenth century when their revenues seemed already at risk, they turned the village main families against them.[74] Nor should it be surprising that one of the leaders of the peasant rebellion of 1297 on the Bec manor of Weedon was none other than John Brockhall, quoted above (p. 106) as a successful accumulator of abbey lands.[75] John Brockhall, although plainly of villein status, had refused services at Weedon on the grounds that he himself was free. And the claims of Brockhall were exactly those that many in his circumstances were likely to be making, as formal servile status came more obviously in conflict with what, for them, was effective economic independence. Seventeen years before, the tenants of the abbot of Burton at Mickleover had followed the lead of their principal families into a refusal to admit their servile status, claiming ancient demesne of the crown. Yet their revolt, although widely supported in the community, had been short-lived, coming to an end in August 1280, just a few months after it began. Exemplifying the reaction of the more oppressive landowners, seriously threatened for the first time, the abbot insisted on formal individual submissions and on a punishing redistribution of village lands. In his brutal phrase, his villeins owned nothing more than their bellies.[76]

Growing tensions of status still provide us, very probably, with the principal explanation for the more effectively conducted rural rebellions of the late thirteenth and early fourteenth centuries. Together with general economic causes and with progressive overcrowding on the manors, these discontents contributed to the substantial rise in the business of contemporary manorial courts, on some manors reaching perhaps three times its level of only a century before.[77] But another reason also for these more numerous fines, characterizing court business at the end of the thirteenth century, was a widespread breakdown of manorial discipline at all levels, both furthered and kept in being by the more serious collapse of public order. In part, this collapse was a local phenomenon, being the work of an unruly rural gentry unchecked by crown or magnates. Yet it took its colour, too, from national reverses, and the one disorder fed upon the other. Significantly, in a history of otherwise cordial relations between the peasants and their lord, the one recorded instance of communal opposition to Merton College at Cuxham occurred in 1327, the year of the deposition, in troubling circumstances, of the luckless Edward II, and this was the opportunity chosen too by the men of Ogbourne to protest against the oppressions of Bec.[78] In the towns likewise, the disorders accompanying the end of Edward II's reign and the violent beginnings of the next were the occasion for damaging riots at the monastic towns of Abingdon, Bury St Edmunds and St Albans,[79] while at Nottingham, it was the French soldiers quartered in the borough in 1328 who were to be the first cause of the serious local troubles of that year.[80]

Certainly, public order, as historians now generally agree, had been deteriorating since the 1290s. The 'immeasurable' increase in felonies said to have occurred already by 1300 was to be followed, in 1304, by the setting up of the first trailbaston commissions, in an attempt to deal with those criminal gangs which were finding support in a discontented countryside sufficient to keep them in being and to make them a nuisance to the crown.[81] Yet a gap was widening all the time between what the king wanted and what, in practice, he could truly afford to do, while ultimately, as we have been usefully reminded, 'good order did not depend on law courts of any sort but on people's attitudes to their neighbours'.[82] Few, indeed, were as profoundly unpopular as those who administered the law. The outlaw sang:

> I will teach them (the judges) the game of Trailbaston, and I will break their back and rump, their arms and legs, it would be right. . . . You who are indicted, I advise you, come to me, to the green forest . . . where there is no annoyance but only wild animals and beautiful shade; for the common law is too uncertain.[83]

Indeed, it was imperfect justice, leading men of spirit everywhere in England to take the law into their own hands, that first drove notorious gang leaders like the Folvilles, of Leicestershire, and the Coterels, of northern Derbyshire, into a life of violent crime and outlawry, placing whole regions under systems of law which rivalled that of the king. In such conditions, Lionel, 'king of the rout of raveners' and one of the more prominent of these scoundrels, might be found addressing a blackmail victim in the style of a royal writ. And although much of this, of course, was parody, it yet reflected a genuine belief in the existence of some form of

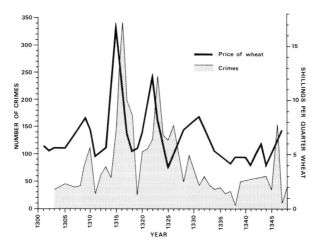

72 Crimes per year, as recorded in the Norfolk gaol delivery rolls, set against the price of wheat in normal and famine years (Hanawalt)

alternative law which many, between the abandonment of the general eyre in the late thirteenth century and the emergence of the justices of the peace almost a century later, might very well have shared. Both the Folvilles and the Coterels were of landed stock, and what made them and their followers particularly difficult to suppress was that they drew their support not from the discontented peasantry of the Robin Hood legends but from men very similar in background to themselves. Among the 'maintainers' of the Folville desperados was Sir Robert de Vere, constable and keeper of the castle and forest of Rockingham, while it was the canons of Lichfield who were to hire the notorious Coterel 'society' as tithe collectors in the lawless parishes of the Peaks. Some decades later, the 'evil deeds' of Sir James Audley, lord of Heighley in Cheshire, were more difficult to correct in one who was himself a serjeant of the peace, the father-in-law of a trailbaston justice, and a companion-in-arms of the Black Prince.[84]

Ultimately, all the king could do with malefactors like these was to strike a personal bargain with them, sending them off to conduct his wars in Wales, in Scotland or in France. However, purely political solutions of this kind could do little in general to reinforce the law, and the real problems of accelerating lawlessness were to continue substantially unchecked. Twice in the mid-fourteenth century the town of Colchester was besieged and held to ransom by the followers of John Fitzwalter, an Essex gang-leader well known for his practice of taking the law into his hands.[85] Nor could the many towns investing in stone walls in the decades on either side of 1300 have been uninfluenced in this by the manifest breakdown of public order. One of the stories told of Malcolm Musard, the Worcestershire gang-leader, is that he conducted a full-scale attack, with bows and arrows, on the rectory at Weston Subedge, in that county, having been hired to do so in 1304 by an aggrieved evicted rector.[86] It would have taken a man of unusual optimism not to have attempted at least some fortification of his homestead when there were scoundrels like Musard and Fitzwalter about. Scarcely surprisingly, this was just what everybody was doing.

Lowland England is scattered throughout with moated sites, the origins and even the purposes of which have been the source of much speculation. However, it has long been recognized that the majority of these moats, where datable at all, must belong to the thirteenth and fourteenth centuries, while a recent count, on the excavators' evidence, has successfully narrowed the dating of many of these to the quarter-century both before and after 1300.[87] Of course, very much earlier than this, there can have been nothing unusual in the digging of defensive moats at both castle and manorial sites, and the employment of moats for drainage on waterlogged sites on clay had been known at least since the twelfth century. Nevertheless, the now obvious association of small-scale moated sites with areas of forest clearance, just where the isolated farmsteads of the assarting peasantry of East Anglia and the west Midlands were most in need of such protection, has established both the very general downward spread of the thirteenth-century moat-building practice and, more significantly, the chief reason why such moats should have been adopted.[88] Licences to crenellate, multiplying already in the reign of Edward I, and concentrated particularly in the reigns of his son and his grandson, are evidence enough of the concern of the military classes with the problems of securing their own.[89] At a very different social level, amongst the assarting peasantry, a site like Gannow Green Moat, in Worcestershire, where the excavators found, on the old ground surface below the platform, a layer of burnt brushwood, wood chips and decayed vegetation, can tell us much of those processes of clearance, colonization and the marking-out of territory which characterized the expansionist moat-building days.[90]

It may well be, as has been the suggested explanation of some Cambridge-shire moats, that one class aped the practices really more appropriate for the other,[91] and certainly the upwards struggle of the village main families must have given them more of value to protect. Homestead moats in a village setting like those, perhaps, at Milton, in Hampshire, and Ashwell, in Hertfordshire, both early-fourteenth-century in date and both requiring the previous demolition of existing peasant houses, very likely recall the social divisions that were beginning to split such communities.[92] Yet it is difficult, for all that, to see moat-building primarily as a response to pressures of status, and a good indication of the true

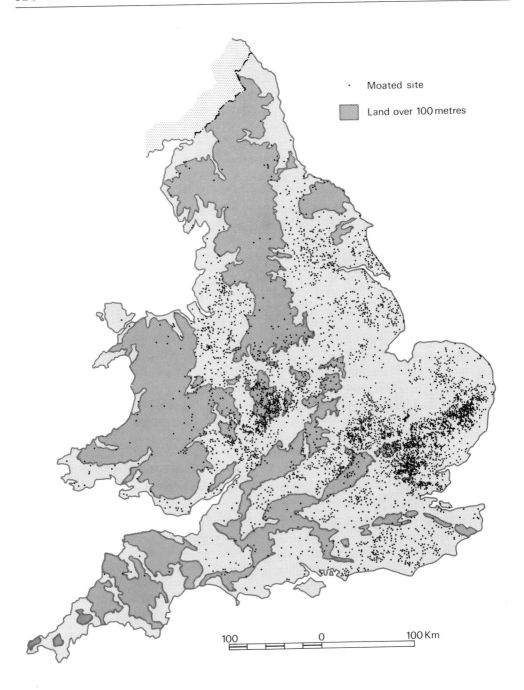

73 A map of the moated sites of England and Wales, updated to 1974 (Moated Sites Research Group)

74 Stokesay Castle, in Shropshire, for which a licence to crenellate was granted in 1291 (R.C.H.M.)

seriousness of its purpose is the way in which defences during this period were elaborated. Particularly, of course, this occurred on the more important establishments, many of which had enjoyed some form of protection from a comparatively early date. There had been boundary ditches, for example, at the Sussex manor of Glottenham since as far back as the eleventh century, yet it was not to be until the very end of the thirteenth century, possibly coinciding with a change in tenancy, that a systematic fortification of the manor-house was attempted. At Glottenham, the substantial gatehouse and stone curtain wall have been dated to the first years of the fourteenth century. Within the wall and set against it, fine new ranges of timber buildings were put up in place of the old.[93]

There are thus two reasons why the immediate explanation for moat-building in this period is also, very probably, the correct one. The first of these is the exceptionally large number of homestead moats, even if some of them were little more than a marking-out of private space, datable to the period of maximum disorder at the turn of the thirteenth and fourteenth centuries. The second is the evidence, everywhere accumulating, of an elaboration and reinforcement of existing moats and kindred fortifications, once again attributable to these decades.[94] It cannot really have been a worsening of the climate which caused the

75 Foundations of the early-fourteenth-century stone-built gatehouse at Glottenham, in Sussex (Martin)

digging of the new moat at Northolt, in Middlesex, any more than this can be the likely explanation of the moats at Milton or at Ashwell.[95] And although problems of drainage probably do account for the moat surviving on the sodden flood-plain of the River Hull at Hayholme Grange, near Beverley, they can hardly explain the fourteenth-century platform moat at Walsall, in Staffordshire, set across earlier buildings and former ridge-and-furrow, where it can only have been by deliberate diversion of the stream that the moat could itself have been flooded.[96] Among many examples of excavated moats, each of them likely to have been of this period, there is the very clear case of Durrance Moat, a Worcestershire site, where a substantial timber-fronted rampart and re-cut ditch took the place of the earlier moat and palisade defences which, before the later thirteenth century, had seemed to offer an adequate protection.[97] At just this time, too, as law and order everywhere disintegrated, the moated site at Shareshill, in Staffordshire, was refortified with a wide ditch and interior bank, the latter surmounted by a stone wall and fronted, additionally, with what was probably a barrier of thorn.[98] Among the buildings of the upper classes, Weoley Castle, now in Birmingham but then, of course, more rural, could scarcely provide a better example of what could happen at a lightly defended manor-house, protected originally by ditch, bank and palisade, after the granting of a licence to crenellate. Here, between 1270 and 1320, the manor was supplied with its surviving moat, with a substantial stone curtain wall studded with interval towers, with its first strongly constructed timber bridge, and with other major rebuildings within the new compass of the walls.[99] At Eltham, in 1315, the works at Weoley had their parallel in the massive curtain wall, within the moats, constructed to protect this important manor-house and later palace, newly acquired by the queen,[100] as they had also in the enclosure wall of the monks of Spalding, enlarged and crenellated after 1333 to frustrate the raids of the men of Deeping, cattle-rustlers from over the fen.[101]

Violence and social change were conditions, clearly, with which the men of early-fourteenth-century England would have had to learn to live. Yet what prompted the aggression of the fenlanders of Deeping was perhaps less their poverty in the face of affluence than that sturdy independence of spirit which the many opportunities of their fenland environment had bred in their kind through the centuries. Fenlanders, even those with very small holdings of their own, had access to great stretches of common land for pasture; they had their fisheries, their wild-fowling, their salterns and their turbaries; they had long enjoyed the freedoms of a locally active land market, encouraged by their custom of partible socage and by the practice of unrestricted sales.[102] Matching these conditions of independence, where a man's hands might be turned to many trades, the royal forests similarly supported an assarting peasantry which might include wood-cutters, turners and charcoal-burners, miners, lime-burners and smiths, tanners and corders, and some of the earliest workers in glass.[103]

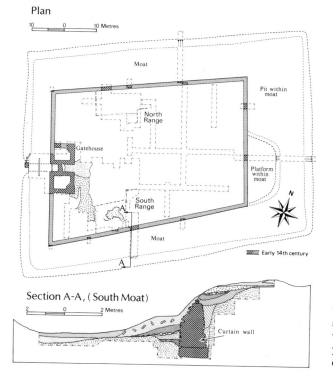

76   A plan of Glottenham Manor, as refortified with a stone curtain wall and gatehouse in the difficult years of the early fourteenth century (Martin)

77 A conjectural reconstruction, now at the Pilkington Glass Museum, of the fourteenth-century glasshouse at Blunden's Wood, in Surrey (Pilkington)

How far each one of these skills, by the early fourteenth century, had become fully professionalized will continue the theme of debate.[104] And at all times, certainly, the rural-based craftsman of medieval England, when an opportunity presented itself or the season demanded, might desert his trade for the land. Yet it was at just this time that the craft movement, after years of suppression, was beginning to take off in the towns,[105] nor can there be much doubt, out in the countryside, of the thorough-going professionalism of the glass-workers of Blunden's Wood, Hambledon, in Surrey,[106] of the salt-boilers of Bicker Haven, in Lincolnshire,[107] or of the iron-workers, only a little later in date, at Minepit Wood, Rotherfield, in Sussex.[108] To add to these, there are many industries for which we have evidence, both documentary and archaeological, of improving technology through the thirteenth century, bringing a more general distribution of the specialized products which, however imperfectly, had hitherto been manufactured at home. Much is known, for example, of changes in the cloth trade during this period, transformed by the spread of the fulling-mill and increasingly rural-based.[109] Contemporaneously, the use of coal as a fuel in iron-smelting and lime-burning brought the coal trade to prominence at Newcastle before the end of the thirteenth century, and was boosted yet again as coal, in the wealthier households, came to be valued for heating.[110] Amongst the older trades, there were the specialist quarrymen and grave-slab sculptors of Barnack, near Peterborough,[111] the brooch- and ring-makers of Chester,[112] the horners and leather-workers of York,[113] and the souvenir-makers at the more popular pilgrimage centres, in particular the Canterbury of St Thomas.[114] Of all of these, the archaeological evidence has been most thoroughly explored in the case of the specialist potter. And whether or not the experience of the potter was shared in other trades, the argument for a revolution in techniques in the thirteenth- and early-fourteenth-century pottery, bringing new status to the craft, would now be very difficult to refute.

0 _____ 5 Cm

78 Pilgrim badges from Walsingham and Canterbury (top left and right), Santiago and Amiens (bottom left and right) (Museum of London)

117

In the older arable-centred village, the status of the individual craftsman had not, it would seem, stood high. Such a man would be out-classed by the land-holding villein, and his skills, although they might keep his family in the village for a generation or two, seldom promoted them to permanent residence. Those, for example, who at Warboys, in Huntingdonshire, occupied themselves as artisans, did so because they could not have made themselves a living on the land. They were smallholders, at best, and migrants, taking their trades to whatever community might offer them a temporary market and the house-room they immediately required.[115] In the pottery industry, particularly amongst tile-makers, this tendency persisted in the migrant workers who set up their kilns, in each case to meet the needs of temporary building campaigns, at such monastic establishments as Meaux Abbey, a Cistercian house, or at the priories of Norton and of Haverholme.[116] Yet the high skill of the tile-makers of Chertsey not only kept them permanently employed at this Surrey abbey for upwards of fifty years, but had reached such a peak of professionalism by the third quarter of the thirteenth century that their products, although imitated often enough, were never subsequently to be improved upon.[117] Moreover, the Chertsey tiles, although certainly the finest of their kind, were no more than one example among many of the local pottery industries which, everywhere in the thirteenth century, were transforming the former village craft into a complex of manufacturing and trading enterprises, each of them serving a region which might be fifty miles across or more. Significantly, the wholly unremarkable cooking-pots of a small early-fourteenth-century village industry at Upper Heaton, near Huddersfield, have been found to have been marketed in the North Yorkshire dales, as much as thirty-five miles from their source.[118] And while it is true that the products of a pottery at Ham Green, near Bristol, were not sold at such other nearby centres as had contemporary pottery industries of their own, they travelled, nevertheless, along the river routes through Gloucestershire and Somerset, and seem to have found their market, most particularly, across the water again in south Wales.[119] One of the more spectacular of the Ham Green products was a 'knight-jug', being a local imitation of the characteristic late-thirteenth-century design known from centres as wide apart as Scarborough, on the north-east coast, Grimston, in Norfolk, and Nottingham, in the East Midlands. With a distribution known to have covered the entire east coast, these English jugs have been found also in Norway, over the North Sea, as well as further to the south in Flanders.[120]

Undoubtedly, what contributed most to the elaboration of pottery techniques was an improvement in the market for the potters' wares which enabled them to practise their craft full-time. Of course, there would always be

79 Chertsey tiles of *c.* 1295, showing a queen, an archbishop and a king (B.M.)

individual part-time potters whether in the Middle Ages or later, nor is it unlikely that part-time working in the industry as a whole should have become the norm again quite quickly, resulting in a widespread lowering of standards in the craft before the end of the fourteenth century.[121] Yet even in the fifteenth century the potters of Lyveden, in Northamptonshire, were socially quite distinct on the archaeological evidence from their neighbours, the peasant farmers: they lived on 'industrial' tenement plots and enjoyed another quality of diet.[122] And the long-lived industry at Lyveden was only one of the many fully professionalized pottery-producing centres, dating from the thirteenth century or earlier, now being identified all over the country as the source of good-quality local wares, including those at Laverstock, in Wiltshire,[123] Sible Hedingham, in Essex,[124] Nuneaton, in Warwickshire,[125] Toynton, in Lincolnshire,[126] and Grimston, in Norfolk.[127] Much, of course, continued to depend on proximity to trade routes and to markets. Thus the industry at Laverstock, although deriving its site initially from the clay, wood-fuel and water supplies of the vicinity, clearly owed its prosperity

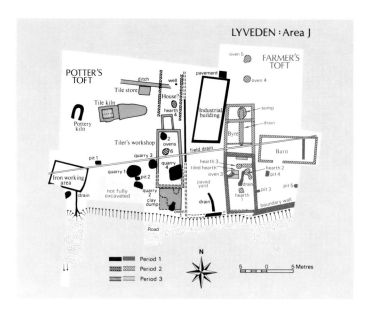

80 Adjoining tofts of a
potter and a farmer at
Lyveden, a long-lived
Northamptonshire pottery-
producing centre (Steane
and Bryant)

in the late thirteenth century to its situation next to the flourishing borough of Salisbury, on the one hand, and to the king's great palace at Clarendon, on the other.[128] Nor were potters reluctant to take their skills to wherever there was an evident need, establishing kilns within a short walk of their market, either next to a borough or, less commonly, inside it.[129] The Orchard Street pottery, being one of the better examples of such suburban pottery industries, was set up in the fourteenth century, and perhaps before, just outside the city wall of Chichester. With a ready market within reach of their kilns, the Orchard Street potters turned their hands to whatever might be most in demand. They made jugs and cooking-pots, storage-jars, lids and pans, with other lines which included roof-tiles, chimney-pots and mortars.[130]

Many potters, like those at Orchard Street, were equally proficient in the making of pots and of tiles, and this might be as true of a small country pottery like that at Hermitage, in Dorset,[131] as it was of a long-lasting industry on the scale of Nuneaton, in Warwickshire.[132] At Binsted, a Sussex pottery in production in the decades round about 1300, a rectangular tile-kiln and a horse-shoe-shaped pottery kiln were built, economically, back-to-back, the one for decorative ridge-tiles, floor-tiles, chimney-pots and ventilators, the other for the handsome jugs of the region.[133] However, there is evidence, too, of specialized industries, with tile-manufactories, at just this period, beginning to operate on what was clearly a considerable scale. The best known of these industries, centred at Penn, in Buckinghamshire, continued in production through both the fourteenth and the fifteenth centuries, being well-placed to send its tiles downriver to what was always the greatest market in medieval England, the growing metropolis of London. And although the craftsmen of Penn never approached in skill the earlier tile-masters of Chertsey, they became known, nevertheless, for a serviceable and consistent product, the success of which must first have come from the development of a new technique for 'printing' the tiles, thus cutting the costs of production.[134] On a lesser scale, those growing markets and improving techniques which had encouraged mass-production at Penn were to bring tile-manufactories of an increasingly specialized kind within reach of many urban centres. Hull, from the early fourteenth century, had a municipal tilery and brick-manufactory of its own, much of the product being subsequently used in the building of the Hull town walls.[135] And it is perhaps significant of the new technology that it was coal, still comparatively novel as a fuel for such a purpose, that was chosen for the firing of the tile-kiln at Boston, operating in the first half of that century.[136] More conventionally, the tile-makers of Danbury, in Essex, made use of the wood readily available locally for their firings, but their professionalism, all the same, was very clearly displayed in their finely built kilns and in the wide variety and technical perfection of their products. Contemporaries of the Boston artisans and just as competent, the Danbury tile-makers produced ridge-tiles, hip-tiles, and decorated floor-tiles with a choice of over a hundred designs. Their market area, although limited effectively to central Essex, included three market towns within less than five miles of their workshops.[137]

Much of the style of the Danbury tile-makers was derivative, it being difficult to be sure how many of the designs sold from the Danbury workshops were genuinely original to these. Yet what is clear, both from this and other contemporary evidence, is that customer demand for variety in the early fourteenth century was high, and that interest in decoration for its own sake, requiring entirely new levels of skill in the producer, was as much a feature of the contemporary trade in pottery table-wares as it was of the building industry, with its stress on the provision of elaborate roof ornaments and on the laying of spectacular tiled floors. In the second half of the thirteenth century and through the first half of the fourteenth, just when the craft of tile-making was reaching new peaks of its own, the potters of Nottingham and Scarborough, Laverstock, Nuneaton, Worcester and Doncaster, with a whole host of others, were competing with each other in the production of ever more elaborate decorated jugs, many of them strongly anthropomorphic in inspiration.[138] One of the more remarkable of

81 A fine early-fourteenth-century tile mosaic at Warden Abbey, Bedfordshire, now moved to the Bedford Museum (Baker)

the products of these industries is the face-jug found on the Old Bailey site in London, so constructed that a rheumy drop will settle on its nose after pouring.[139] But it is of interest, too, that peasant potteries like those of Audlem, in Cheshire, and Winksley, in north-west Yorkshire, should have felt called upon also to experiment contemporaneously in these forms, borrowing their motifs, if not always very successfully, from the wider-selling industries of the towns.[140] Certainly, the more sophisticated products of the urban industries were greatly sought-after, and we know that they could travel a long way. Thus the fine knight-jug from Dartford, in Kent, is almost certainly an import from the North Midlands potteries, brought there by the coastal trade.[141] And intriguing evidence of pottery trading, only a little earlier in date, has survived in the many glazed jugs found broken together in a pit on the London Guildhall site, perhaps placed there eventually to help drainage in the pit but originating, very probably, in a failed consignment smashed while in transit to the capital.[142]

In a wealthy port like Southampton, doing a great part of its business with Bordeaux, there can have been nothing unusual in the evident preference of

82 An early-fourteenth-century face-jug from the Old Bailey site, London (Museum of London)

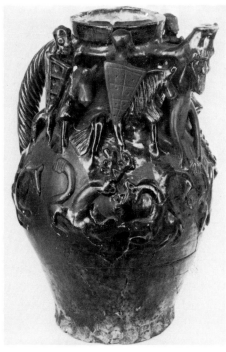

83 A knight-jug, probably from a North Midlands pottery, found at Dartford, in Kent (Museum of London)

84 Jugs of the late thirteenth century, found broken together in a pit on the Guildhall site, London, and perhaps part of a failed consignment (Museum of London)

Richard of Southwick, a propertied burgess of the late-thirteenth-century town, for the richly decorated wine-jugs of the Saintonge, just to the north of that city.[143] And at least one of these now famous polychrome jugs, by early in the next century, had been brought as far as Nottingham, the very heart of the native decorated pottery industry, to be found on the property of William de Amyas, one of the wealthiest traders of the borough. Yet it is a tribute to the skill of the local Nottingham potters that it was their products, chiefly, that William chose to use. Among the eventual rejects of his household, found in a cesspit on the site, decorated Nottingham jugs held their own alongside fine vessel-glass from the Mediterranean and other remarkable discoveries.[144] Like Richard, the burgess of Southampton, William de Amyas both wanted the best he could buy for his household and evidently could afford to pay for it. The difference only was that, in pottery at least, he could make his purchases closer to home.

It is no doubt the case that such finer wares as these, whether imported or locally produced, would have found a market more readily in the prospering towns than they might ever have done in the countryside. In the Scarborough district, for one, the more expensive glazed wares actually produced in the port have been shown to have occurred almost three times as often at Scarborough itself as in its

85 Jugs and other vessels from France and Spain found with the seal of Richard of Southwick, a late-thirteenth-century burgess of Southampton (Stirling)

adjoining villages.[145] However, this is not to say that the peasantry, in thirteenth-century England, was always so poor as to be unable to indulge in such purchases, nor was this in fact to be the case. We know, for example, from the excavated evidence, that the peasants of Barton Blount, in Derbyshire, although poorer even than those at Goltho, an equivalent Lincolnshire settlement, were nevertheless able to buy at least some of their jugs from the professional potters of Nottingham, while at Goltho itself, alongside the local wares from Toynton, there were face-jugs, probably from Scarborough and Lincoln, with a cooking-pot from the Netherlands and a wine-jug from the Saintonge.[146] Just such another Saintonge jug has been found recently, too, in what has been described as the 'extremely rural' setting of the Norfolk village of Welborne,[147] and although, of course, such isolated communities never matched the rich accumulations of imported wares that we can see, for example, at ports like Stonar and Southampton, it is yet significant that the villagers of Wharram Percy, in Yorkshire, more secluded even than their Norfolk brethren at Welborne, could obtain their pottery not just from the obvious sources at Scarborough and York, but less directly from south-west France, from the Rhineland, and even from the eastern Mediterranean.[148]

The advice addressed by Bishop Grosseteste in the early 1240s to the widowed countess of Lincoln might not have suited many at the time. However, it does at least remind us of the essential mobility of both purchasers and sellers at a period characterized, it is so often thought, by obstacles in the way of such exchanges. The bishop counselled:

> Make your great purchases on two occasions in the year: buy your wine, wax and wardrobe at the fair of St Botulf, what you consume in Lindsey, Norfolk, or in the value of Belvoir; when in the county of Caversham and of Southampton buy at Winchester; when in Somerset at Bristol. Your robes purchase at St Ives.[149]

In effect, the countess bought her household supplies in the rich agricultural land which lay nearest to her estates, but she did better to save her other purchases for those great annual fairs to which either she or her agents might travel – at Bristol and at St Ives, at Boston (St Botulf) or at Winchester (St Giles). At a humbler level, men even of moderate means in thirteenth-century England, whether in search of bargains or, more probably, of variety, would try to do the same. And these, of course, were precisely the conditions that would promote changes in taste and the rapid spread of fashions: those developments, indeed, which the archaeology of the period is so helpfully beginning to chart.

4   After the Black Death

We are unlikely now to view the Black Death in the same way as did its contemporaries. This 'wretched, fierce, violent' pestilence, in the words of the Ashwell Church inscription, after which only the 'dregs of the populace live to tell the tale',[1] can be coolly revalued by the historian of today as 'more purgative than toxic'.[2] And, indeed, with surplus population to be disposed of whether in this way or another, the famines of the early fourteenth century, the Black Death of 1348–9, and the succeeding pestilences of 1361 and 1368–9, all had their part to play in remedying the social ills which, from the reign of Edward I and earlier, had increasingly beset the kingdom. Yet, as we now know, the Black Death and its immediate successors carried off, within the space of a generation, between a third and a half of what had been the mid-century population.[3] Both in the short term and in the long, the consequences of these epidemics were momentous.

Naturally, the incidence of each epidemic varied, and there were some communities in every case that escaped virtually unscathed. Nevertheless, the experience of the villagers of Cuxham, in Oxfordshire, struck by the Death in the early months of 1349, cannot have been untypical, being one example among many of the devastations of a plague which, however we care to view it, placed its mark on the community for centuries. At Cuxham, in 1349, all twelve of the lord's villeins died within the year. And although, inside six years, new tenants were again found for every vacant holding on the manor, it is clear that they had not been come by easily: they were turbulent now and undisciplined, reluctant to perform labour services and, wherever an opportunity offered, insistent on their right to a high wage.[4] It was explicitly 'because of the death of men' that the issues of the mill at Ibstone, another of Merton's manors, were said to be so small in 1349,[5] while the decline of the college's receipts at Ibstone, already visible before the Black Death, was matched on the estates of many contemporary landowners, to whom the disaster of 1348–9 brought a permanent diminution of income. Between 1347 and 1351, and directly attributable to the Black Death, the monks of Battle lost fully 20 per cent of their pre-plague revenues, which fell again by

86   Lead plague crosses, found with the bodies of the victims in a mass grave at the Greyfriars cemetery, London (Museum of London)

another 7 per cent before stabilizing in the early 1380s at a new low level, virtually unchanged up to the date of the suppression.[6] During that same period, the receipts from spiritualities of the monks of Durham, being the income they drew from their tithes, are known to have suffered what has since been described as a 'really catastrophic collapse'.[7]

Other landowners, it may well be, evaded the consequences of the first great pestilence with more success than either Battle Abbey or Durham, to enjoy, rather, a last 'Indian summer' of prosperous demesne farming while, for perhaps as much as another two decades, prices kept up with rising wages.[8] But when the exceptional harvest of 1375 ushered in a new era of low prices, that balance between prices and wages, always precarious, was at last permanently upset. The movement away from demesne farming, already beginning on some estates as much as a century before,[9] became general, hastened by the development of accounting techniques which for the first time made the real profitability of an individual estate immediately apparent to the landowner.[10] At Christ Church, Canterbury, the reform of the priory accounts coincided, significantly, with the leasing of the demesnes between 1391 and 1396, within the first five years of the priorate of Thomas Chillenden. No cloying sentiment or foggy economic preconceptions impeded the 'outstanding financial acumen' of Prior Thomas. As a former treasurer of the cathedral priory, he had seen the way that the balance of advantage, in economic terms, had swung against continued control of the demesnes. Once he was prior and treasurer rolled into one, enjoying the absolute power that centralization of the accounting system had brought to his new office, he hurried to lease out the estates.[11]

The drastic solutions of Prior Thomas Chillenden did not appeal to everybody, and even at Christ Church, from early in the next century, the more cautious practice of preserving at least one manor in demesne was adopted by his successors in the priorate.[12] With the identical purpose of household supply, the archbishops of Canterbury continued, as late as 1444, the direct exploitation of their demesne at Otford,[13] while the monks of Battle were not finally to get rid of the demesne at Alciston until just before the end of the century.[14] However, the profitability of Otford, it must have been obvious to all, had been in decline since well before its leasing, and both there and, eventually, at Alciston, the advantages of home production, whatever these might be, were outweighed decisively by its cost. On other estates, not as amenable to household exploitation, the decision to lease was usually taken much earlier. Few, perhaps, moved as fast as the monks of Selby, whose abandonment of demesne cultivation on at least some of their manors followed within six years of the Black Death.[15] And there is some evidence elsewhere, in restocking and building on the Titchfield estates, and in the programme of works carried out during 1360–3 at the Surrey manor of Oxted, of a determination, not yet shaken, to continue direct exploitation of the demesne.[16] But the secular trend of declining profitability, the product of low prices and high wages, was against it. Following the example of many identically situated landowners, the canons of Titchfield, who had still been investing as late as the 1380s in new stock and buildings at Inkpen, leased this manor before 1425.[17] Their conversion to leasing in just these years fell in with the national pattern.

Reversing the experience of the pre-plague years, this pattern owed nothing to the exhaustion of the soil and very little to a failure in techniques. Indeed, at precisely the time that the monks of Battle were abandoning their demesnes, the crop yields on those estates were exceptional.[18] Yet the return on farming the demesne was failing to match up to the effort. Even on the exceptionally prosperous Cornish manors, long-term leases, held from the duchy, were granted from 1434,[19] while full-scale leasing programmes, frequently beginning in the 1380s and gathering momentum as wages continued to climb in the early fifteenth century, had been adopted well before this date at such great religious houses as Durham and Westminster, Ramsey, Leicester and Bolton.[20] In 1291, the Cistercians of Dieulacres, in Staffordshire, had derived no more than 8 per cent of their temporal income from rents; yet in the 1530s, for which the same sums can be done again, the equivalent figure had risen to nearer 70, as grange after grange had been lost to them.[21] Significantly, the greatest expansion of the barns and other facilities at Waltham Abbey's home farm can be seen, on the archaeological evidence, to have occurred only in the fifteenth century.[22] It was a development presumably designed to compensate for the contemporary contraction of the demesne on the abbey's outlying estates.

The principal cause of the rise in wages had been, of course, the shortage of labour, and as that shortage persisted in England, so wages continued to rise. The increases were no worse in the decades immediately following the Black Death than they had been already at several points earlier in the century. However, major wage-rises occurred particularly in the 1370s and 1380s, with a further spurt to all-time highs beginning in the 1420s, and it was this that put the demesne farmers out of business, then and (on the old pattern) for ever. Contemporaneously, labour shortages left their mark even on the more profitable manors in vacant tenement plots, cottage dilapidations, and unchecked reversions to waste. On the less hospitable soils, they might frequently result in a total and irrevocable desertion.

Such desertions are unlikely to have happened very quickly, and we have long since ceased to see the Black Death as the sole agent in the massive abandonment of hamlets and villages that we know to have occurred during the course of the later Middle Ages. Thus although most of one such settlement, at Caldecote in Hertfordshire, had been abandoned by the early fifteenth century, there were peasants still resident on the former village site for another two centuries at least, while, with plentiful land to keep them there, they were plainly comparatively well off.[23] Similarly, although Keighton, a Nottinghamshire village, drops out of the historical record as early as 1387, there is yet firm archaeological evidence in the pottery recovered there for continued occupation well into the third quarter of the fifteenth century,[24] nor would it be easy to place the final abandonment of such other marginal settlements as Upton, in Gloucestershire, or Barrow Mead, in Somerset, before the late fourteenth century at earliest.[25] In practice, what most of these poorer villages and hamlets suffered was an extended period of more or less continuous attrition, losing population all the time to their more favourably situated neighbours. Eventual village desertions, as it has been observed of some of the better-studied counties, peaked not in the immediate post-plague decades but after the late 1420s.[26] And it can surely have been no accident that this movement away from the marginal lands should have coincided with the exactly contemporary abandonment, by most of the greater landowners, of any further cultivation of the demesne, thereby bringing good land on the market in such unprecedented abundance as to make pointless the continued ploughing-up of poor.

It remains far from clear what percentage of the fifteenth-century desertions, as finally completed at this time, may be attributable to the initiative of enclosing landlords, becoming depopulators in the process. And it is no doubt true that the heavier profits deriving from the still buoyant wool sales of that century were sufficient inducement to convert much arable to pasture.[27] However, it is also the case that these market forces would not have had such obvious effect if they had not been preceded already by a widespread retreat from the arable as the peasantry regrouped on the land. If the landowner, in other words, was not the depopulator he has sometimes been made out to be, it was because his work had been done for him already by the peasant. What made the bishop of Worcester into a sheep grazier at Upton, late in the fourteenth century, was his inability to find tenants for his arable.[28] Like the similarly marginal Woollashill, in Worcestershire, on Bredon Hill's northern slopes, Upton had become unattractive to new settlers both because of the inhospitable soils of the region and as a consequence of the unfreedom that persisted there. And Woollashill, too, was turned over to grazing as one tenant after another abandoned it.[29] We know of Landbeach, a Cambridgeshire fenland village, that the most drastic depopulation of this long-lived settlement occurred on the initiative of Richard Kirby, a tough-minded mid-sixteenth-century grazier. Yet already, as far back as 1350 just after the Black Death had visited the village, there had been cases at Landbeach of the looting of doors, shutters and other surplus timber from deserted and ruinous cottages, nor was there much else surviving in the village when Richard Kirby flattened its centre.[30]

In the villages of England, whether deserted or merely shrunken, the consequences of this retreat of settlement are still plain for all to see, and it was accompanied, from the late fourteenth century and before, by a swelling tide of cottage dilapidations which, occurring over many years of persisting neglect, has left us with the earthworks of today. At Chalfont St Peter, in Buckinghamshire, from the 1360s, and at Chippenham, in Cambridgeshire, from the 1380s, there is clear evidence of a decay of tenements certainly to continue in later generations and already the cause of concern to the lord.[31] And as, in the late 1380s and the 1390s, villein land-demand shrank on the Ramsey manors, the abbot's court rolls came to contain the reports of ever-increasing dilapidations in the villages, themselves no doubt an important factor in his decision to lease out these demesnes for good.[32] Just as, on the one hand, the decay of the building stock at

Brookend, in Oxfordshire, hastened the progress of the steady depopulation which had already set it in train,[33] so a great deal of the success of the bishop of Exeter in holding his tenantry at Bishops Clyst, in Devonshire, must have been owed to his practice, not so common on other manors, of financing repairs and new building. Amongst these repairs, one large item in the bishop's accounts concerned the re-erection, in 1406, of a cottage row, typical enough of the contemporary artisan housing in some of the more prosperous towns, but rare in the country in that form.[34] Yet the bishop, unlike the urban developer, cannot have been interested primarily, if at all, in what such cottages would bring him in rents. Above all, what he needed on his land was men.

It should be obvious – and recent studies of the deserted villages of Hertfordshire and Oxfordshire, Norfolk, Berkshire and Northamptonshire have made it still more so[35] – that the peasants, when they abandoned the land, must have left the smallest settlements first. Thus where, in the great age of clearance for arable during the twelfth and thirteenth centuries, a forest-edge village like Whiteparish, in Wiltshire, had flung out satellite settlements of its own, it drew back these resources again in the later Middle Ages, to prosper where the smaller communities had failed.[36] And although, even at this later period, an active market in land may still be easy to find on many of the more favoured manors, such activity could usually be expected to continue, as had certainly been the case at Whiteparish, only at the expense of poorer neighbours. In effect, it was the failure of the poorer manors like Helston-in-Kirrier, in Cornwall, which served to prop up the economy of the rest.[37] That analogy of the lifeboat so frequently used in discussions of the world economy of today, has its application too in the regions of late-medieval England. If the lifeboat, that is, should remain afloat, not all who wish to join it may safely be allowed aboard. Poor manors, like poor nations, might have to swim – and could perish – on their own.

There are, of course, other parallels with today just as apposite, and one of these was the ability of well-off men in late-medieval England, as in every generation since, to turn the misfortunes of their less lucky contemporaries to their own immediate advantage. As war or a natural disaster will always do, the Hundred Years War, with the plagues to hasten it, promoted social change. In the villages, as we have seen already (pp. 105–6), such change had begun substantially before the Black Death. But the consolidation of holdings which wealthy peasant families in the pre-plague years had struggled so hard to achieve, could be come by much more easily after 1348–9, the first qualification for taking a part in this market being often no more than survival. Not every village would show an identical pattern. At Brookend, for example, not even the consolidation of holdings, beginning at this Oxfordshire hamlet in the early fifteenth century, could reverse its slide into insolvency.[38] Nor is it clear that it was the peasant consolidators who were always the winners in such transactions, for, as it has been pointed out of Cuxham, another Oxfordshire village, those villeins who had once been the employers of landless labourers, standing at least one rung up the social ladder as both they and their contemporaries saw it, now stood on the lowest rung themselves.[39] Nevertheless, none could doubt the evidence, everywhere abundant and compelling, of a transformation of English peasant society which, gathering momentum in the late fourteenth century, shook out the yeoman at the top. That unique wooden effigy of Walter de Helyon, preserved at Much Marcle Church, in Herefordshire, and dating to about 1360, can show us what such a man might have been like.[40] Walter lies, like a knight, with a lion at his feet, yet the contrast with other almost contemporary magnate effigies in the same church could scarcely be more striking. Walter de Helyon, franklin of Much Marcle, was as proud of his status, and as concerned to record it, as those who could afford a monument in stone.

In Walter's day, it was still unusual to achieve such high social status in a rush. At Oxted, in Surrey, the rise of the Stokets, another franklin family, had begun at least as far back as the late thirteenth century, many years before Katherine Stoket left a monument of her own at Lingfield Church, in her case in the form of a brass.[41] Katherine, in 1369, had been the principal chamber-woman to the lady of the manor, and what recommended such families, very obviously, to the leading landowners of their localities was their own continuity as dominant figures in the parish, inviting partnerships that would be forged and extended over the years. Not unnaturally, it was these families who came to inherit the demesnes. When leasing was eventually resolved upon, it was the 'ministerial' class on the Westminster Abbey estates — the former reeves, rent-collectors and other

87   The effigy, in oak, of Walter de Helyon, dating to c. 1360 and preserved at Much Marcle Church, Herefordshire (Museum of London)

88   Effigies at Much Marcle of a knight and his lady, *c.* 1400 (R.C.H.M.)

manorial officials – who took up the leases for the first time.[42] And similarly, when the labour and expense of running their own manors became too much for the canons of Leicester, it was their richer peasants, in almost every case, who had the skill and the resources to take over.[43] Certainly, it was men of this class, far more than the local gentry, who were to be the choice tenants of the more substantial Canterbury demesnes, at one end of the country, as of the Durham Priory manors, at the other.[44]

These solid men, many of whom would lead off the great farming dynasties of early-modern England, could afford to live very well. More sophisticated building standards, whether in town or country, were a feature of the later Middle Ages, and it was then, undoubtedly, that the once-aristocratic tradition of the hall-centred house spread downwards to reach the well-off peasantry. Most particularly, this can be seen to have been the case in the Wealden houses and in the Pennine aisled halls characteristic of fifteenth-century England (below, pp. 202–3). But something of the new life-style can be recognized already at a site like the late-fourteenth-century Hambleton Moat, Scredington, in Lincolnshire, as it can be too at Caldecote, in Hertfordshire, or at the Lincolnshire and Derbyshire clay-land villages of Goltho and Barton Blount. At Hambleton, the particular interest of this moated site, with its rather old-fashioned aisled hall and other buildings all dating between 1350 and 1450, is the association with the Pylets, a village main family first identifiable in Scredington as far back as the late twelfth century and still prominent there in the fifteenth.[45] And while there is little to place the final-period buildings at Caldecote, Goltho and Barton Blount as early as the moat at Hambleton, they nevertheless reveal the relative prosperity of the post-plague survivors, owed presumably to a consolidation of plots at what was, in each case, a substantially shrunken settlement. Thus the peasant farmer of late-medieval Goltho, although still not the builder of a hall-house, could afford for the first time the good-quality timber that enabled him to put up a traditional long-house in a very much more durable form.[46] At Caldecote, rather later, a farmhouse of the fifteenth and sixteenth centuries might be equipped with a hall and a first-floor solar, the buttery and pantry being separated from the hall by the cross-passage first seen in both more elaborate and socially superior buildings.[47]

'Riches', so went the near-contemporary saying, 'oft bring harm and ever fear', and the growing prosperity of families like the Stokets of Oxted and the Pylets of Scredington would not be achieved without cost. Since the late thirteenth century and even before, there had been clear signs at the top of village society of an emergent yeomanry, emphasizing inequalities within it. However, it was the free availability of land, most of all, in the post-plague period that gave the already-propertied families their major opportunity and that drove such social divisions much deeper. With all its disadvantages and inequities, feudal land-holding in the English villages had yet promoted both equality of plot-size among the villagers and a stable pattern of inheritance. It had been within the reach of most villein families – as, indeed, it was usually to prove their ambition – to 'keep the name on the land'. Together, they had co-operated in the mechanics of community land-use which a shortage of arable had made essential; they had made fair apportionments among themselves, and had conducted their business as a fellowship. At the Death, all this changed.

Inevitably, the pace of such changes varied, nor would peasants readily abandon their practice of conveying their lands to their children. Yet the flexibility of land-holding in late-medieval England, where plots might be bought and others freely exchanged, came to mean that it was not invariably the *family* land which

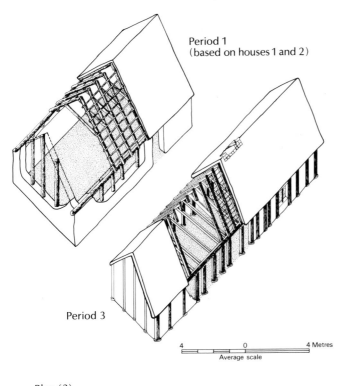

Period 1
(based on houses 1 and 2)

Period 3

4   0   4 Metres
Average scale

Plan (3)

89 Conjectural
reconstructions of peasant
houses at Goltho, in
Lincolnshire, showing an
improvement in structural
techniques already evident in
houses of the later thirteenth
century (period 3) (Beresford)

descended from father to son. And whereas the thirteenth-century court roll had
recorded, as a matter of routine, the peasant's inheritance as being 'his father's
land', land-transfer documents of the post-plague period quite as commonly list
earlier tenants unconnected with the family of the new one.[48] In field archaeology,
the late-medieval instability of the village, as the sense of community dissolved,
may be recognized plainly enough in the change of house-plot patterns, in
consolidations of holdings, and in the disuse or rebuilding of individual
tenements. Yet its implications, at the time, were much larger. Those village
communities which had felt themselves able, in the late thirteenth century, to
band together in collective opposition to the lord, fell a victim, bit by bit, to the

enclosers of fifteenth-century England.[49] And when, in due course, the great demesne farms became available for leasing, it was individuals, and only exceptionally the communities, who took them.[50]

An obvious by-product of the dissolution of traditional community ties was the breakdown of manorial discipline. A significant post-plague increase in trespasses and other felonies, noted both at Warboys and Holywell-cum-Needingworth, was accompanied, understandably enough, by the disappearance of the practice of personal pledge by which one villager, in more settled times, had willingly supported another.[51] And although, perhaps, the absolute level of violence was no higher at Holywell in the later Middle Ages than it had been during the worst years of social unrest at the turn of the thirteenth and fourteenth centuries, there can be little doubt that its social distribution had changed. Increasingly, by the late fourteenth century, it was the village main families themselves, formerly the prop of manorial discipline against the landless migrant labourer, who were taking the law into their own hands.[52] Indeed, it was just such a climate of violence, as this, taking hold on a higher social level in the localities, that was needed to set the scene for peasant unrest on a national scale. And this, in 1381, meant rebellion.

There have been many explanations, some particular and some general, for the violence of the Peasants' Revolt. Nor should it be seen out of context with those other popular rebellions in Germany and France, Italy and the Netherlands, all of them concentrating in the 'years of revolution' between 1378 and 1382.[53] Yet the English revolt, the only truly national movement of them all, was also, in most respects, very local. In England, that is, the so-called Peasants' Revolt of 1381 had been immediately preceded, as it was accompanied and succeeded too, by what were essentially village rebellions on such contemporary issues as the local re-exaction of labour services.[54] Moreover, it had frequently been these village-felt exactions, mounting suddenly over the country as a whole as the individual landowner reacted instinctively to the movement of prices and wages against him, that had driven the main families into a flurry of violence, setting the scene for the national rebellion.[55] There may be some truth still in the general theory of an awakening class-consciousness as the back-cloth to disorder in the villages, and there is certainly no reason to doubt the verdict of contemporaries that it was the poll-tax collections of 1380/1 that sparked-off the eventual rebellion. However, it would be difficult now to see the Peasants' Revolt as anything more than a passing incident, albeit a particularly striking one, in the long-drawn-out sequence of socio-economic change that characterized late-medieval England. Like the Black Death itself, the revolt has its own particular importance, and every schoolboy must know of it. But again like the Death, its effect was restricted, while its long-term consequences, although certainly to be detected in fifteenth-century society, are not easy to assess with precision. In late-medieval England, plague, war and social rebellion were so woven into the fabric of everyday life as to transform many attitudes and values. As we shall see in the next two chapters, the archaeology of England in the later Middle Ages would be quite impossible to interpret without them.

5 Stability at a Reduced Level: the Church

Nowhere in English society were new departures more evident than in the late-medieval Church. Except as great landowners and, occasionally still, as builders, there will be little to report of the mighty possessioner houses which, in pre-plague years, had dominated the monastic Church. Yet this is not to say that the Church itself was unappreciated, or that its institutions were in a state of disarray. There had been, of course, many signs of religious unrest, with a stepping-up, early in the fifteenth century, of the crown's campaign against heresy. But the association of Wycliffe's Lollardy with the social discontents of the Peasants' Revolt, as with other lesser rebellions, had done nothing but harm to its supporters, and if, indeed, there were to be any turning-away from the traditional institutions of the Church, this would take the form of a realignment of allegiances within the existing fabric of the Church, not a search for new alternatives outside it. In staying away from the great religious houses which their ancestors had favoured and endowed, the devout men and women of late-medieval England were voting with their feet for something a little nearer in spirit to themselves. They found this something in the parish church and the friary, the hospital and almshouse, the chantry and fraternity, with the Carthusians standing out among their fellow monks as most deserving of patronage for remaining most consistently austere.

In post-plague England, there is some risk of over-emphasizing the role of the typical parish church as the mortuary chapel of its parishioners. As the most notable public building in the locality, it had a purpose as much in the business and social life of the community as in the cure and remembrance of souls.[1] Nevertheless, it was generosity in the face of death which contributed most to the very heavy expenditure on parish church fabrics that characterized fifteenth-century England, both in the countryside and in the towns. And the marks of this abiding late-medieval obsession with death are still stamped very firmly on the landscape of today. One of the more striking records of contemporary communal piety, as it found full expression in church-building, is the remarkable parish church of Swaffham, in Norfolk, remodelled almost from the ground at the

90   The parish church of Swaffham, Norfolk, reconstructed in the fifteenth and early sixteenth centuries with the help of individual parishioners' contributions (R.C.H.M.)

expense of its parishioners during the course of the late fifteenth and early sixteenth centuries. To this work, we are told in the *Black Book of Swaffham*, John Chapman and Catherine, his wife, contributed the north aisle, with the glazing, seating and paving of the same, and with the further gift of £120 'to the makyng of the New Stepyll'. Among the many other donors whose contributions were recorded individually, John and Margaret Plummer financed the repair of the old Chapel of the Trinity, 'to the glory of God'; the Stywards provided seating in the north part of the old church and paid for the glazing of four windows; the Langmans seated the middle aisle and Raffe Hammond the Trinity Chapel; the Taylors roofed the church from the chancel back to the cross alley, and the Coos did the same for the porch.[2]

    We are not told, at Swaffham, how many of these contributions had anything directly to do with the death cult. However, Simon Blake, 'gentylman', and Jane, his wife, were among the more important patrons of the new work at Swaffham

91 The porch roof at Swaffham Church, financed by William and Anne Coo who 'did make the Roffe of the porche'; fifteenth-century (R.C.H.M.)

Church, and it had been Simon Blake who, in 1489, had founded a personal chantry there. Of course, chantries, which might require permanent endowment of the stipend of a priest to celebrate memorial masses for the departed, would remain beyond the means of most. But there were many substantial men, in late-medieval England, who could afford to endow the annual memorial mass known to contemporaries as an 'obit', and if this were beyond them, they had some substitute still in the co-operative chantry of the parish fraternity or the guild. In 1497, to their evident dismay, the Goldsmiths of London, being one of the wealthier of the city companies, found themselves keeping, with services and solemn processions, the obits of twenty-five goldsmiths once of their fellowship, in effect one working day in twelve.[3] And although the dilemma of the London Goldsmiths was not, perhaps, that common, it was nevertheless the case that the

G   The sophisticated tower keep at Conisborough, in Yorkshire, a baronial castle of the late twelfth century (Department of the Environment)

H *left* Multiple defences at Dover Castle, Kent, considerably strengthened in the thirteenth century to the order of Henry III (Department of the Environment)

I *above* Excavations in the south transept of Bordesley Abbey, in Worcestershire, showing raised floor-levels in the exposed section at the rear (Rahtz)

J *right* A windmill of post-mill type, perhaps similar to the mill built at Ibstone, on the Chilterns, for Merton College, Oxford; Flemish, *c.* 1340 (Bodleian, Bodley 264, f.81)

K   An important hoard of pewter tokens, found in August 1971 on the Winetavern Street site, Dublin (National Museum of Ireland)

Opposite
L *above*   A peasant long-house of the late thirteenth and early fourteenth centuries at Upton, in Gloucestershire, with its adjoining cobbled yard (Rahtz)

M *below*   Faxton, Northamptonshire: the stone walls and interior floor of a peasant long-house, later the barn of an early-fourteenth-century farmstead on the site (Butler)

N   A mid-fourteenth-century tile-kiln at Nuneaton, Warwickshire, being one of many excavated at this important Midlands pottery (Mayes)

O   Inlaid floor-tiles from the pottery at Penn, in Buckinghamshire, one of which has lost its white clay filling; fourteenth-century (Museum of London)

Opposite
P *above*   An early-fourteenth-century tile-kiln, just missed by the 1939 water-main, at Danbury, in Essex (Drury)

Q *below*   Warden Abbey, Bedfordshire: a tile-mosaic pavement uncovered for the first time in 1974 in what may formerly have been the lodgings of the abbot; early-fourteenth-century (Baker)

R   Six wine-jugs from the Saintonge, north of Bordeaux, thought to have been the property of Richard of Southwick, a late-thirteenth-century burgess of Southampton (Stirling)

memorial mass, considered as a potent means of intercession with the Almighty that both required and deserved heavy investment, was familiar all over the country. Moreover, the fashion was growing. Something like three-quarters, and perhaps more, of the Yorkshire chantries, as recorded in the mid-sixteenth century, were foundations of the post-plague period, nor is there any indication of a falling-off of such chantry foundations in the late fifteenth century when, indeed, the pace of new creations was quickening.[4] At Norwich, over the same period, as a useful recent study has shown, citizens of every will-making category left more money for the financing of memorial masses and other prayers for the dead than for any other purpose, apart from bequests within the family. And interestingly too, the next ranking beneficiary in these citizen's wills was the local parish church, whichever that might be, much going as bequests to the fabric fund for further embellishments or repairs.[5] In Norwich, as in many other towns, the extensive rebuilding and enlargement of almost every parish church, which is known on other evidence to have occurred between the late fourteenth and the early sixteenth centuries, could scarcely have been conceivable without them.

There were other ways also of financing rebuilding, and when, for example, in the early sixteenth century, All Hallows-on-the-Wall fell into 'grete Ruyne and dekeye', the rector of this London church petitioned for the licence to hold a stage play which, with the parish collection run alongside it, would successfully raise a fair sum.[6] No doubt, too, the increasing fifteenth-century practice of sharing-out manor court fines equally with the village church, 'one half to the fabric of the church and the other to the lord of the fee', contributed substantially to the routine expenses of keeping many churches in repair.[7] Yet, whatever the source of the finance might be, the fact is that there were many in fifteenth-century England most actively concerned in the embellishment and refurnishing of the local parish church, and that this concern could be both competitive and imitative. Besides, that is, the so-called 'wool' churches at which the wealthier cloth-manufacturing communities vied with each other in the financing of ever more extravagant constructions, there were the 'war' churches with which successful captains, rich on the ransoms of France, sought to augment their fame.[8] And there were gangs of specialist craftsmen, working a region and leaving their mark in a characteristic arch-mould or a window, ready to do the bidding of whoever might raise the finance to employ them.[9] Helmingham, Framsden and Brandeston are Suffolk villages with less than five miles between the three of them, and it was at Helmingham, in 1487/8, that the villagers entered into a contract with Thomas Aldrych, a Norfolk mason, to build them a tower at least sixty feet high, perhaps higher if they felt they could afford it. He was to build it, at the west end of the

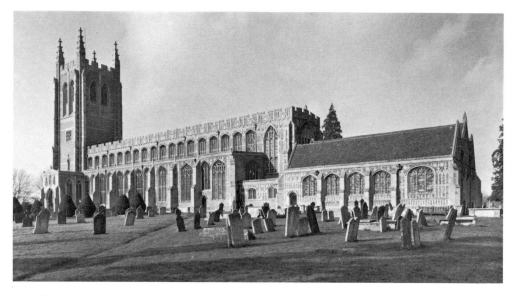

92   The 'wool' church at Long Melford, Suffolk, built on the profits of the fifteenth-century cloth trade (Hallam Ashley)

church, 'after the brede wydnesse and thicknesse of the stepyll of Framesden', with a door, windows and buttresses 'after the facion of the stepyll of Bramston'. And if, in the event, it would suit his employers to have the tower built higher than they had specified in the original contract, 'thanne the s^d Thomas shall make or do to be mayd the s^d stepyll as many fote heyer as they wole haue yt'.[10] They were to take it as high, on this occasion, as was necessary to overtop their neighbours.

Several such fifteenth-century building contracts survive, among these an unusually explicit contract of 1412 by which a mason bound himself to demolish the old church at Catterick, in Yorkshire, and to re-use the stonework in the construction of an entirely new church on a fresh site.[11] But the circumstances at Catterick were exceptional, and what happened, for the most part, in fifteenth-century rebuildings was a reconstruction of whatever there might be of an existing fabric to suit the needs or the fashions of the moment. Occasionally, as was to be the case at Wharram Percy, in Yorkshire, the decline of a community would lead to the demolition of aisles put up originally to house a congregation on the increase in the twelfth and thirteenth-century,[12] while elsewhere an economical response to competing pressures might be that, for example, of the parishioners of Angmering, in Sussex, whose southern tower, in the brave new fashion, replaced half an aisle now surplus to their needs as the congregation which had required it had diminished.[13] More usually, fifteenth-century parishioners, if they had any

St Mary's Church
Framsden
Suffolk

St Mary's Church
Helmingham
Suffolk

All Saints Church
Brandeston
Suffolk

93 Three adjoining parish-church towers in Suffolk; Helmingham, being the last to be built, incorporates features both of Framsden and Brandeston (Hallam Ashley)

money to spare, would spend it, as at Hadstock in Essex, on a western tower and, probably, on a porch.[14] They would build a new roof, as we know they did at Halstead in the same county in 1413, deliberately copying the roof already supplied to another nearby church;[15] and they might take the opportunity that such roof-building presented to improve the lighting of an over-dark nave by the insertion of clerestory windows, or to decorate the exterior roof-line with new battlements. When a chapel was built at St Mary-on-the-Hill, Chester, the contract of 1433 provided for the embattling of the roof in the modern manner, as well as for great windows in the latest fashion, 'faire and clenely wroght . . . full of light'.[16]

At St Mary, Chester, the chapel was sited next to the chancel, on its southern side, being an extension very common in the later Middle Ages as more space was needed for a mortuary chapel or for the particular purposes of a guild. One of the earlier of these chapels was the one recently investigated at Bradwell Priory, in Buckinghamshire, probably erected only a little after the Black Death for the use of pilgrims attracted to the priory by a miracle-working image of Our Lady.[17] And many still remain today as the most obvious manifestations of a devotional cult which, to whatever saint or mystery that cult was directed, must clearly have been of great power. An evocative reminder of the lasting appeal of the pilgrimage, even in late-medieval England, is the list of relics and other holy souvenirs which the noted traveller, William Wey, brought back with him from Palestine, the rich

94   The chapel at Bradwell Priory, Buckinghamshire, before restoration (R.C.H.M.)

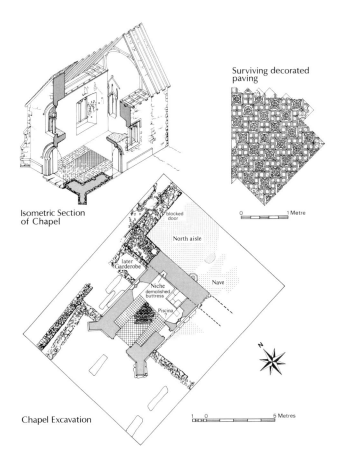

Surviving decorated paving

Isometric Section of Chapel

0   1 Metre

blocked door

North aisle

later Garderobe

Niche
demolished buttress

Nave

Piscina

Chapel Excavation

1   0   5 Metres

95   The chapel at Bradwell after excavation and conservation, showing the niche in the east wall, next to the altar, which would have held the miracle-working image of Our Lady (Woodfield and Mynard)

harvest of two mid-fifteenth-century excursions. William Wey, after the second of these, spent his last years with the Bonshommes of Edington, in Wiltshire, and it was in their chapel of the Sepulchre at Edington that he intended his collection to be preserved. With the maps of the world and of the Holy Land which Wey must have purchased for his journeys, there were many devotional objects acquired in the souvenir bazaars of Jerusalem, including a reproduction of the handkerchief of St Veronica with which she had wiped the sweat from the brow of Our Lord, and a 'clothe stayned wyth the tempyl of Jerusalem, the Movnte of Olyvete, and Bethleem'. Probably the pride of the collection was Wey's gathering of holy stones:

> a relyquary of box in the wheche be thys relyks. A ston of the Mownte of Calvery, a stone of sepulkyr, a stone of the hyl of Tabor. A stone of the

pyler that ovre Lord was stowrchyd too (scourged at). A stone of the plase wher the crosse was hyd and fvnde. Also a stone of the holy cave of Bethleem.[18]

All these curiosities, to our great loss, were swept away by the reformers at the Dissolution.

Churches elsewhere built up similar collections, from the rich relics and fine church-plate of a city church like St Mary-at-Hill, London, to the more modest assemblages of the village churches, among them that of Little Waltham Church, in Essex, a feature of which was the gift of livestock to sustain services there, with

96   The fable of the Three Living and the Three Dead, partly represented in a wall-painting at Peakirk Church, Northamptonshire, with flies, slugs, beetles and worms to drive home the lesson of corruption; mid-fourteenth-century (Kersting)

'a cow for the parson to synge with every day'.[19] However, the wholesale dispersal of church goods, occurring at the Reformation, rid the parish churches of all but a few of their vestments and an item or two of church plate, and what is left to us now of these 'cults of the folk' is limited, for the most part, to such survivals as the carved bench-ends of East Anglia, the elaborate choir-screens of the West Country, or the occasional wall-painting and church glass. It is in these, though, that the links between folk art and popular religion are still to be seen very clearly. Thus the well-known fable of the Three Living and the Three Dead, confronting the more fortunate of the painter's generation with what was certain to be their fate, was to be a favourite theme of many wall-paintings, a particularly unpleasant example of which is the mid-fourteenth-century version at Peakirk, in Northamptonshire, perhaps inspired by the Black Death itself, where flies, slugs, beetles and worms are used to emphasize the lesson of corruption.[20] And it was precisely these moralizing reminders of death and of retribution which were brought out again in the great Dooms, or Last Judgement scenes, placed centrally over the chancel arches of such village churches as Penn, in Buckinghamshire, or Pickworth, in Lincolnshire, in full view of the preacher's captive audience.[21] There were Dances of Death, a popular mortuary sequence of a peculiarly grisly kind, in the guild chapel at Stratford-upon-Avon, at Newark, at Hexham and elsewhere,[22] with individual creations like the 'Pricke of Conscience' window at All Saints, York,[23] or the specially commissioned 'Ymage of Deth' roundel in the chancel window at Stanford on Avon, Northamptonshire, by which Henry Williams, vicar of Stanford in the late fifteenth century, hoped to be remembered in perpetuity.[24]

At Stanford, the particular interest of Henry Williams's 'Ymage of Deth' roundel is that the instructions for its making have been preserved. By the terms of the vicar's will, there were to be at least two such roundels in the church windows at Stanford, to have in each case 'my ymage knelyng in ytt and the ymage of deth shotyng at me', and to be made of 'as gude glasse as can be goten'. Evidently, the roundels were to take the place of the funerary monument which Williams might otherwise have built for himself in the church, and it was one of the provisions of his will, again, that his body should be laid to rest in the churchyard. At the other extreme, there were those, of course, for whom the church itself was scarcely an adequate memorial.

For the great magnate who had accumulated riches in the government service or who returned with a fortune from France, one of the most obvious methods of perpetuating his memory would be the foundation of a hospital or an almshouse.

97   A Dance of Death scene in a fifteenth-century window at the church of St Andrew, Norwich (Hallam Ashley)

98   Henry Williams, a late-fifteenth-century vicar of Stanford on Avon, Northamptonshire, portrayed in a window of his church with 'the ymage of deth shotyng at me' (Marks)

Of course, this had long been a purpose of hospital foundations, some of which had originated as far back as the twelfth century. But the growing popularity of the chantry, on the one hand, as set against the waning appeal of conventional monasticism, on the other, had had the effect of turning many potential founders in late-medieval England to just those institutions of the secular church which could promise them elements of both. Of the new colleges, hospitals and almshouses of the later Middle Ages, very few would have come into existence at all without a memorial purpose to inspire them, this belief in the perpetuation of memorials for the dead being shared by magnate and priest, merchant and war-captain alike. Sir John Fastolf, one of the best known of these last, spent his declining years at Caister, in Norfolk, there deploying an appreciable part of his large fortune on the works at his fortified manor-house. But he had no heirs, and it became his intention to set up a college and an almshouse at Caister which would do duty as a chantry for himself. Plentifully endowed and richly housed, the college at Caister would no doubt have been successful had it not been for the stratagems of Fastolf's man of business, John Paston the elder, as ambitious and as ruthless as himself.[25]

Among the earliest of the great 'war' hospitals of which Caister, in luckier circumstances, might have been one, was the new collegiate establishment at Leicester, a lavish re-endowment in 1356 of Henry of Lancaster's hospital and

99 The Yorkist collegiate church at Fotheringhay, Northamptonshire, established in the early fifteenth century as a well-endowed chantry for the family; the chancel at Fotheringhay was demolished in the late sixteenth century (R.C.H.M.)

149

chantry of 1330, built up as a family memorial by his son.[26] And there were many others also which Fastolf might have taken as examples, including the Fitzalan hospital, college and chantry at Arundel, established in the 1380s, the Yorkist collegiate chantry and almshouse at Fotheringhay, founded in 1411, and the duke of Suffolk's hospital at Ewelme, in the heart of rural Oxfordshire, set up in 1437 at a village especially dear to Alice, his duchess, being the home of her family, the Chaucers.[27] One such project of which Fastolf would certainly have known was the college at Tattershall, in Lincolnshire, established by Ralph, Lord Cromwell, in 1440, immediately next to his great new castle. It was to be here, in the collegiate church at Tattershall, that John Taverner, perhaps the greatest of our early-sixteenth-century composers, would come to perfect his art.[28] But although Tattershall Church survives, to be one of the finer examples of such single-dated structures of the period, little else remains of the great collegiate establishment which Cromwell projected and which Taverner was to use as a staging-post on the way to a career at Oxford. What little there is, includes the gatehouse, with the merest suggestion of the characteristic double-courtyard plan of the colleges and hospitals of Tattershall's generation, as of virtually all domestic building projects conceived at that time on any scale.[29]

In hospitals especially, such courtyard plans were still something of an experiment. Traditionally, the sick had been lain in the body of the church with the chancel serving as their chapel, and this had been the arrangement in 1330 at the earl's hospital at Leicester,[30] as it would remain at many of the more old-fashioned establishments through the rest of the late Middle Ages. Alternatively, a

100   The collegiate church at Tattershall, Lincolnshire, built for Ralph, Lord Cromwell, in the mid-fifteenth century to complement his new castle at Tattershall (Hallam Ashley)

150

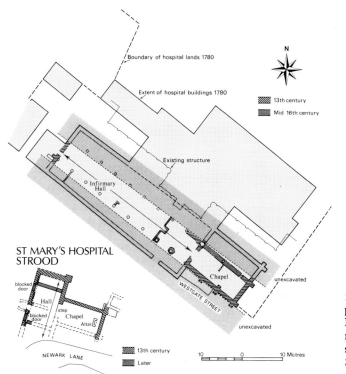

101 The nave-and-chancel plan at St Bartholomew's Hospital, Gloucester (above right), and the cross plan at the smaller St Mary's Hospital, Strood (Hurst and Harrison)

chapel might be set centrally, at right-angles to the infirmary hall, and there are good recent excavated examples of both these plans at St Bartholomew's, Gloucester (the nave and chancel), and St Mary's, Strood (the cross).[31] However, at Strood there is already some evidence of the disuse of the original infirmary hall, in the late fourteenth century, with a refashioning of the hospital on the modern quadrangular plan. And there can be no doubt at all that this was the plan selected at the new Fitzalan *Maison Dieu* at Arundel in the 1380s, as it would be again at Ewelme in the late 1430s, the Chaucer and de la Pole foundation.[32] Both old and new are present at Browne's Hospital, Stamford, founded in 1476,[33] while at the Savoy Hospital, in London, Henry VII's spectacular work of piety on a staggeringly munificent scale, there would be something of a reversion to the ancient and traditional techniques.[34] But whereas the dormitory at Browne's Hospital had been placed, traditionally enough, with a square chapel to complete the range at its eastern end, the infirmary hall had been divided, as was already common practice at monastic houses of this date, into private cubicles, while an enclosed court to the north of the hall included accommodation for the warden.

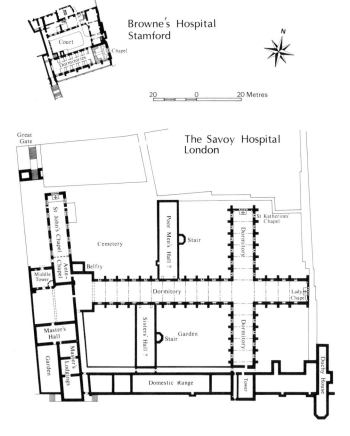

102 Browne's Hospital, Stamford (founded in 1476), with Henry VII's great charitable foundation at the Savoy (Spittle and *King's Works*)

And the Savoy Hospital, as it has been convincingly shown, was built on a continental and not on a native model.

More familiarly, the pious foundation of the later Middle Ages took the form of a church and common hall, but with individual lodgings such as those still in use at St Cross, near Winchester, an ancient hospital rebuilt extensively by Cardinal Beaufort before the middle of the fifteenth century. At Ewelme, indeed, it was the expressed intention of William de la Pole that the inmates of his hospital should have

> a certeyn place by them self . . . that is to sayng, a lityl howse, a celle or a chamber with a chemeney and other necessarys in the same, in the whiche any of them may by hym self ete and drynke and rest.[35]

And when, in 1485/6, the almshouse at Tattershall was eventually contracted-for

103   St Cross Hospital, Winchester, rebuilt in the mid-fifteenth century with individual
lodgings for the bedesmen situated in the range west of the church (Aerofilms)

104   Part of the hospital buildings, with the church behind, of William de la Pole's foundation at
Ewelme, in Oxfordshire (R.C.H.M.)

153

in fulfilment of the wishes of the late founder of the college, it was to be built, adjoining the churchyard, with a common hall and chapel of its own and with thirteen separate chambers, each for a bedesman's use.[36] Characteristically, many private chambers are listed in the surviving inventory of the wealthy *Maison Dieu* at Dover, taken shortly before the suppression of that house,[37] and these no doubt included the separate apartments of the relatively well-to-do who would have bribed their way, as they certainly did at Leicester, onto the roll of this comfortable foundation.[38] It was precisely to secure the exclusion of 'persons rich and not poor, strong and not weak, healthy and able to work', that the men of Saffron Walden provided that no fewer than twenty-four of their number should serve as the governors of the local almshouse founded on 5 August 1400, 'with the consent and help of all and in the presence of the whole assembly' of the parish. At Saffron Walden on that day, 'advantageously providing for the remedy of their own souls', the parishioners 'decided piously to build certain houses of a durable kind to the honour of God and of his glorious mother for the refuge and upkeep of 13 poor persons', these to be chosen by common consent of the two custodians, the governors, and 'two or three of the senior men of the vill', with 'impartiality and without any bribe or carnal affection . . . so that they be the more indigent persons namely if they be such as are decrepit, blind, lame'.[39] Although lacking the wealth of the great magnate and royal hospitals, these almshouses at Saffron Walden were to be maintained, nevertheless, by a steadily increasing endowment in property and by the parish collections which, since their foundation, had been allowed as a weekly round.

At Saffron Walden, as the first statutes carefully prescribed, these things should be done without prejudice to the rights and revenues of the existing church in the parish. Yet the new focus of charitable loyalties presented by such institutions as the Saffron Walden almshouses, could scarcely do otherwise than erode the revenues of the older religious bodies, in particular of the possessioner houses, and these, as we have seen already (above, pp. 126–9), had long since come upon hard times. Of course, few independent religious houses went out of business altogether at any time in the late Middle Ages. However, almost all suffered a decline of activity that came close, in some cases, to bankruptcy, and among those that went were the alien priories, the cells and other very small foundations, with an occasional 'cradle-sick child' like the diminutive Benedictine community at Alcester.[40] Perhaps the most obvious sufferers in the face of competition were the Austin canons, a relaxed and comparatively loosely organized order that had grown up in the twelfth century with many small independent communities, seldom adequately endowed. Of these, in fifteenth-century England, nine disappeared, while another seven were deprived of their original autonomy.[41] Among those that survived, the little priory of St Denys, near Southampton, cannot have been alone at its suppression in 1536 in being judged to be in a condition of 'extreme ruin and decay'.[42]

Just as had been the case among the post-plague villages and occasionally even in the towns, it was the smallest and the weakest of the monastic houses which were obviously the first to collapse. The Augustinians of Selborne, another Hampshire house just a little poorer even than St Denys, who had been in trouble from soon after the onset of the Black Death, held out till as late as 1484, when the sole surviving canon in residence (the prior, aged 72) consented to the appropriation by Magdalen College, Oxford, of his ruinous buildings and their lands.[43] But for many establishments, weaker even than this, the collapse came very much earlier. Particularly at risk were the alien priories: victims not only of their economic insufficiencies but of the politics of the Hundred Years War. These communities, as dependencies of monastic houses controlled by foreign powers, had already suffered brief confiscations before the Hundred Years War under both Edward I and his son. However, it was not until the 1370s, when the war, after a full generation, was beginning to turn against England, that the demand grew for the permanent expulsion of all aliens, whoever they might be, subsequently formalized in the Commons petition of 1377 and resultant government orders. From this time, although few alien priories or foreign-held manors passed irrevocably into lay hands, the processes of lease, and even of sale where the king might permit it, stepped up. It was the war, the pestilences and the harshness of the times that were put forward in 1379 as the reasons why the monks of Bec had drawn nothing for fifteen years from their lands in England, 'where great part of their property was', and why they wished now to lease whatever they had there, 'if any could be found to take it'.[44] And it may be that it was the poverty of St Neot's Priory, one of the more important of Bec's English possessions, that prevented the completion of the cloister court in stone, a timber-built west range having to make do where, in better circumstances, stone would surely have been preferred.[45] But at St Neots, at least, the community survived by going independent, with the blessing of the mother house, in 1409, just before the final confiscations of 1414. Others were certainly less lucky.

Among the lesser priories of Bec, both Steventon (Berkshire) and Wilsford (Lincolnshire) were disposed of comparatively quickly, the former to Westminster Abbey in 1399 and the latter initially to the nearby Augustinians of Bourne, the abbot and convent of Bec being persuaded that it was 'more desirous to alienate the priory to the abbot and convent of Bourne than to any secular person, as more conformable with law'. But Wilsford, later temporarily in the hands of Ralph, Lord Cromwell, became part of the endowment of the Yorkist collegiate chantry at Fotheringhay, before being returned in 1486 to Bourne Abbey following the Lancastrian restoration.[46] And its uncomfortable fate is a useful illustration of the extent to which the alien priories had come to be looked-upon as the rewards and playthings of magnate families, a precedent for what would happen again, on an altogether grander scale, in the suppressions of 1536–9.[47] With so much land permanently in the hands of the Church, or of prominent landowning families almost equally unwilling to dispose of it, Henry V's courtiers and military associates saw opportunities in the confiscations of 1414 that might never be repeated. Formally and in the short term, very few of the alien estates were irretrievably lost by the Church. But local magnate interests were both pervasive and difficult to deny, and just as Wilsford, the former alien priory, came to Lord Cromwell in 1440, another of the Bec manors, at Swyncombe near the priory at Steventon, had become the possession of Thomas Chaucer before his death in 1433, and passed to his daughter Alice, countess of Suffolk, shortly afterwards co-founder of Ewelme.[48]

What had brought difficulties to the alien priories, almost as much as the greed of the king and his friends, was their continuing short-fall in recruitment. At Bec, the monks had found it hard to keep their representatives in England, where they belonged, complaining in 1379 that their own numbers at the home abbey had been impossibly increased 'because those in England had returned to the monastery and had been admitted out of compassion'.[49] Nor were they alone in their predicament. That severe overcrowding which had been such a problem, for example, in the late-thirteenth-century nunneries (above, p. 65), had yielded less than a century later to failures in recruitment of an even more burdensome kind. For a great monastic house like Battle Abbey, it might still be possible to make a virtue of necessity by deliberately restricting the numbers of the community, matching shrunken assets against a reduced establishment.[50] And this, again, is the probable explanation of the shrinkage at Kirkstall, one of the richer Cistercian communities, evidenced archaeologically in the reduction in scale of the kitchen facilities which had occurred there by the fifteenth century.[51] At Studley, in Oxfordshire, the nuns, who for similar reasons had kept their establishment down, were rebuked severely in 1531 and ordered 'to augment your nombre of ladyes within the yere'.[52] But it was easier said than done. We do not know whether the Studley Benedictines were successful in following these instructions, and this uncertainty itself is indication enough of one of the great recurring dilemmas of almost every late-medieval nunnery in England, the problem of fluctuating numbers. When, in 1511, the prioress of Minster, a Kentish Benedictine house, was asked about the number of her nuns, she replied that 'she had heard there were seventeen; she knew of fourteen; she herself wished to increase the number to fourteen if she could find any who wished to enter into religion'.[53] Thus, it was not always that an enclosed community might seek to keep itself and its fortune inviolate, but that nobody might want to get in.

Where recruitment even at the monastic house was running into difficulty, the maintenance of a religious life on its cells or other dependencies was likely to be especially at risk. Like many of the alien priories, the dependent rural cells of a great house like Durham Priory were always very small, and became, as recruitment waned at the mother house, a source of continuous embarrassment. It would always be easy, as the priors of Durham found, to discover monks willing to serve at Finchale Priory, the nearby rest-house of their community, or at Durham College, in Oxford. But to get them to go to one of the remoter cells, with perhaps no more than a single companion to share their exile, was another matter altogether.[54] Moreover, that permanent dislocation of the religious life, brought on the dependencies of Durham in the fifteenth century, had been even quicker to occur elsewhere. From the beginning, there had been those houses like Denney, in Cambridgeshire, which had gone by fits and starts as one community came to take the place of another. Originating as a Benedictine priory, being then a dependency of Ely, Denney had become a Templar preceptory and hospital, was converted, after the suppression of that order, into a house of Franciscan Minoresses, or Poor Clares, and exhibited every one of these stages in its plan.[55] But much more common than this was the slide into failure of an individual community, which became in due course irreversible. A principal reason for the abbey of Bec's eventual sale of its dependent priory at Wilsford had been the irremediable dilapidation of its chapel and other buildings, already too far gone by the 1380s to be worth the cost of repair.[56] Nor was there, after all, so much to distinguish such establishments from the farmhouses by which they were replaced. Bec's other so-called 'priory' at Steventon, in Berkshire, sold before the end of the fourteenth century, appears to have lacked even the chapel we know to have existed at the abbey's manor-house at Wilsford. Like another alien priory at Minster Lovell, in Oxfordshire, of which some details survive, Steventon would have resembled rather a contemporary parsonage, with the hall, chamber and kitchen arrangements of the typical domestic plan. Both at Steventon and at Minster Lovell, the monks would have worshipped at the parish churches which, as appropriated by their houses, were in truth the main reason for their presence there.[57]

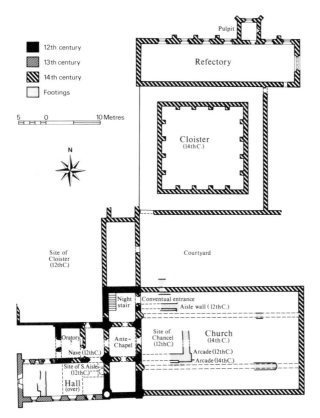

Pulpit

12th century
13th century
14th century
Footings

5   0   10 Metres

N

Refectory

Cloister
(14thC.)

Site of
Cloister
(12thC.)

Courtyard

Night
stair

Conventual entrance
Aisle wall (12thC.)

Oratory
?

Nave (12thC.)

Ante-
Chapel

Site of
Chancel
(12thC.)

Church
(14thC.)

Arcade (12thC.)
Arcade (14thC.)

Site of S. Aisle
(12thC.)

Hall
(over)

105   Changes in plan at Denney
Abbey, Cambridgeshire, as the house
was converted from a Benedictine
priory to a Templar preceptory, and
then to a house of Poor Clares
(Spittle)

Indeed, it was precisely on this grey frontier between what was and what just
was *not* a monastic house that failures were most likely to occur. In the twelfth and
thirteenth centuries, optimum conditions for the religious life had scattered the
land with small cloistered buildings, inexpensive adaptations to local resources of
the more sophisticated plans of the great monasteries. But times were changing,
and although some of these buildings survived in fair condition, maintained in
repair by the mother houses to which they were usually attached, many had long
lost their purpose even before 1400, to be turned to alternative uses. It seems, for
example, a reasonable assumption that the strictly non-conventual buildings of the
Suffolk 'priory' at Walton, a dependency of the cathedral priory of Rochester,
were a fourteenth-century rebuilding on a new site and to a new plan, close by the
parish church, of a cell which had ceased to maintain a full monastic community
and at which communal buildings on a claustral plan were no longer either
necessary or economic.[58] At Gorefields, in Buckinghamshire, the Cluniac nuns of
De la Pré, Northampton, seem to have kept in being, perhaps right up to the

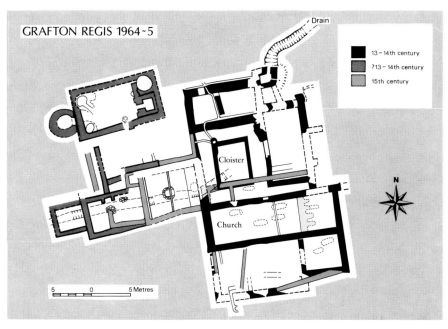

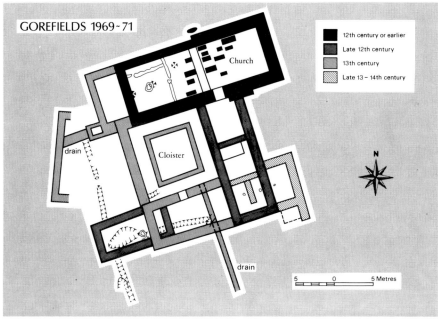

106   Lesser monastic establishments, built on a simplified claustral plan, at Grafton Regis, Northamptonshire, and Gorefields, Buckinghamshire, the former overlain by the fifteenth-century buildings of the Woodville manor at Grafton (Mahany and Mynard)

dissolution of their house, the diminutive claustral buildings they had put up on this property as far back as the thirteenth century.[59] But without the support of conservative-minded nuns, and with lay patrons of a very different inclination, the transformation of the small Augustinian hospital, or 'hermitage', at Grafton, in Northamptonshire, was certain to be much more complete. Here the Woodville family, which had helped the Hermitage prosper in the thirteenth century, when it assembled a reasonable endowment, were to move in upon it from the mid-fourteenth century, just as soon as it fell upon hard times. By the end of that century, in a not uncommon change of function, the chapel at Grafton had become a Woodville chantry, perpetuating the name of the hospital's tenacious founder-patrons. And although transferred in the 1430s to the Augustinians of Northampton, according to the terms of Thomas Woodville's will, Grafton was back in the family's hands again by the 1470s, at which time Anthony, Lord Rivers, brother of the queen, was probably responsible for the construction of the new lay manor-house which Grafton's recent excavators found, somewhat to their surprise, to be sealing the original monastic buildings.[60]

Of course, not all religious orders were doing badly during the later Middle Ages, and there were even those, among them the friars, the Carthusians and the Bridgettines of Syon, who fared remarkably well. Nevertheless, the very general drying-up of new endowment at the more traditional monastic houses had the effect, at the more active of these, of encouraging a planned redeployment of resources, while others achieved the same security by cutting down. On a small scale, many communities came to engage in the 'industrial' enterprises of which evidence has been recovered recently on several excavations. Thus there have been finds in the immediately pre-Dissolution levels at the priories at Stamford, Pontefract and Selborne of distilling apparatus in pottery and glass, establishing the practice of chemistry at these houses and perhaps even the study of alchemy.[61] At many such establishments, too, the ancient crafts of copying and illuminating manuscripts continued as before, sometimes developed as commercial enterprises serving more than the needs of one house. At Mount Grace, for example, a Carthusian community remotely sited in northern Yorkshire, the monks have been shown to have been experimenting with printing shortly before the Dissolution, complementing what is known of the Benedictines of Tavistock, whose more sophisticated printing venture was operating commercially.[62]

However, of obviously much greater importance than any effort of this kind was the deliberate campaign of the more energetic of the monastic administrators both to diversify their resources and to enlarge, or protect, their endowment. The

107 A drain sump at the south-west corner of the cloister at St Leonard's Priory, Stamford, found to have been filled in the late fifteenth century with material which included glass distilling vessels, crucibles and mercury, probably used in alchemy (Mahany)

prior of the Hull Charterhouse, in a less lucky example of such strivings, drove himself almost to the point of breakdown in an effort to recover his lost rents, and it was his brother prior at Mount Grace, among others, who in 1440 rebuked him for over-concern with the things of this world, urging him, rather, to seek first the kingdom of God.[63] Very evidently, when it came to the law, a great corporation like Tavistock Abbey was in a much better position to defend itself, nor did it neglect such other opportunities as the economy of its region provided. If Tavistock's interest in the tin mines of Devonshire was not, in point of fact, very direct, there can be no doubt that the monks drew at least some profit for themselves from this booming late-fifteenth-century industry. Among other things, it was on their press at Tavistock in 1534 that the statutes of the tinners' parliament were printed, both establishing and publishing the laws of an industry which, to the monks themselves, was undoubtedly a matter of concern.[64]

Where the Benedictines of Tavistock might look to tin as a means of enlarging their revenues, their brethren at Durham, since the early fourteenth century, had been interested in the commercial exploitation of coal.[65] Yet those houses, it is obvious, with access to such valuable natural resources were always to be very much in the minority, and perhaps more typical of the solutions generally sought by monastic administrators was quite another venture of the monks of Durham, the setting-up of the new collegiate church at Hemingborough. Prior Wessington's college at Hemingborough, in the East Riding, established in a hurry in 1426–7 to forestall other claims to this rich benefice, did not prove a financial success. However, the reasons for the college's foundation, being the formal appropriation of the rectory, the prospect of more patronage to meet the demands of influential place-seeking clerks, and the collection of further revenues to swell those of the cathedral priory itself, were exactly those most likely to appeal to the monastic administrators and chief executives of whom Prior Wessington is himself one of the better examples.[66] Indeed, for a good many monastic houses, the appropriation of a wealthy benefice, with the immediate access this might promise to new revenues, had long been seen as quite the most reliable specific for their ills. And when, for example, the monks of Glastonbury had embarked, in 1391, on the appropriation of the parish church of Longbridge Deverill, in Wiltshire, they would have done so with many good precedents before them, including the successful appropriation by Westminster Abbey, almost a century before, of Longdon Church, in Worcestershire (above p. 63). Nevertheless, the use they made of their latest acquisition was very much of their own generation. At Longdon, the revenues had been specifically assigned to the repair of the fabric at Westminster, and when Glastonbury, in its turn, asked for Longbridge Deverill, the reasons advanced were those usual for the time, being the debts and declining revenues which had followed on pestilence, murrain and flood. But unlike Longdon, the profits of Longbridge Deverill were not used to make good a disaster, nor even, in a more general way, to prop up the finances of the monastery. They were committed instead to the supplementation of the individual cash doles of the monks.[67]

Glastonbury was a very wealthy abbey, and its cash doles, like those indeed of Westminster, were already very high. However, even a rich community might feel the pinch of a genuine economic recession, differing only from the run of its contemporaries in having the resources to seek remedies. At Longbridge Deverill, the appropriation, although eventually well worth its cost, had started by being very expensive. Among other methods of diversifying investment for which Glastonbury again became known, there was the purchase and development of town lands. We know, for example, that Glastonbury's holdings at both London and Bristol were built up considerably before the mid-fifteenth century, in part compensation for what must have seemed an irreversible decline in receipts from its rural estates.[68] And it is from London, once more, that we have contracts surviving for shop-row developments of 1369, 1370 and 1373, the first two as investments of the dean and chapter of St Paul's, the last of the prior of Lewes.[69] One of the more successful of such investment decisions must have been that taken by the dean and chapter of Exeter Cathedral to rebuild for leasing in 1394–5 a newly acquired High Street tenement, for which they subsequently had many good tenants.[70] A similar enterprise, although at the other end of the market, was the abbot of Tewkesbury's terrace of twenty-four cottages, constructed together

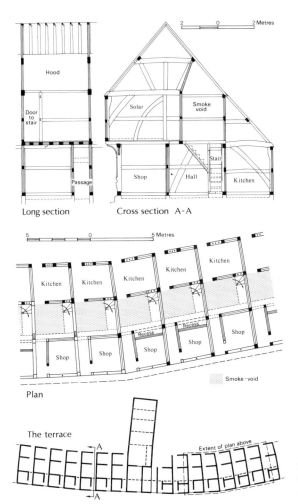

108   The abbot of Tewkesbury's mid-fifteenth-century cottage-row development, originally of twenty-four cottages (Jones)

163

in the mid-fifteenth century and each, presumably, available for letting.[71] At lesser houses, without such resources, there might be other expedients to be tried. One of these we have seen already (above, pp. 144–5) in the rebuilding, almost certainly for investment, of the pilgrimage chapel at a poverty-stricken Benedictine house, Bradwell Priory in Buckinghamshire. With a similar purpose, the canons of Walsingham built themselves a chapel (the so-called 'New Work' of the mid-fifteenth century) completely to enclose the famous Holy House, with its cargo of crowd-drawing relics.[72]

In difficult times, an obvious reaction will always be to put the bulk of one's investment into building. And it was no accident, certainly, that Prior Thomas Chillenden, the hard-headed business-man who had leased at a stroke the Canterbury demesnes, was also 'the greatest Builder of a Prior that ever was in Christes Church', being largely responsible for the final completion of the

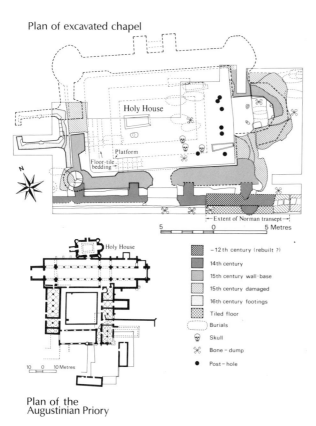

109   The 'New Work' at Walsingham Priory, a mid-fifteenth-century chapel built totally to enclose the original crowd-drawing Holy House (Whittingham)

110 The nave at the cathedral priory of Bath, a work of the very end of the Middle Ages, still incomplete at the Dissolution (Kersting)

cathedral's magnificent nave.[73] Nor was he, even at Christ Church, the last of such builder-administrators, for the celebrated Angel Tower, the crowning glory of Canterbury Cathedral, also known as Bell Harry, was a work of the later fifteenth century, its final details being debated well into the 1490s.[74] Almost contemporary were the great works at Bath Cathedral Priory or at Fountains Abbey under the energetic Abbot Huby (1494–1526), one of the most active builders of them all, while a century earlier the monks of Durham had either remodelled or rebuilt entirely from the ground every major conventual building of their priory, leaving only the refectory untouched.[75]

At Durham, the exception was a significant one, and it tells us much already of the improved domestic standards which the monks had become accustomed to demand. The right to privacy, claimed first by the monastic obedientiaries and then by the monks themselves, had increasingly usurped the place of more primitive ideals of a life lived entirely in common. Thus, when the monks of Durham had contracted in 1398 to rebuild the dormitory of their house, they had

165

Later blocking wall

111 The church and
claustral buildings at Sawley
Abbey, Yorkshire, showing
the wall inserted in the later
Middle Ages to cut off the
greater part of the nave,
presumably on the reduction
in size of the community
(Cambridge: Committee for
Aerial Photography)

made provision for separate sleeping cubicles within the body of their new
dormitory hall, and if they neglected the reconstruction of their old-fashioned
refectory, it was because it was so rarely in use.[76] At all but the most austere
religious communities, relaxed dietary rules had led everywhere to the more
regular use of the *misericord*, the room originally designed for the infirm where
meat and other luxuries had been permitted. And it was quite common, in these
circumstances, for the refectory itself to be divided, a new floor being inserted in
such a way as to leave an upper chamber to serve as a meatless frater, conforming
with the ancient Rule, while a lower might do duty as a misericord. Such
arrangements, for example, were well-known at fifteenth-century nunneries,[77]
while another contemporary example has recently been explored at the Cistercian
abbey of Kirkstall. What the excavations at Kirkstall have shown was evidence for
the transformation of the original refectory, including the insertion of a new floor
and the building of a chimney to warm the lower chamber at just that point where
the *pulpitum* had once been. Associated with these works, there had been a
remodelling of the kitchen quarters of the abbey, a new meat kitchen in the latest
fashion taking the place of the much larger cooking areas for which the community,
now much reduced, no longer had any need.[78]

Those declining numbers which, in every order, had made the great halls of
the common life echo so cheerlessly, would have taken their toll of Cistercian
communities especially, as lay brethren ceased to be recruited. In the late
Middle Ages, well before its suppression although the date has yet to be

112   The luxuriously remodelled early-sixteenth-century refectory at Cleeve Abbey, in Somerset (Batsford)

established, the monks of Sawley, another northern Cistercian community, let the great nave of their church fall into ruins, abandoning that part of the church which the lay brethren had used and concentrating resources on the crossing, transepts and chancel which might still be of service to the monks.[79] Already, by 1381, there were only two lay brethren at Sawley, and before the late fourteenth century, in Cistercian houses generally, the lay brethren's quarters in the west claustral ranges were becoming redundant, to be turned to a new purpose or neglected altogether, according to the resources of the community. Cleeve Abbey, in Somerset, which was to be one of those houses where in the early sixteenth century the western range would come into service as a newly improved and enlarged abbot's lodging, had seen also, just a few years before, the thorough-going conversion of the south cloister range, now redesigned to hold a handsome, well-heated first-floor frater very much on the model of the great halls of the wealthier laymen.[80]

The almost total rebuilding of the domestic quarters at Cleeve, as a phenomenon of the late Middle Ages, was far from unique to the Cistercians. One

113   The prior's lodging, guest chambers, and infirmary at Much Wenlock, in Shropshire, being a late-fifteenth-century domestic building of exceptional distinction and comfort (Batsford)

168

114   Prior Crauden's personal chapel at Ely, built in the early fourteenth century (R.C.H.M.)

of the best examples of late-medieval domestic architecture, dating to the final years of the fifteenth century, is the magnificent surviving range at Much Wenlock, in Shropshire, a former Cluniac priory, which probably combined the functions of prior's lodging and redesigned infirmary, having provision for guest chambers in addition.[81] Nor are there lacking other fine examples of such improved official lodgings, from Prior Crauden's fourteenth-century work at the great cathedral priory at Ely, through similar elaborate provision at Rievaulx or Castle Acre, and down to the more modest but still comfortable buildings of the prior of Bicester, an Augustinian house, or of the Premonstratensian abbot of Bayham.[82] From 1460, we have striking evidence of the comfort of such establishments in the surviving inventory of the abbot's effects at Peterborough Abbey which, though one of the greater Benedictine houses, was yet far from the wealthiest of its order. At Peterborough, the abbot kept a great stock of silver vessels, many of them gilded, with spoons and candlesticks also of silver and with three large platters for spices; he had rich supplies of table- and bed-linen, fine towels and napkins, and soft feather beds; his kitchen was well equipped with cauldrons and pots, his larder with chargers, platters, dishes and saucers of pewter or of wood; in his stock-house, there were earthen pots for the storage of flour, with barrels for fish, and with shelves for setting-out his cheeses, providently guarded with a mousetrap.[83]

The ostentatious luxury of such a private household as this, in plain contravention of both the letter and the spirit of the Rule, continued to excite the wrath of clerical reformers, contemporary bishops urging the errant houses in their dioceses to return to their original pure practices, 'etyng and drynkyng in oon house, slepyng in oon house, prayng and sarufyng (serving) God in oon oratorye', and, to that end, 'levyng vtterly all pryuate hydles (hiding-places), chaumbres and syngulere housholdes'.[84] In 1421, advised by a Carthusian, Henry V had placed this issue high on the list of the other malpractices for which he scolded the Benedictine establishment.[85] Yet even Henry's cherished Carthusians, before the Dissolution, furnished their cells with modest additional comforts, while at other houses, less professedly austere, there was little to hold the monks back. Brother William Ingram, monk of Christ Church, Canterbury, and custodian of the shrine of St Thomas, bought new bedding and furniture all his life, sometimes with the priory's money, and what he did not spend on his private property might go instead into his garden, on the sunny side of the cathedral church, where he had built himself a little gazebo.[86] Nor were the canonesses of St Sexburga, at Minster in Sheppey, any more reluctant to protect themselves from what they must have regarded as thoroughly outmoded austerities. At Minster, before the inventory taken at the suppression of that

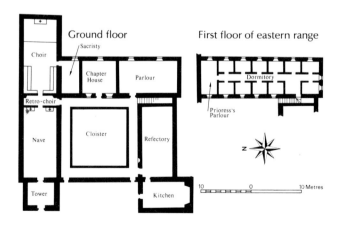

115 The dormitory and other buildings at Littlemore Priory, Oxfordshire, showing late-medieval partitioning of the dormitory into separate chambers, with the prioress's parlour at one end (Pantin)

116 Finchale Priory, County Durham: a choice rest-house and retreat for the monks of the neighbouring cathedral priory at Durham (Aerofilms)

house, the original common dormitory had been partitioned, to become instead both the treasury of the priory and a range of private apartments. In one of these, Dame Agnes Browne's chamber, there was a feather bed, with bolster, pillows, blankets, sheets and coverlets, and with other 'stuff given her by her frends'. Dame Agnes, like her namesake Agnes Daye in the same convent, had brought with her painted hangings, furniture, silver, brass and pewter, few of their sisters in religion being without their own small piece of silver, their painted wall-cloth, their feather bed, candlestick and picture.[87]

One of the chambers in the dormitory at St Sexburga, probably set across the end of it, had been the private apartment of Dame Ursula Gosborne, sub-prioress of the community. And this was the position of the prioress's chamber in the similarly divided dormitory of the much smaller house of Benedictine nuns at Littlemore, in Oxfordshire, suppressed as early as 1525 to become part of the endowment of Wolsey's new collegiate foundation.[88] Standing sentinel at the end of the dorter range, the prioress's parlour may recall at least the remnants of a monastic discipline which, even with this light rod, both men and women in the religious life were usually very ready to evade. Perhaps the best known of the holiday retreats maintained for such a purpose by the monks, was the priory of Finchale, a dependency of Durham, captivatingly placed on a bend of the River Wear, just a few miles downstream from the priory. It had become the function of Finchale, when its own small community had diminished, to take four monks regularly from the cathedral priory, giving each a three-week break. Accordingly, its buildings underwent a transformation, from the early fifteenth century, entirely in keeping both with its new purpose and its period. Already, in the middle 1360s, the over-large church at Finchale had lost its aisles, and as work progressed on the new domestic quarters, the former priory began to resemble less a house of religion than the grand country mansion which it had, in truth, become. Work concentrated particularly on the prior's lodgings, east of the cloister, where the monks spent much of their time. Here there was a handsome first-floor hall, next to the kitchen, with a fine suite of rooms for the prior himself, well-heated, wainscoted and adequately lit by bay and oriel windows. Visiting monks had their own heated day-room, known as the Player Chamber, and while some may have slept in the former dormitory, over the chapter-house, others would have used the more comfortable room, also with beds in it, adjoining the prior's private chapel. The original frater, already rebuilt once in the early fourteenth century when the permanent community at Finchale had remained still fairly substantial, was altered drastically in the later Middle Ages by the insertion of a new upper floor, the vacationing monks from the mother house at Durham no doubt preferring the greater comfort and more obvious convenience of the prior's refurbished hall.[89]

6 Conspicuous Waste

The ease and comfort of the monks of Durham, taking their rest at the priory of Finchale, were perhaps no greater than their well-endowed community could very well be expected to provide. Yet there are visible here, too, the strong pressures of a life-style thought appropriate for men of their rank and position: a style which demanded generosity, or *largesse*, and which was characterized by conspicuous waste. Contemporaneously, on the far side of the Pennines, their brethren at Whalley, a Cistercian house, were spending as much as two-thirds of their considerable annual income on the purchase of food and drink, much of this to feed an over-large household which outnumbered the monks by a factor of between four and five.[1] Similarly, if there was one thing that the monks of Battle, in a programme of economies, evidently refused to cut down, it was their expenses at table.[2] Where such a style, in the late Middle Ages, was important to men of religion, the same pressures would operate – and even more so – on the lay magnates. Indeed, little of how they rewarded themselves in the post-plague period is truly understandable without it.

As had certainly been the case with the monks themselves, many prominent landowners in fifteenth-century England found themselves the victims of high wages and low rents, to the permanent deterioration of the income they could get from any one property on their estates. However, whereas the monks had been restrained by law and custom from adding to the stock of their property, those of Durham complaining, by the mid-fifteenth century, that 'except for the manor of Houghall, which is hardly worth twenty marks when put to farm these days, we have not acquired any lordship, land or military fee for 160 years',[3] the position of the magnate could be very different. Although hampered too by a sluggish land market where every family held onto its own, the magnate nevertheless enjoyed opportunities denied to the monks to extend his patrimony by marriage or by the fortunate placing of his heirs. And if these horizons, for whatever reason, were closed, there might always be the alluring prospect of an office of profit under the crown. Accordingly, with the props of inheritance and royal patronage to support them, and with an advantageous marriage always round the corner to rescue the noble family on the brink, there were few magnates in fifteenth-century England who, if they kept intact politically, would come financially to grief. In very many respects, as members of a dwindling caste able to put much pressure on the king, the older aristocracy had seldom been better off.

These processes, both of the preservation of old lands and the accumulation of new ones, are still traceable in a number of fifteenth-century families, from great aristocratic clans like the Percies of Northumberland, through the dramatically rising middle-rank nobility like the Nevilles and the Woodvilles, to such humbler gentry families as the Mainwarings of Over Peover, in Cheshire, the Willoughbys of Wollaton, in Nottinghamshire, or the Plumptons of Spofforth, in Yorkshire, themselves long-term clients of the Percies.[4] Nor can it be doubted that there were others of whom it could have been claimed, as it has been of the twenty-two children of Ralph de Nevill, first earl of Westmorland (d. 1425), that their careers 'made up an almost interminable series of matrimonial triumphs'.[5] However, once that is said, there were yet many differences both between and within these groups, whether in taste, in industry, or just in the basic ability to succeed, and something of this is visible still in what they chose to leave behind. It is perhaps an over-emphasis to see the period of the Hundred Years War as the 'first great flowering of English *domestic* architecture', which is how one of its most knowledgeable historians has described it.[6] And, certainly, the evidence of really conspicuous expenditure on building in the grand manner, if this is all that was meant, is restricted to a small and not even a very representative class.[7] The Percies themselves were not great builders, at least in the fifteenth century,[8] and the same might be said of the careful Greys of Ruthin, earls of Kent,[9] as again of the Bourgchier earls of Essex, the exception in their family being Thomas Bourgchier, archbishop of Canterbury (1454–86), who began the rebuilding of Knole.[10] However, the Percies, like their neighbours the monks of Durham, had completed most of their work on the castles at Alnwick and Warkworth before 1400, and the Bourgchiers, if they spent little on building, proved much more generous to themselves when it came to internal furnishings, to plate and jewels, to fine costumes, and to the more ostentatious forms of patronage, including the support of drama.[11] Indeed, whether or not it would take the form of new building, a substantial part of the resources of England's late-medieval aristocracy was assigned to the improvement of personal living standards and accommodation. And if this could be done with a maximum of public ostentation and display, so much greater would be the honour of the builder.

The castles of the period, as few have neglected to point out, were usually

117 The keep at the great Percy fortress at Alnwick, in Northumberland, completed in the late fourteenth century (Hallam Ashley)

118 Bodiam Castle, in Sussex, for which licence to crenellate was granted in 1385 (Aerofilms)

militarily inadequate. But this judgment, while it does them some injustice even as strongholds, more seriously overlooks their true purpose. In fifteenth-century England, the fortress-palaces of the old aristocracy were to be seen as badges of rank at least as important to their magnate owners as were fine claustral buildings to the monks. Of course, as demonstrations of magnificence, they would be tricked-out too with all the latest military gimmickry from the Continent, such continental models no doubt explaining, as little else can, the expensive and inconvenient pseudo-keeps of Tattershall and Raglan, or the great artillery tower at Sir John Fastolf's new castle at Caister. Nevertheless, the function of a castle in late-medieval England could scarcely have been more different from that of its equivalents in the war-torn areas of the Rhineland or of southern and central France. And although Caister, briefly, endured a siege, Raglan was threatened,

119 The water defences and great artillery tower at Caister Castle, Norfolk, built for Sir John Fastolf in the mid-fifteenth century (Hallam Ashley)

and Tattershall, during the alarming Tailboys affair, clearly derived some advantage from its defences,[12] it would be difficult to see a primary emphasis on impregnability at any of these buildings, if this were truly to incommode the owner. Furthermore, what all three castles shared was the role, highly characteristic of the century, of a prop to personal dignity, all the more essential where the dignity itself was new. Fastolf of Caister, Cromwell of Tattershall, and William, Lord Herbert, of Raglan were all largely self-made men. Significantly, it was only in Fastolf's later life when, at the age of 46, he had become both knight of the garter and baron of France, that he set about refashioning the family manor-house at Caister on the coast of Norfolk, making it, after very heavy expenditure and a long building campaign, a setting appropriate to himself.[13]

Neither Fastolf nor Caister were unique, and there are close parallels, for example, between the building of Caister to the order of Sir John and the work begun contemporaneously by his friend Sir Andrew Ogard, another soldier of fortune, at the Hertfordshire manor of Rye, near Ware.[14] Nevertheless, what Caister shows so clearly is that combination of roles, at once palace and fortified retreat, to which such buildings might commonly be adapted so long as political uncertainties persisted. Initially, that is, the decision to build at Caister had had nothing to do with the war in France, yet when Burgundy changed sides in 1435, jettisoning its long-standing English alliance in favour of reconciliation with France, the threat to the Norfolk coastline, via Flanders, became immediate, with repercussions, of course, at Caister. Soon after this, Sir John's agents were dispatched to London to buy up a stock of arms for his mansion, while his builders were directed to alter their designs, improving the defensibility of the postern gate and increasing the fire-power of the great tower.[15] Yet, through it all, Sir John and his successors referred to Caister as a 'mansion' at least as often as they called it a 'castle' or a 'fortalice', and this characteristic mixture of views is well brought out in William Worcestre's assessment of Caister in 1468, being a 'ryche juelle' which was yet much 'at nede for all the cuntre yn tyme of werre' – or as Margaret Paston would have it for her family, recent expropriators of Caister, the fairest flower in their garland and one obviously worth great efforts to defend.[16]

In all, Fastolf is known to have spent over £6,000 on the works he financed at Caister, yet there is little to suggest, whether at Caister or at his many building projects elsewhere, that the old knight was seeing these activities as a form of investment from which, in due course, he might expect an adequate return on his money. In his other roles, especially in the cloth trade, Fastolf had earlier shown himself as acute in business as he was undoubtedly daring in war. But when it came to manors, his collecting mania (for that is what it seems to have been) was such as to render him heedless of advice, however good, and it was this same spirit, very obviously, that guided his approach to more building. Both manors and new building would increase his name, and both would be pursued for that reason.[17]

Fastolf's fortune and his reputation had been won abroad, this background explaining why he chose a design for his castle at Caister that was founded on no local precedent. Caister, it has been argued, followed the pattern of the so-called *Wasserburgen* of the lower Rhineland, much emphasis being placed on the elaboration of its water defences,[18] and the great keep at Tattershall, in just the same way, can be seen to have been inspired by the very latest military thinking of contemporary northern France, owing nothing to Anglo-Norman or Angevin prototypes.[19] In addition, both castles shared, in brick, a new building material still uncommon in England in the early fifteenth century, but known to Fastolf and Lord Cromwell from their travels in northern Europe, as it would have been also to their contemporaries and fellow-campaigners, Sir Roger Fiennes, the builder of Herstmonceux, or Sir Andrew Ogard of Rye. Brick, of course, had already been used in England for some time before the Agincourt campaign. Nevertheless, it is plain that the new fortunes and sophisticated continental tastes of those who had fought with Henry V encouraged them to look overseas for craftsmen in a material which, if not yet familiar to local builders, could readily be manufactured on their own estates, at Caister as again at Tattershall.[20] Thus when, in the 1430s and 1440s, the fashion for building in brick caught on generally among those who at that time could afford it, the imported traditions were already highly developed, shown well in the sophisticated detailing of Sir Andrew Ogard's gatehouse at Rye, the subject of a recent study.[21] Much later, at Kirby Muxloe Castle, in Leicestershire, begun by Lord Hastings in 1480 and left unfinished following his execution in 1483, the bricks were still fired by Antony 'Docheman', paid more for his labour than his English assistants and known from the evidence of later accounts to have been a bricklayer as well as a brick-maker. In 1481, it had been to Tattershall that Lord Hastings had sent both his master-mason, John Cowper, and Cowper's principal assistant, Robert Steynforth, no doubt to study, for re-application at Kirby, that combined treatment of brickwork and masonry which was among Tattershall's exceptional achievements.[22]

Little remains at Caister now and still less at Kirby Muxloe, while at Tattershall Castle, besides the church, the only surviving building of importance is the great tower-keep, designed also as the residence of the lord. Yet enough is preserved in each case to show that what they all had in common was a handsome courtyard layout, being a development on a grander scale of the courtyard plan familiar already at manor-houses much earlier in date, with something also of the

120 The keep of Ralph, Lord Cromwell, at Tattershall Castle, Lincolnshire, remarkable especially for the high quality of its mid-fifteenth-century brickwork (Hallam Ashley)

traditions of a college. In practice, although the movement was still uncertain towards the regular quadrangular plans familiar to us all in the great-house architecture of the sixteenth century and later, the most advanced new building, from early in the fifteenth century, had begun to display those elements of symmetry which we more usually associate with the Renaissance. Henry V's palace at Sheen, which was also the first royal residence to have made extensive use of brick, seems likely to have been laid out in quadrangles, as was certainly the plan adopted at Ralph Cromwell's other great mansion at South Wingfield Manor, in Derbyshire, the direct contemporary of Tattershall.[23] Not very much later, this was the layout again at Knole, in Kent, much developed, of course, by Archbishop Bourgchier's successors, but surviving still as undoubtedly the best example of the genre.[24] At Caister itself, only the great tower of Fastolf's imitation Rhineland fortress mars the symmetry of a plan otherwise developed originally in two regularly laid-out courtyards, while there is much of symmetry, too, in the plan of Sir Andrew Ogard's moated manor-house at Rye, as there would be, still more obviously, at Lord Hastings's Kirby Muxloe. When, in 1426, the decision was taken to rebuild, in a more modern fashion, the mansion known as the Manor of the More, near Rickmansworth in Hertfordshire, the plan then adopted was a symmetrical three-sided courtyard, enclosed on the fourth side by a boundary wall pierced centrally by a handsome gate. In due course, the More was to become a favourite residence of George Nevill, archbishop of York (d. 1476), and would be used again both by Cardinal Wolsey and then by Henry VIII. On rebuilding, much emphasis had been placed, as was to be the case at Ogard's Rye House in the same county, on the construction of a substantial moat, completely encircling the

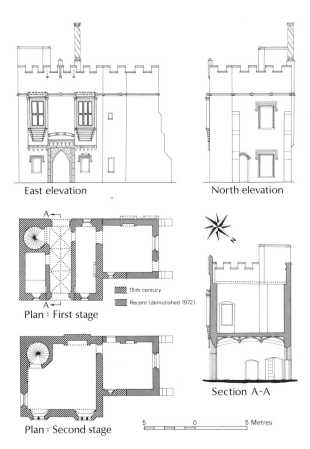

East elevation

North elevation

15th century

Recent (demolished 1972)

Plan : First stage

Plan : Second stage

Section A-A

5   0   5 Metres

121 The surviving gatehouse of Sir Andrew Ogard's lightly fortified mansion at Rye House, Hertfordshire (T. P. Smith)

122 Archbishop Thomas Bourgchier's late-fifteenth-century mansion at Knole, in Kent, with sixteenth-century extensions and improvements (Aerofilms)

123 Symmetrical planning at Lord Hastings's unfinished late-fifteenth-century castle at Kirby Muxloe, Leicestershire (Aerofilms)

site, with a gatehouse to round off the defences. At both mansions the material chosen to give lustre to the work was the newly fashionable brick.[25]

One of the things we know about the More, being informed of it in Warkworth's *Chronicle*, is that Archbishop Nevill, in the 1470s, had fitted it out 'ryghte comodiusly and plesauntly'. And it was there, according to Warkworth, that the archbishop gathered together, in anticipation of a visit by the king, all the plate and fine furnishings from his other manors and town houses, which he had hidden away after the battles of Tewkesbury and Barnet, and of which the king now deftly relieved him.[26] No doubt the More, just before the archbishop's arrest, was unusually richly arrayed, for Nevill had understandably gone to great lengths to do the king particular honour. Nevertheless, the jewels, plate and fine fabrics we know to have been removed from the More on Nevill's arrest for treason were just those that, among the archbishop's contemporaries, would have been regarded as appropriate to his rank. Nevill himself, to greet the king, had furnished the More 'as rychely and as pleasauntly as he coude'. In their own houses, and to the limit of their means, men of middling to great wealth would be competing to do the same.

Among the more complete surviving inventories of household effects at one of the great mansions of the period is the list of goods and furnishings compiled at Caister in 1459, shortly after the death of its builder. Much of Fastolf's ready cash, and a good deal of his plate, had been entrusted for safe-keeping to the monks of St Benet of Hulme, a nearby Benedictine community of which Sir John was also a patron. Yet what remained at Caister was still very formidable, and it is plain that the old warrior had lived in considerable state at his newly completed castle, to die amid splendour which, for one man alone, even his associates might have considered excessive. There were many stirring military memorials at Caister, including a pair of silver-gilt basins bearing the device of Sir Robert Harling, a former companion-in-arms, with a gown in the livery of Ralph, Lord Cromwell, and a tapestry of the siege of Falaise. In his own chamber, Fastolf had made himself comfortable with a feather bed, blankets, sheets and a bolster, with bed-hangings of tapestry and curtains of green worsted, with cushions, two chairs, a folding table, and what was probably a pewter candelabrum. And there are similarly complete lists for the many separate chambers of Fastolf's considerable entourage, as there are too for the halls, the chapel and the other family chambers at Caister, including that of Lady Milicent, the deceased wife of Sir John, in which the last item recorded was a set of two 'lyttyll Ewers of blew glasses powdered withe golde', very probably imports from Venice.[27]

When Fastolf died, the Wars of the Roses had already begun, and it could be said that the disgrace and deprivation of Archbishop Nevill were to be among their more salutary consequences, 'such goodes as were gaderide with synne' being 'loste with sorwe'.[28] However, the wars were to have another effect of great utility to the archaeologist, for inventories such as Fastolf's, illuminating though they are, can convey to us no more than the flavour of the lavish setting in which a man of his class might place himself, whereas in the jewelry hoards of the civil-war period we have the objects themselves to guide us. Sir John, we know, owned a diamond collar, given to him by Richard of York for services in France, which is said to have cost 4,000 marks, or as much as Fastolf's nine Suffolk manors.[29] And although, of course, nothing has survived to us of anything approaching this value, there is more than a touch of comparable magnificence in the Dunstable swan jewel, found there at the site of a Dominican friary to which it may have been entrusted for safe-keeping, as there is too in the personal jewelry of the Thame and Fishpool hoards, both likely to have had Wars of the Roses associations.

The Dunstable jewel, which is probably of Parisian workmanship, could have been commissioned originally by the Duc de Berry, a descendant of the Swan Knight and consequently fond of the symbol. However, the swan, along with the better-known red rose, was also a badge of the house of Lancaster, and it may very well have been as a livery badge of Margaret of Anjou, Henry VI's queen, that the swan jewel found its way to Dunstable, a centre of Lancastrian activity in both 1459 and 1461, just before and just after the dynasty's initial collapse.[30] The rich enamel-on-gold of the Dunstable jewel, with its fine representational quality, have made it a discovery of the first importance to the history of jewelry at this period, and the same could be said of the remarkable reliquary ring from the Thame hoard, of gold set with amethysts, recently redated on the associated coin evidence to the war years 1457–60.[31] Linking the story of the Wars of the Roses with the final episodes of English commitment in France, the Fishpool hoard, from the Nottinghamshire village of that name, included jewelry of Flanders or northern French inspiration, with coins that were certainly Burgundian. The value at burial of the 1,237 gold coins from Fishpool, just over 80 per cent of which were English, has been calculated at approximately £400 – to contemporaries a generous fortune. The associated jewelry, moreover, was of very good quality, in particular the heart-shaped brooch from the Fishpool hoard which, in its contrasting use of white enamel and gold, resembles the Dunstable jewel. Again, as was probably the case with the Dunstable badge, the Fishpool jewelry is likely to have been the property of a Lancastrian supporter, recently returned from the wars on the Continent, who never survived to recover it. On 15 May 1464, the Battle of Hexham brought to an end the Lancastrian resistance in the north. At Fishpool,

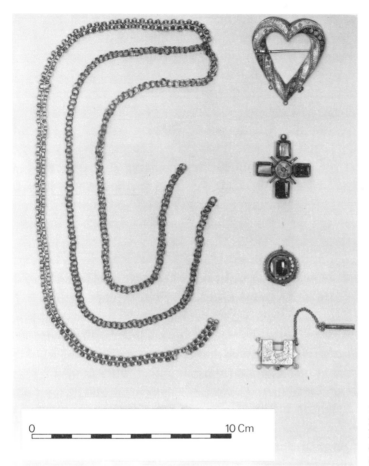

0   10 Cm

124   Jewelry from a hoard found at Fishpool, in Nottinghamshire, probably concealed there in 1463/4 (B.M.)

on the coin evidence, the hoard could not have been concealed earlier than the last months of 1463 nor later than the following spring, a reasonable assumption consequently being that the events were closely connected.[32]

That strong sense of personal style which, against all caution, had encouraged great expenditure on building in late-medieval England, and which had led to the purchase, no more than incidentally as an investment, of excessive stocks of personal jewelry and of plate, found another outlet in household consumption on what was frequently an exaggerated scale. Of course, thrift in the right places continued to be admired almost as much as generosity, and something of this is uniquely displayed in the very modern calculations of John Walsch, steward of the Talbot household of Blakemere, in Shropshire, who systematically broke down his year's expenditure in 1417–18 to arrive at an average cost per meal consumed there of $2\frac{1}{8}$d.[33] However, there is little to suggest, even at Blakemere, that such calculations were made in order to bring about economies. Walsch's year of stewardship, as he says himself, was far from being a usual one. His lord was away, fighting with the king in France, and the household at Blakemere was much reduced, although still not to the point where *largesse* would be totally forgotten. Of the 15,700 meals served over the year at Blakemere, itself only one of several Talbot households, Walsch records that as many as 2,172 meals were 'for strangers who turned up at various times', as recorded in the day-book of the household.[34] Had Gilbert, Lord Talbot, been in residence at Blakemere, these totals would have been very much larger.

With so many to feed, another characteristic of the Blakemere accounts is the formidable variety of the purchases. To achieve it, the Blakemere provisioners would go as far as London to shop for their luxuries, especially their spices and fine wines. They bought much, of course, at the local market-town at Whitchurch, but went regularly also to Nantwich and Chester, Shrewsbury, Worcester and Gloucester.[35] Indeed, for those lucky enough to belong to such a household, the daily fare would be far from monotonous, being sustained at a high level of quality and variety even in the more difficult years. There is little, as it has been pointed out, in the household accounts of Elizabeth Berkeley, countess of Warwick, to tell us of the troubles which, in 1420–1, were besetting her Berkeley inheritance. Instead, what they record is the great number of visitors dining or supping even then with the countess, whether at Berkeley Castle or at her favourite manor-house at Wotton-under-Edge, revealing also the very considerable extra expenditure generated in the household at every visit of Earl Richard from France. At Berkeley Castle, on one such occasion, the number of meals consumed at a sitting rose to as many as 200, while throughout the year such large-scale catering would require massive purchases of wine and ale, meat and fish, cereals, dried fruits and spices.[36]

Richard Beauchamp, earl of Warwick, as one of the wealthiest landowners in early-fifteenth-century England, could maintain a state at table rivalled by few of his own generation. Nevertheless, the domestic accounts of late-medieval households of very different conditions again show this same year-long pursuit of variety at table, limitations being imposed less by any shortage of commodities than by the willingness of the purchaser to travel. Thus the monks of Battle and of Glastonbury, like the victuallers of Blakemere, were accustomed to send to London for their better-quality stockfish, their spices and special wines, and it appeared to make little difference that many of these journeys would have had to be scheduled for deepest winter, when the roads were difficult but when the carts and the carters, freed from the farm, were available for such employment.[37] More locally, Battle Abbey bought its meat at the market by its gates, with fresh fish from Hastings, less expensive wines from Winchelsea, and other provisions from Sandwich and Canterbury, or from the markets and fair of Faversham. Just as the archbishop of Canterbury contemporaneously used his Sussex manors to supply his London residences, so the monks of Battle would draw their supplies of fresh game, chickens and eggs from their demesnes at Appledram and Wye.[38] Although great beef-eaters always, as they would have to be in the cattle-raising lands of the Weald, they ate lamb and mutton also, with pork and sucking-pig, veal and kid, and with as many varieties of game-bird and poultry as they could purchase in the markets of their region.[39] In the closely comparable circumstances of Kirkstall Abbey, a Yorkshire Cistercian house situated, like Battle, in a region known for its cattle herds, it is scarcely surprising that a recent analysis of the bones found associated with the fifteenth-century meat kitchen should have shown a great preponderance of ox bones in the sample, rising to as much as 90 per cent. Against this, sheep bones totalled only 5 per cent, pig bones just 3 per cent, and deer bones no more than 2, with variety in diet deriving, more obviously, from other meats, among these domestic fowl, duck and goose, rabbit and hare, heron, woodcock and blackcock.[40]

Understandably enough, there are marked differences to be observed in the content of bone groups from households at extremes of the social scale, though these cannot always be taken to mean quite what at first they suggest. At Battle Abbey, for example, not known for the economy of its diet, the monks were yet content to keep for their kitchens the old and unsaleable cattle, the 'sick and dying', culled from their herds as unsuitable for work or for market.[41] And just this preponderance of aged, work-weary animals has been noted in the bone evidence from Kirkstall.[42] But the monks, of course, could take their pick of the finer meats as well, and a more accurate reflection of contemporary taste at the more exalted social levels might be, rather, the recently recovered bone group from Hadleigh Castle, in Essex, where vertebrae and rib fragments, occurring in disproportionate numbers, have suggested a preference for the finer cuts – the chops and the steaks – which this particular late-medieval household could evidently very well afford.[43] At Hadleigh, there are some indications also of hunting by the garrison, with the bones of pheasant, plover and teal, alongside those of a male merlin, one of falconry's best-known birds.[44] And it is in no way remarkable that such birds of the chase should be prominent again in the bone recovered from late-medieval deposits at Writtle, also in Essex, a former royal hunting lodge held from the crown by the Stafford dukes of Buckingham. Here, with the pheasant, plover and teal of Hadleigh, there was heron and gull, woodcock, swan and partridge. Both goose and duck, in the same assemblage, may either have been domestic or wild, whereas the pigeon, also found at Hadleigh, is certain to have been domestic.[45]

The differences, usually, are evident enough, but if all else were lacking, the occurrence or not of game bones in an archaeological deposit might well serve as an indicator of wealth. Thus whereas there are few traces of game among the bones recovered, for example, from Wharram Percy, a remote Yorkshire village visibly in decline through the later Middle Ages, a similar analysis of the bones from Southampton has shown its burgesses, at least those of the wealthier sector, capable of making purchases in the market which included venison and a choice selection of wild-fowl.[46] And bones, too, may have their value in underlining the particular emphasis of an economy. On diet alone, if this were all we had, the monks at the abbeys of Kirkstall and Battle might reasonably have been judged to be cattle-farmers. Just as certainly, the peasants living by another sort of agricultural regime at Wharram Percy, were clearly dependent upon their sheep. In proportions that were to be almost exactly reversed at York, their nearest city, the Wharram Percy families enjoyed a meat diet that was 60 per cent mutton, 30 per cent beef, and 8 per cent pork.[47] In contrast, the villagers of Upton, in Gloucestershire, for whom sheep were not as important, left bone deposits which suggest a meat consumption of 53 per cent beef, 31 per cent mutton, 13 per cent horse-meat, and 3 per cent pork. At Upton, the cattle were slaughtered young, fully 60 per cent of the cattle-bones examined coming from beasts less than three years old. Sheep, on the other hand, were kept until an advanced age, to be killed, as was usual at other medieval settlements, only when no longer any use for their wool. The Upton assemblage, like that of Wharram Percy, showed little evidence of wild animals hunted for the pot.[48]

Fish bones are absent in the Upton record, and perhaps, indeed, fish was never more than an occasional delicacy at this remote northern Cotswolds settlement. However, at Wharram Percy, somewhat nearer the sea, the bones of cod have been found in amongst the other kitchen debris of the village, and there can be no doubt that fish, at this level of society almost as much as at any other, constituted an important part of the late-medieval diet, rich in protein and almost indispensable for good health. Among the fish bones recovered from medieval contexts at Southampton have been plaice, cod, gurnard and conger eel, while we know, too, from other evidence, that Southampton's burgesses were great consumers of herring, as they were certainly fond of shell-fish of all kinds, in particular cockles, mussels and oysters.[49]

All these, of course, and a great deal more besides, are to be found listed in the domestic accounts of representative fifteenth-century households, a rare 'middle-class' example of which is the account book of Munden's Chantry at Bridport, hard by the Dorset coast. By 1453, at which date William Savernak, as warden, began to record their daily expenditure, the chaplains of John Munden's century-old foundation were not especially well-off. Nevertheless, in fish alone, they made their purchases of ling, hake, cod and whiting as salt-fish for their store, whilst at Lent, with meat forbidden, they sought extra variety in haddock, conger and herring, supplemented by shell-fish in considerable quantity with a preference, clearly, for oyster.[50] What the chaplains of Bridport could not have afforded would have been the fresh salmon enjoyed by Elizabeth Berkeley, countess of Warwick, only as an expensive Christmas treat,[51] nor is there much evidence at Bridport of those other fresh-water fish, the pike and the trout, which the countess undoubtedly favoured for herself and which, in the case of the richer monastic establishments, would be worth considerable investment. Fish-ponds, even today, are a common enough survival from the medieval landscape, occurring at many manorial sites where they frequently doubled as moats. At one of the earlier of these, a Templar establishment at Washford, near Redditch, recent excavations have uncovered the remains of a fish-house and curing furnace, associated with the ponds and breeding-tanks of the thirteenth-century enterprise, and constituting

125   The abbot of Glastonbury's early-fourteenth-century fish-house at Meare, in Somerset, next to one of his favourite personal manor-houses (R.C.H.M.)

S   The fifteenth-century
Doom, or Last Judgment
scene, painted over the chancel
arch at Combe Church,
Oxfordshire (Pemberton)

T   A fifteenth-century
portrayal of Winchester
College, with its characteristic
courtyard plan, taken from a
life of William of Wykeham,
its founder (Bodleian, New
College 288, f.3)

Opposite

U *above*   Fifteenth-century gold rings from London (Museum of London)

V *centre*   The Dunstable Swan Jewel, perhaps used as a superior livery badge and lost at Dunstable in *c.* 1460 at the time of the Lancastrian dynasty's collapse (B.M.)

W *below*   A reliquary ring and other rings from the Thame hoard, deposited in the war years 1457-60 (Ashmolean Museum, Oxford)

X *above*   Pages from a twelfth-century English herbal, discussing hound's tongue, sundcorn and ground ivy (left), with organy and wormwood (right) (Bodleian, Ashmole 1431, fos 25v-26)

Y   A timber-built
water cistern of the late
fifteenth century, found
to adjoin a contemporary
dock at Portsmouth's
Oyster Street site
(Portsmouth Museums
and Art Gallery)

Z   Remains of a winged
glass-furnace of
Lorrainer type, found
at Hutton, in Yorkshire;
late-sixteenth-century
(Aberg)

in their modest way the ancestral equivalents of the abbot of Glastonbury's still surviving stone-built fish-house, as preserved at Meare, in Somerset.[52] On another great monastic estate, shortly before the Dissolution, we have Prior More's record of expenditure on the fish-ponds of the Worcester manors, showing him to have stocked his tanks at regular intervals with eel and perch, roach, tench and pickerel.[53]

Of course, such luxuries as the monks and the magnates continued to share were beyond the resources of the 'middle-class' chaplains of Bridport. Yet they lived, at least, in a coastal town, and their grievances would not have been those of the fifteenth-century schoolboy, wistfully writing 'wolde to gode I wer on of the dwellers by the see syde, for ther see fysh be plentuse and I love them better than I do this fresh water fysh.'[54] Even he, moreover, in his own generation, might have profited from recent improvements. By the early sixteenth century and probably before, the sea fisheries at Rye, for example, had become so well organized that fish on offer at the early-morning market at Rye might be resold that same evening in London.[55] And although, naturally enough, not everywhere in England had access to such facilities, whether in markets or in pack-horse routes, as London and the Cinque Ports enjoyed, there had been, nevertheless, major developments, particularly in the late fourteenth century, in the curing and transportation of fish, making it possible to dispatch herring from the seaports – gutted, heavily salted, and packed tightly head-to-tail in sealed barrels – wherever the market demanded.[56] These, indeed, were the necessary preconditions for a rapid fifteenth-century expansion of the east-coast fishing industries, being further encouraged by the contemporary reopening of the Icelandic fisheries to those with the capital to finance long-distance fleets. Briefly, Scarborough, in north-east Yorkshire, was to take its part in this same expansion. No more than twenty miles distant from Scarborough by road, it would have been from this market, almost certainly, that the peasant community in the isolation of Wharram Percy must have drawn its supplies of cod (above, p. 187).

If we know rather little of peasant fish-consumption in fifteenth-century England, and must return to Wharram Percy for what we do, there is still less to be said of the many local markets in fresh fruits and vegetables, as essential for the contribution of vitamins to diet as fish might be of protein. In household accounts of the period, such supplies feature only very rarely, for they were usually locally grown on the demesne. Yet gardening, of course, has always had its literature, and it is in the *De Naturis Rerum* of Alexander Neckam that we can consult one of our earlier gardening texts. Alexander Neckam, who wrote this work at the turn of the twelfth and thirteenth centuries, was not always careful to distinguish between plants that would grow in a northern environment and others which could never have sown seed there. Nor does his interest in the herbs considered so essential to much medieval cooking recommend his advice to modern users. However, those he addressed would have shared the same priorities, and even if they could not always have cultivated the plants he listed, they would have known them well enough by name. Neckam urged:

> The garden should be adorned with roses and lilies, the turnsole or heliotrope, violets, and mandrake, there you should have parsley, cost, fennel, southernwood, coriander, sage, savery, hysop, mint, rue, ditanny, smallage, pellitory, lettuce, garden cress, and peonies. There should also be beds planted with onions, leeks, garlic, pumpkins, and shalots. The cucumber, the poppy, the daffodil, and brank-ursine ought to be in a good garden. There should also be pottage herbs, such as beets, herb mercury, orach, sorrel, and mallows.

In a 'noble' garden, although scarcely in a garden of northern Europe except in some particulars, the fruits to be found might be 'medlars, quinces, warden-trees, peaches, pears of St Riole, pomegranates, lemons, oranges, almonds, dates, and figs'.[57] The rare surviving garden-accounts of medieval England, while lacking the variety of Neckam's catalogue and neglecting still the more ordinary items which the gardener himself thought unimportant, yet provide us with what is certainly a more accurate guide to what grew in most northern gardens. At Rimpton, north of Sherborne, the bishop of Winchester's garden, greatly enlarged there in the mid-thirteenth century, was used principally as a pear and apple orchard, with vines as well, and with some ordinary field crops like flax, beans and peas. A century later, at Glastonbury, the produce of the abbey garden, listed in the gardener's account of 1333–4, included garlic in great quantitites, with wine from the vineyard, hemp, madder and flax, apples and pears, beans, leeks and onions.[58]

To lists such as these, until now drawn exclusively from the records, archaeology is beginning to make some contribution of its own. Whereas we can know no more, for example, of the chaplains of Bridport than that they bought almonds and some dried fruits, like raisins and figs, to see them through the rigours of Lent, with peas, beans, pears and apples in season,[59] there is good archaeological evidence from late-thirteenth-century Southampton of a diet which, at least in the wealthier households, included hazelnuts and walnuts, raisins and figs, strawberries and raspberries, plums, cherries and sloes.[60] Similar abandoned cesspit deposits from medieval King's Lynn have yielded evidence, which would otherwise certainly not have been recorded, of the consumption there of walnuts, hazelnuts and cherries,[61] while we know that Dubliners, besides being importers of figs, also ate strawberries, blackberries and rowan-berries, apples and plums, cherries, sloes and hazelnuts.[62]

Alexander Neckam, although interested in the garden as a source of fresh vegetables and fruit, saw there also a useful facility for the cultivation of medicinal herbs, among them saffron and thyme, borage and purslane, hazelwort, cole-wort and ragwort, valerian and myrtle.[63] And again, from a Chester cesspit thought to date to the turn of the thirteenth and fourteenth centuries, unambiguous evidence has recently been recovered of plants which, if deliberately collected, can only have been present in the fill of the pit because of their medicinal properties. Most prominent among these was corncockle (*Agrostemma*), a poisonous plant which, appropriately for this context, was commonly used in the Middle Ages as a laxative. Many of the corncockle seeds had been crushed, as if in an apothecary's mortar, and this again had happened to a high proportion of the other seeds also included in the fill, some of them from plants not normally edible but thought, like the others, to have been medicinal. With stinking mayweed, cornflower, hair-moss and bracken, none of them commonly eaten, there were seeds of orage and black mustard, goosefoot and hawthorn, sorrel, penny-cress and whortleberry. Hazelnuts and sloes, occurring in the Chester cesspit as they had done also both at Southampton and at Dublin, might have been collected there either as a food or a medicine.[64]

It must be chance, and certainly no more, that the bulk of the dietary evidence from archaeological sites has come, to date, from the towns. However, what the Southampton cesspits have additionally shown is an improvement in the *quality* of urban diet, occurring there not later than the thirteenth century, which was one factor alone in a more general advance of living standards. The many fruits which were represented in the fills of late-thirteenth-century pits at Southampton, have not been found in equivalent contexts of less than a century before. And while this, of course, may be nothing more than an accident of archaeological recovery, it has the further support of animal-bone analysis, the earliest bone groups recovered in the port having little of the variety of the later.[65]

Like their contemporaries in every other social order, the burgesses of late-medieval England experienced an economic recession of their own. But this is not to say that individual standards of living need have suffered. Although programmes of street paving, for example, had already begun during the thirteenth century, this particular improvement in the urban environment was pursued most actively in the later Middle Ages.[66] To this period, certainly, have belonged the paved and cobbled lane-surfaces recently identified in excavations at Bedford and at York,[67] and we can surely expect more evidence of this kind, just as we can of those other typically late-medieval municipal enterprises: the public buildings, the wharves and cranes, the water conduits, almshouses, and perhaps even the common latrines. Some of the more interesting material bearing on this activity has come recently from the excavation of waterfronts, where strongly-timbered wharves have survived very largely intact from the late Middle Ages, preserved in the waterlogged silts. Prominent among these have been the London examples, including wharves dating to the thirteenth and fourteenth centuries at Seal House, the Custom House site, and Trig Lane.[68] But there have been other wharves too, both of stone and of timber, excavated at Pevensey and King's Lynn, Harwich and Lincoln, while one of the most interesting associated structures on the Portsmouth waterfront has proved to be a timber-built cistern, probably a ships' watering-tank, datable to the fifteenth century.[69] Some of these were conceived as municipal enterprises, others being certainly private. However, a good indication of the amount the towns themselves were prepared to invest has survived to us in a contract, dated 1432, by which John Marwe, freemason and citizen of Norwich, bound himself to rebuild in stone the decaying common quay of his city. In works that were to be completed within ten months, Marwe undertook to remove the old timbers of the original construction, using a crane where necessary. He agreed to provide a new foundation of timber piles and planks, setting on this his ashlar wall, and filling-up behind with layers of rammed gravel and marl. With Marwe's own remuneration, the new quay at Norwich cost the common purse the then considerable sum of £53 6s. 8d., or almost three times as much as that committed by the dean and chapter of St Paul's in 1347 to a similar Thames-side project of their own, although in this case their wharf was of timber.[70]

Such major municipal projects as the new town quay at Norwich were the product, it could be argued, of over-government. Ever since, that is, the achievement of effective independence at many towns from the early thirteenth century, borough officers had multiplied, to bring predictable consequences in public spending. It may well be that London's new Guildhall, rebuilt at very great expense in the two decades following 1411, was a luxury which the capital's wealthy citizens could very well afford.[71] But, of course, the Londoners were not alone in this particular municipal extravagance. And although it is to the early-modern period that the great movement of town-hall building has more usually been seen to belong, its origins go back much further than this, into the fifteenth

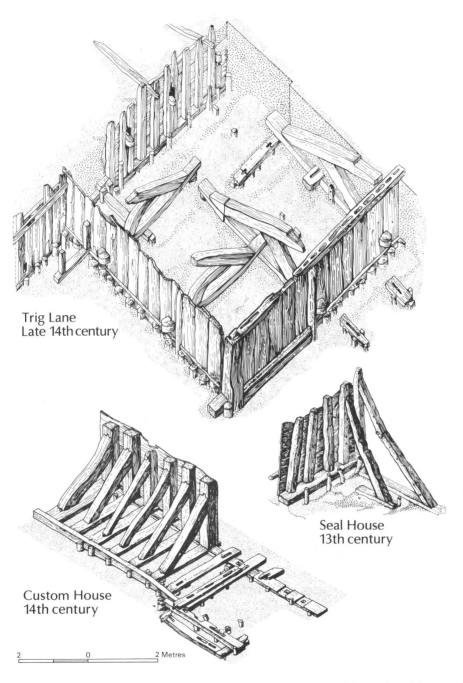

Trig Lane
Late 14th century

Seal House
13th century

Custom House
14th century

2   0   2 Metres

126   Wharf-timbering on the London waterfront, dating to the thirteenth and fourteenth centuries (Harrison, Schofield, and Tatton-Brown)

127 The excavated timbers at Trig Lane, London, showing the back of the fourteenth-century waterfront (left), with the braces of a thirteenth-century wharf (right) (Museum of London: Department of Urban Archaeology)

century and earlier, giving expression then, as later, to rich sentiments of corporate pride. One of the more striking examples of this pride was the major rebuilding of the Guildhall at Bury St Edmunds, already long a symbol of the townsmen's unity in their struggle with oppressive abbots. During the second half of the fifteenth century, this locally significant building was supplied with a handsome king-post roof, a new kitchen, and a fine crenellated porch over which, in the so-called Evidence House, the burgesses kept securely their collection of charters, being the best ammunition available to them in their continuous battles at law.[72]

At Bury, what financed the rebuilding of the fifteenth-century Guildhall was the rich trade in East Anglian cloth in which its burgesses were then profitably engaged. And similarly it was the Italian trade, at Southampton in the same century, that brought wealth to the port, helping to pay for a programme of works that would radically transform the environment. As at Bury, it was in the fifteenth

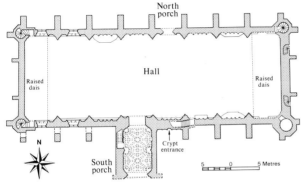

North porch

Hall

Raised dais

Raised dais

N

Crypt entrance

South porch

5   0   5 Metres

128   The early-fifteenth-century Guildhall, London, built on a scale appropriate to the size and dignity of the capital city (Barron and Ball)

century that Southampton rebuilt its Guildhall; it was then that the walls were strengthened and redesigned for guns, and that a new public quay, equipped with its crane, improved the port's facilities. The paving and proper drainage of Southampton's streets was the work, in large part, of its fifteenth-century administrators; it was a former mayor of Southampton who, early in that century, left money to the town to repair the friary water conduit and to preserve it thereafter as a municipal water supply; common latrines, down by the quays, are first mentioned in Southampton in the fifteenth century; while it was in the fifteenth century, again, that extensive investments in urban property were made by the municipality, and were put out very profitably to rent.[73]

Public order, as was only to be expected, reflected a greater fastidiousness in private habits which at least the governors of the town could afford. Thus, in late-

129 The porch, with first-floor
'Evidence House', of the
guildhall at Bury St Edmunds;
late-fifteenth-century
(R.C.H.M.)

medieval Southampton, the better-off burgesses lived in comfortable timber-built houses, with well-heated halls, and with garderobes, or lavatories, fitted internally, designed for regular cleaning. Those backyard cesspits which, for earlier centuries, have told us so much of the dietary and other household standards of the town, disappeared at Southampton in the fifteenth century, and were replaced by properly built latrines and by the regular cartage of night-soil and refuse for which there is good evidence elsewhere. At Exeter, too, there are internal lavatories, dating to this period and paralleling those at Southampton.[74] Both there and at every other centre of population in a countryside haunted by plague, the natural inclination of all wealthy men to keep their privies sweet was much reinforced by contemporary medical theory, identifying odour, not unreasonably, with disease.

While there is still much truth in a general theory of the so-called 'Great Rebuilding' that would date it no earlier than the sixteenth century, some of its characteristics being indeed familiar only in that period, the new insistence on improved domestic standards in late-medieval England, both urban and rural, was already preparing the way for alterations in house-plans and better facilities which are usually thought of as much later. In the towns, such changes might have been held back by restrictions in plot-size, or by the difficulty, common to all developers, of acquiring control of tenements in multi-occupation. Nevertheless, Norwich is thought to have undergone one of its cyclical major rebuildings no later than the decades 1470–1530, and it is, even so, to the first half of this period that the interesting Pottergate houses belong. At these Pottergate houses, excavated recently on sites little disturbed by later rebuildings since the general conflagration of 1507, there is good evidence of improvements, including internal

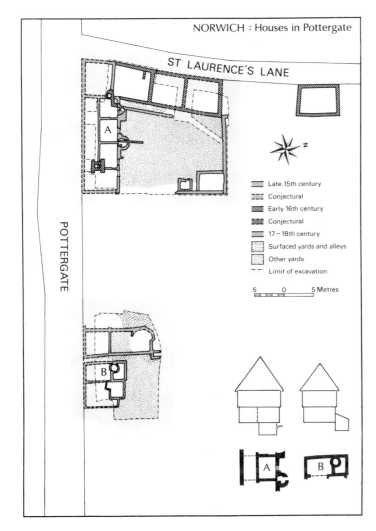

130 Recently excavated late-fifteenth-century houses at Pottergate, Norwich, showing evidence of improvements in the early sixteenth century, to include indoor staircases and lavatories (Carter)

staircases and garderobes, occurring as secondary features in houses which, on other evidence, were already no earlier than the late fifteenth century in date. Clearly, what they show at rentable properties of no great size put up very probably for investment, is the pressure of lifting domestic standards in improvements now required of the landlord. Where, less than a generation before, such facilities had been considered unnecessary, the better of the Pottergate houses, by 1507, had been equipped with proper staircases, as well as indoor lavatories of their own,[75] no better demonstration surely being required of the shift in contemporary taste.

Most obviously, of course, the introduction of new standards took its effect in contemporary rebuildings of the manor-house. While less remarkable, certainly, than the great fortress-palaces of the magnate classes (above, pp. 174–82), the fifteenth-century manor-house, wherever a rebuilding occurred, could promise considerable comfort. In almost every case, the traditional hall-and-chamber plan, not to be shaken off for another full century at least, was still recognized as the only pattern truly appropriate for such a building. Yet when, in 1474–6, the Oxfordshire manor of Great Milton was rebuilt, its hall, for all its traditional placing between chamber and kitchen wings, was a most modern and comfortable apartment, with great bay windows on either side of the dais, and with a handsome end-wall fireplace.[76] Again, the disproportionate width of the hall at Great Milton, as compared with its restricted length, can be said to exhibit another sign of the times in the tendency, frequently lamented by contemporaries, for the old-style common hall to lose ground to the private apartments of the lord, it being within the second half of the fifteenth century, once more, that the original great hall at Manor Farm, Wasperton, in Warwickshire, was reduced to half its former size, the space saved being then redesigned as a two-storey solar block.[77] For as long, of course, as central hearths remained in favour, traditionally the social gathering-point of the household, a lofty hall would continue to be essential if the smoke were to make its escape. And even in a hall, for example, as handsomely rebuilt as the late-fifteenth-century specimen at the Old Manor, Askett, in Buckinghamshire, provision for this, in an open timber roof, remained the precondition of its planning.[78] However, the side-wall or end-wall fireplace, with its great chimney of stone or brick, was commonly beginning, even in the fifteenth century, to make such precautions unnecessary. Thus the comfortable hall of the abbot of Glastonbury's manor-house at Ashbury, in Berkshire, rebuilt in the late fifteenth century, had become a low-ceilinged, single-storey apartment, very much in the modern manner, with the end-wall fireplace that had made this possible and with two fine chambers above. Other characteristics also of this remarkable building

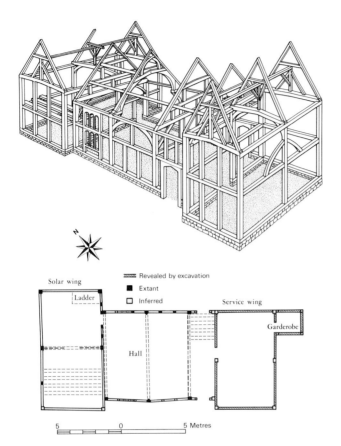

Solar wing

Ladder

Revealed by excavation

■ Extant

□ Inferred

Service wing

Garderobe

Hall

5   0   5 Metres

131   A late-fifteenth-century manor-house at Askett, in Buckinghamshire, built to the traditional hall-and-chamber plan (Beresford)

include a staircase linking the hall at the abbot's end with his chamber immediately above it, the heating by wall-fireplaces of several of the upper chambers, and the first-floor indoor lavatory, personal to the abbot, which had preserved until recently ('precious relic') its original fifteenth-century seat.[79]

It would not be easy to find, among other manorial buildings of fifteenth-century England, an example as sophisticated as Ashbury, and the standards of the wealthy abbot of Glastonbury, whether in hall or lavatory provision, were not those of the majority of his countrymen. But if the ultimate refinements of luxury were still restricted to men of his rank and position, the pursuit of comfort was not. The modernization of older housing, in a manner until recently considered characteristic only of the sixteenth century, was in fact proceeding, it is now usually argued, as much as a century before. In an old house, one obvious improvement might be the flooring-over of the hall, to make better use of a space which, in contemporary opinion, had begun to seem too large. Yet feeling, clearly,

132 The indoor lavatory of the abbots of Glastonbury at Ashbury, in Berkshire, being one of the facilities newly provided at this late-fifteenth-century retreat (R.C.H.M.)

was still divided on the abandonment of the central open hearth, and a compromise, recognized as late-medieval both in Devonshire and the south-east, seems to have been no more than a partial flooring-over, with a new upper chamber jettied over half the hall, the other half left open still to permit smoke to escape into the roof.[80] In more modest houses, newly built in the fifteenth century, an identical effect might be achieved more economically by the progressive reduction in size of the hall, to occupy, as at St Katherine's Cottage, Shorne (Kent), no more than a bay and a half, or even as little as a single bay.[81] Interestingly, the quality of building at the Old Shop, Bignor (Sussex), one of the better-known examples of this last arrangement, is such as to suggest that economy was not there the primary consideration in the reduction in size of the hall. At Bignor, by the mid-fifteenth century, the four chambers of the service and solar wings had all but taken the place of the hall which still, by tradition, divided them. With the insertion subsequently of a floor in the hall, a six-chamber house in the modern style was to take the place, with only the minimum disturbance, of the old-fashioned hall-house put up by the original builders.[82]

The Old Shop, Bignor, in all but the excessive contraction of its hall, is a typical 'Wealden' house of the style most familiar in Kent and in Sussex but occurring also wherever, in fifteenth-century England, a migrant carpenter might have taken it. Essentially, the Wealden tradition suited middle-class housing in particularly prosperous areas, being a remarkable demonstration of the high domestic standards which the better-off yeomanry of late-medieval England had come, in their turn, to expect. Characteristically, the Wealden house has the lofty central hall of the traditional medieval manor-house, sandwiched between symmetrical service and chamber wings under a single hipped roof. Usually, too, the hall is recessed, the wings are jettied, and considerable elaboration of detail is displayed both in carving and other specialized timberwork. The men who built such houses, according to one plausible suggestion, had been encouraged to do so by the local practice of partible inheritance, keeping younger sons on the family land and promoting the development of home industries.[83] Yet such equal division of family lands among the testator's heirs was not generally the practice in late-medieval England, being in fact comparatively rare, and it is just as likely that the Wealden houses were an expression, once again, of the exceptional energy of the

133   A Wealden house of classic plan at Synyards, Otham, Kent, the gable being an addition of 1663; early-sixteenth-century (R.C.H.M.)

peasant land-accumulators whose exploitation of land surpluses following the Black Death had raised them up into a new yeomanry. It was men of this class who, when the time came, were both ready and willing to take on the leases of the archbishop of Canterbury's demesnes, and although some were required, by the terms of their leases, to keep the old manorial buildings in repair, most would have accepted only what they needed of those buildings, preferring for themselves the modern timber-built farmhouses which they could now very obviously afford.[84] At Yardhurst, in Kent, a representative yeoman holding of almost 80 acres survived until recently virtually intact, being a compact small-scale farm which, while workable with nothing more than the labour of the family, could yet support a fine house and a three-bay barn, the first in the Wealden style. The farmhouse at Yardhurst, as was to be the case everywhere in Kent and Sussex in buildings of comparable standing, underwent the familiar sequence of early-modern improvements, with a flooring-over of the hall at first through one bay only and then, after the insertion of a new chimney stack, along the entire original length. But, this apart, the building has remained until today as convenient and well-designed for its purpose as it was on the date of its completion. Furthermore, the detailing at Yardhurst demonstrates very clearly the considerable attention that the yeoman farmer, even of modest wealth, might give to the work he was financing. In a building that dated, very probably, no later than the third quarter of the fifteenth century, the windows at Yardhurst were traceried, equal care being shown in the finish of other mouldings, including those of the roof. The close-studding of the walls was expensive and structurally unnecessary, but it was also very up-to-date.[85]

Close-studding, like the use of the jetty in a rural building, was little more than a decorative fashion. However, it is exactly this quality of manifest self-indulgence, at Yardhurst as at other buildings of its type, that tells us most both of the wealth and of the values of the class that could afford it, being the product of a land market that had seldom been more favourable to the peasant of enterprise and initiative. Such men, of course, were not confined to southern England, nor were they invariably specialists in agriculture. A group of Pennine aisled halls, for example, only recently identified in houses of the Halifax and Huddersfield region behind the characteristic stone cladding of late-sixteenth-century rebuildings, can be attributed to the growing wealth of an area much advantaged in the fifteenth century by the expansion of the cloth-finishing industry. Significantly, considerable emphasis was placed in these halls on the status of their newly rich builders, both in the choice of a building-style as grand as this, already out of fashion in the south, and in such details as the massive timber-and-plaster

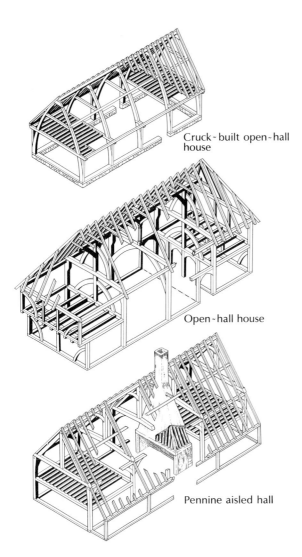

Cruck-built open-hall house

Open-hall house

Pennine aisled hall

134 House types of late-medieval England, with a typical Wealden house in the centre (Mercer)

firehoods frequently taking up one end of the hall, while a pompous canopied dais, following the local gentry fashion, as often occupied the other.[86] In the Vale of York, the more modest single-aisled halls, only a little later in date, would seem to have constituted an intermediate class, neither as expensive as the houses of the Halifax clothiers nor as poor as those of the common generality of peasants.[87] Yet theirs was an isolated and a strangely old-fashioned group, and more importance attaches to the cruck-built, open-hall house of central and western England, the direct contemporary of the Wealden house and the Pennine aisled hall, although certainly their poorer equivalent. This, while larger and more sophisticated than the broadly earlier peasant long-house, has been claimed as its typological descendant.[88] Yet both styles, of course, persisted in the countryside, the cruck-built house meeting the needs of the richer peasantry while the long-house, in its many different guises, continued in use among the poorer. In essence, what the crucks reproduced was a more economical, if head-cracking, version of the classic central hall, with its two-storeyed end-blocks, developed originally in the stone-built manor-house and transmitted thence via the more commodious box-framed hall-houses of both gentry and yeomen in the richer farming areas, down to the better-off peasantry. Quite obviously a *peasant* house, the cruck-built hall-house, of which there are many variants, is as representative of new standards at the lower levels of fifteenth-century society as the fortress-palace of a knight like Fastolf might be of those at the higher. It has survived in such numbers for the very good reason that, like the Wealden house, it had attained a standard which, although certainly regarded as quaint today, is nevertheless thoroughly acceptable. It was the first peasant house to do so.

7 Reorientation under the Tudors

It is not as easy now, as once it seemed to be, to draw the dividing line between medieval and early-modern England at Bosworth Field on 22 August 1485. And the clear architectural antecedents of the Great Rebuilding, now recognized as much as a century before its late-sixteenth-century florescence, are but one of the many examples of this blurring. Nevertheless, the problems that the Tudors both met and created for themselves in their own generation were not those that had confronted their predecessors. The stagnant population and the relatively stable price-levels of the fifteenth century had been converted, by the mid-sixteenth century, into what we have come ourselves to recognize in more recent contexts as a 'population explosion' and 'galloping inflation'. In the Church, the discontents only dimly perceived in the fifteenth century broke through under the Tudors in the Reformation. There were fresh developments in the local home-based industries that owed much to new patterns of trade, partly explained also by the greater receptivity of English society to Continental influences, at last allowing in the Renaissance. In one significant particular, familiar to every archaeologist, Henry VII's accession in 1485 indeed constituted a watershed. From as early as 1493, Henry's coinage begins to make use of Renaissance motifs even in this most traditional of mediums, while in 1502–4, for the first time, profile portraits were introduced on the coinage, representing the king as a Renaissance prince in what was something approaching a true likeness. Alexander of Bruchsal, the king's chief engraver at the London Mint, who may have been responsible for these portraits, was a citizen not of London but of Antwerp.[1]

There were many other ways, too, in which England's rulers responded to the magic of the Renaissance, and we shall see these most obviously in the architectural novelties and other strange conceits which, once adopted by the crown in sixteenth-century England, would be grasped at enthusiastically by the aristocracy. But as striking a manifestation of the mood of the period, and one that showed through rather earlier, was the innovatory zeal of Henry VIII throughout his reign in the proper defence of the realm. Of course, for centuries adequate

135 Groats of Henry VII, showing the transition from the traditional medieval full-face portrait (left) to the 'Renaissance' profile portrait of the king (Metcalf: *SCBI Ashm.* 90 & 807)

136 Effigy of Henry VII at Westminster Abbey, being a fine portrait in the new 'Renaissance' realism (Warburg Institute)

coastal fortifications against the French had been the continuing concern of the Plantagenet kings, Edward III's fine castle at Queenborough, on the Isle of Sheppey, anticipating by two centuries, in its advanced concentric plan, many of the more obvious characteristics of the much better known Tudor works.[2] And more recently, in the 1480s, Dartmouth's burgesses had already fortified their harbour to such good effect that Henry VIII's surveyor, reporting in 1522, could enthuse with his colleagues that he had never seen a 'goodlier haven after all our opinions', strongly guarded by new stone blockhouses on either side of its entrance, with a chain ready to be tautened between them.[3] Nevertheless, it was Henry's clear vision of himself as a Renaissance prince, to be expressed in so many other ways in his patronage of architecture and the arts, that gave new direction to a coastal defence system so hastily conceived and so vigorously forwarded that, in many particulars, it was outmoded just as soon as it was built. Henry's personal involvement in these works is beyond question, whether instanced in his own 'devyse made by the kinges highenes', worked out for the fortification of England's bridgehead at Calais during a visit there in 1532,[4] or by his systematic viewing of the defences of Hull, in Yorkshire, where he stayed five days in 1541 during the course of a progress through the North.[5] At Nonsuch Palace, perhaps the clearest expression of Henry's developed tastes, the raised and bastioned platform of the detached banqueting house, a work of the early 1540s, burlesques the military architecture of that day.[6] However, enthusiasm alone for the new artillery fortifications currently being perfected, above all, in northern Italy, was no compensation for the inexperience of the king and his advisers. At Camber Castle, on the Sussex coast, a building programme of 1539–43 was interrupted, even during this short time, by a major change of plan, requiring expensive

137   The artillery fort at Camber Castle, Sussex, representing up-to-the-minute military thinking towards the end of Henry VIII's reign (Kersting)

demolitions and rebuilding.[7] In much the same way, Henry's blockhouses on the Thames, five of them completed with great dispatch in 1539–40 to meet the same anticipated attacks, were disarmed already by 1553, outmoded in current military thinking by the new angle-bastioned artillery defences only recently developed by the Italians.[8]

These same uncertainties, in subsequent reigns, continued to handicap royal works. Before his death, Henry VIII had already been employing Italian engineers on such projects as the strengthening, with angle bastions, of Portsmouth's artillery defences, or the rebuilding of Tynemouth Castle in Northumberland. Yet the fort at Tresco, in the Scilly Isles, as built for Edward VI, marked a return to earlier traditions, entirely outmoded by the end of the century and considered by many, even in the 1550s, to be archaic.[9] At Berwick-upon-Tweed, the massively bastioned star-shaped citadel of Edward VI's engineers was to be abandoned incomplete in the last year of Mary's reign shortly after the appointment there of Sir Richard Lee, the noted military architect. However, Sir Richard's own plans for a total defensive system at Berwick were later to come under criticism from Italian consultants, appointed in the 1560s by Elizabeth, and the final compromises reached at Berwick accorded neither with economy nor with the better military thinking of the day.[10] England, enjoying 'remarkable advantages with the sea as its wall and moat',[11] continued on the fringes of the fortification expertise contemporaneously developing on the Continent. It was very much cheaper to remain so.

Military expenditure, no doubt, was seldom the main cause of the financial difficulties of mid-sixteenth-century governments. Nevertheless, it remained, as it does still today, a vitally important element in the fiscal policies of the Tudor state, and there were occasions, in Henry's reign as in Elizabeth's, when military priorities very obviously overrode all others. There are monetary explanations, surely more important than the burden of coastal defences, for the catastrophic 'Great Debasement' of 1542–51, which was the cause of so much anxiety to its contemporaries. Yet the king, certainly, was collecting a substantial profit from the currency manipulations of the decade, milking the coinage of a silver content worth over a million-and-a-quarter pounds, nor is it clear how, without such expedients, he could have raised any comparable sum.[12] Indeed, it was the high cost of coastal defence, beginning to bite particularly in the early 1540s, which exposed the king uniquely to irresistible temptations to use the Mint to perpetrate the deliberate fraud of the Debasement, just as it would be the Edwardian recoinage of the early 1550s which would come to require a looting of

138 'Old Coppernose' coins of the Great Debasement, in which the silver content had been reduced by as much as 75 per cent (Museum of London)

parish church plate, done in the name of reform and the king's necessity, but bringing before many, for the very first time, their personal loss by the Reformation. Both the excuse for the one and the precedent for the other had already been long in the making. Henry VIII's military troubles, inherited by his son, had much to do with the political manoeuvrings which accompanied the later stages of the Reformation. And before Edward's advisers steeled themselves to raid the parish churches of England, Henry had plundered its monasteries.

The Dissolution and its circumstances are already well known, there being much truth in the contention that the course of events at the suppression of the monasteries – first the lesser houses in 1536 and then the 'great and solemn' monasteries in 1538–40 – was dictated only marginally by the logic of genuine reform. Nevertheless, the conditions for such changes had not been created overnight, nor would it be easy to interpret the archaeology of the Church in late-medieval England without some appreciation, at least, of these processes. Revolutionary heresies, tainted already as politically dangerous by their association with the Peasants' Revolt, had made little progress in fifteenth-century England, and it would be difficult to find many later parallels, even in the larger population centres, for the small-town Suffolk tradesmen in the Norwich diocese who, in 1429–31, were standing trial for their Lollardy.[13] But the Lollards themselves had started with powerful friends at court, and there were many Lollard principles which continued to command wide acceptance even when the movement itself had been forced to go underground. Henry V, in the early decades of the century, did not live long enough to carry through the reform of corrupt Benedictine practices he had projected in 1421. Yet he had already shown his preference clearly enough before his death for houses of the more austere observance, supporting lavishly the two new foundations, originally promised by his father, of the Carthusians at Sheen and the nearby Bridgettine nuns at Syon, both 'houses of strict life'. And it is not without significance that a large part of the wealth of both these houses should have been drawn from the former possessions of the recently suppressed alien priories, most of them Benedictine or Cluniac and at many of which the life of religion had failed.[14] At the very end of the century, it was Henry VII who welcomed the Friars Observant to England, being the reformist wing of the Franciscans. As Henry V had set up his new houses of Carthusians and Bridgettines, so the Observants were to be set up initially at the king's expense next to a favoured royal palace and retreat. Although nothing survives of their friary at Richmond, of which even the site is unknown, it was certainly very expensive.[15]

The austerities practised by the Carthusians and the Observants, which had brought them to the notice of the king, attracted a wide public audience. Bequests to all the Charterhouses of England and all the houses of Friars Observant feature, for example, in the will of Sir Henry Willoughby (d. 1528), itself described as a 'model of conventional medieval piety'. Yet Sir Henry left nothing to his Cluniac neighbours at Lenton Priory, with whom he was accustomed to deposit his valuables, nor would any others of his family.[16] Very similar in their preferences to these Nottinghamshire knights were the citizens of London and of Norwich, the collected wills of whom have been the subject of recent careful studies. Throughout the fifteenth century, and persisting through to the Dissolution, both Carthusians and friars featured regularly in the London wills, while it is noticeable that the Observants, just as soon as they were introduced, very rapidly built up their own following.[17] Whereas at London some 36 per cent of the wills included gifts to the friaries, the proportion at Norwich rose to as much as between 44 and 47 per cent, the greater part of these testators leaving money equally to each of the city's four friaries. Furthermore, among the very few monastic establishments outside Norwich which still featured in its citizen's wills, there was an identifiable swing within this period towards the houses of stricter observance: the Carthusians of London, for example, and of Mount Grace, in Yorkshire, with their brethren at Sheen and the Bridgettine nuns of Syon.[18] Inevitably, this success of some houses in attracting benefactions resulted in the failure of others. Among the more traditional of monastic establishments, the unusual favour of the Benedictines of Norwich probably owed itself to their custody of the city's fine cathedral.[19] More commonly, the old-fashioned regular houses both at Norwich and at London had fallen (on the evidence of the wills, and a full century or more before the Dissolution) very low in the popular esteem, particular sufferers also being the hospitals and colleges of the secular clergy, caught up in the same descent. Indeed, while the overall receipts of the Church had remained quite steady and its wealth was still obvious to predators, the altering patterns of popular devotion had hit certain of its revenues especially hard. Brother William Ingram, the comfortably-off custodian of the shrine of St Thomas at Canterbury (above, p. 170), watched over an asset of the cathedral priory once vital to its fortunes but, by his time, seriously eroded. During Brother William's long term of office, from 1504 right through till 1533, only two men of note visited his altar, and neither gave generously to the shrine. Except at its greatest festival, the Vigil and Translation of St Thomas, the premier pilgrimage church of medieval England had come to be woefully neglected.[20]

While declining receipts, in one form or another, did not prevent continued extravagant building expenditure at many of the greater houses, even Bell Harry,

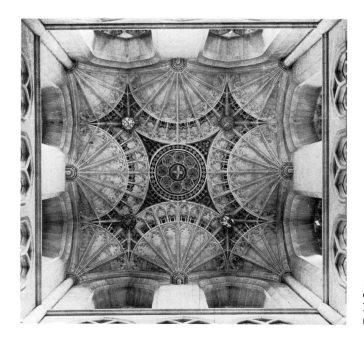

139 The late-fifteenth-century fan vault of Bell Harry, Canterbury Cathedral (R.C.H.M.)

the crowning glory of Canterbury Cathedral, being completed only a decade or so before Brother William took office, a sure consequence of the new concentration of public interest on the friars and the more austere orders was to give these the resources, with both excuse and encouragement, to embark on building programmes of their own. Many friaries, at the major centres of population, had benefited especially from the Black Death and its aftermath, provoking the sour observation of a Benedictine near-contemporary that 'without more ado, little heeding their profession and their rule, which consist in mendicant poverty, they gathered from all sides superfluous equipment for their rooms, their tables and their horses, being tempted thereto by the devil.'[21] And it was the Black Death again, certainly, which had provided the initial stimulus for the foundation of London's Charterhouse.[22] But this impetus did not decline with the plagues. Still, in the last decades of the fifteenth century, an abbot of the great Cistercian house at Fountains contrasted unfavourably the sluggish progress made by his own order on its new collegiate buildings at Oxford with the very different experience of the friars. Passers-by, he observed, among them the great and the powerful, had been heard to remark on the inability of the wealthy Cistercians to finish just one college of their own while the Mendicants everywhere were putting up magnificent buildings.[23] Nor could the Cistercians, in the face of such competition, have viewed these works with generosity. In the accounts of Whalley Abbey for 1520, chiefly remarkable for the lavish household expenditure of the monks, the recorded gift of a shilling each to the four principal orders of friars is less a gesture of charity than an insult.[24]

If insult it were, the friars were well placed to ignore it. As confessors, particularly, and as buriers of the dead, their popularity among townspeople had brought them the wealth that set up, for example, an establishment as magnificent as the Carmelite house at Coventry. And while their Benedictine critic of post-plague days had disagreeably remarked that 'the friars always spoil their penitents',[25] they evidently did so to very good effect. When, in 1467, the Dominicans of Chester found themselves in need of extra buildings, they were able to persuade 'that devout woman Dame Cecily de Torbock', relict of a knight already a benefactor of their house, to bequeath them a sum sufficient to cover the full cost of the new work.[26] And it was local notables like Dame Cecily and her spouse who successfully maintained the friars against their critics,[27] just as the Carthusians, too, drew upon their favour to finance the steady expansion of their own establishments, which has been noted, for example, at Hinton Priory, in Somerset, or at the very much larger Charterhouse in London.[28]

In the final event, however, this very popularity of the more austere orders was itself a symptom of a general malaise in the pre-Reformation Church which would end by carrying both the friars and the Carthusians, along with their defeated competitors, into the same oblivion. The evangelical mood of those 'retired army officers', the Lollard knights, with its strong anti-clerical bias, did not evaporate following the death of their leader, Sir John Oldcastle.[29] Henry V, it is true, repudiated his former friendships, strongly condemning the heresies of Oldcastle and his supporters. But Henry himself, impatient with the slow pace of change in the Church, did his best to accelerate reform, and for those who, unlike the king, were unable to influence events, there was always the option of withdrawal. At Norwich, there is little evidence of Lollardy, or of any other heresy, openly on display in the fifteenth century. Yet in this important city, the emphasis on private devotions, which had been one of the beliefs of the Lollard knights before their suppression in 1417, was to gather strength much later in the century as, starting in the 1470s, citizen bequests to the recluses of Norwich (the anchorites, hermits and beguines) became almost a matter of routine.[30] These self-same citizens, now the admirers of an individual religion somewhat akin to Protestantism, had been the props of the Mendicants and the Carthusians.

Support for the friars, at Norwich as elsewhere, dropped appreciably in the short interval that separated the English and the Continental Reformations, this being the period of such heresy stories as that of the sailors of Hull, corrupted at Bremen in 1528 by the sight there of Lutheran practices.[31] However, the brief run-up to the Reformation in England, too abbreviated to leave a mark of any consequence on the landscape, is not something on which we need pause. In the story of the religious communities of medieval England, the next archaeologically verifiable event would also be, with few exceptions, the last.

Broadly speaking, the violence done everywhere to the buildings of the monasteries was not applied at the Dissolution to their inmates. In Yorkshire, for example, the sparing of many of the lesser houses in 1536, during the first round of suppressions, was dictated quite simply by the impossibility of finding adequate accommodation in the greater houses for the monks and nuns who would then have been displaced. This was to be true particularly of the houses of nuns, commonly both poverty-stricken and very small. But it applied as much to communities such as the Carthusians, unable to adapt the cell-by-cell plan of houses like Mount Grace to a sudden, uncatered-for expansion.[32] Of course, in 1538–9, the option of remaining in the life of religion was not any longer to be considered. In the choice between martyrdom and a government pension, many opted, very sensibly, for the second.

140   The great cloister and its surrounding individual cells at Mount Grace Priory, Yorkshire
(Aerofilms)

In doing so, the pensioners immediately joined the ranks of those with an
interest in maintaining Henry's final solution, and the first priority, to all in their
position, was to make a return to the old ways impossible. One new owner, of
Repton Priory in Derbyshire, explained his demolition of the priory church as a
destruction of the nest 'for fear the Birds should build therein again'.[33] And
elsewhere, for very similar reasons, it was usually the church and the east claustral
buildings, essential for the religious life, that were the first to be demolished, the
farm buildings of the outer court and the more comfortable abbot's lodging more
commonly being permitted to survive.[34] We have long had before us the grim
historical record of the pre-demolition on-site auctions of 1538–9, most poignant
of which is the sad tale of the monks of Roche, standing-by individually to sell off
the contents of their cells.[35] But there is now, also, a growing body of archaeological
evidence for the form these destructions took. Of other Cistercian houses as
wealthy as Roche, there is evidence at Bordesley, where the auction of iron-work,
glass and tiles took place on 23 September 1538, of lead-melting and the casting of
ingots, preserved on the floor of the church.[36] And four such ingots, stamped with

the Tudor rose and crown, were found together some years ago on the church-floor at Rievaulx, buried under a masonry collapse.[37] Hearths and furnaces, also for the processing of lead, have been found similarly on the floor of the refectory at Durham Priory, on the church-floor of the Franciscans of Northampton, at Fountains Abbey, in the nave, and at Muchelney (Somerset), Sopwell (Hertfordshire), and Pontefract (central Yorkshire).[38]

At each of these houses, as at all the rest, the more useful fittings and other furnishings were carefully preserved for resale. However, lead was as valuable then as it continues to this day, and much would be sacrificed to obtain it. At Roche certainly, and presumably at Fountains too, to judge by the ash-heaps noted by the excavators, stalls, screens, and other interior woodwork were used in this process as a fuel. And although orders, we know, were given at Rievaulx to preserve the best glass from destruction, it was window-lead, almost as much as the lead from roofs, which drew the attention of the demolishers. Great quantities of broken glass have been found next to the infirmary at Monk Bretton Priory, one of the last to be dissolved, associated with fire-fused fragments and such broken lead calmes as had fortuitously survived the blaze.[39] At Pontefract and again at Sopwell, the thick demolition layers characterizing both these priory sites were found to hold painted glass and fragments of window-lead, with the destruction sequence at Pontefract showing especially clearly in the discovery of the glass

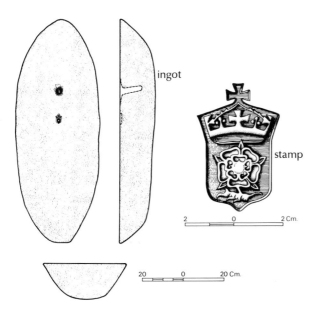

ingot

stamp

2   0   2 Cm.

20   0   20 Cm.

141   A lead ingot, carrying the royal stamp, which survived, concealed by debris from the post-Dissolution lead-melting at Rievaulx Abbey, Yorkshire (Dunning)

between the mortar bedding of tiled floors, already removed, and the stonework of the final collapse. Very little of this glass, at Pontefract at least, was found outside the church, the suggestion being that the priory windows had been 'systematically shattered' by stone-throwing vandals outside the church immediately its interior fittings had been salvaged.[40]

Frequently, as was certainly the case at Sopwell Priory, a former Benedictine nunnery, some of the thoroughness of the post-Dissolution demolitions must have followed from the desire of the new owners of the sites to turn them to better use, whether by the reconstruction of the vacated buildings or by their total razing. Sopwell, in Hertfordshire, had been granted in 1544, with the very much richer St Albans Abbey, to Sir Richard Lee, the military engineer, and

First plan (Lee I)
Final plan (Lee II) and later alterations

water pipe

fireplace

eavesdrip gullies
water pipe
drain

Cobbles   Above ground
Mortar floors   Above ground (later)
Tiled floors   Foundations

5   0   5 Metres

142 Sir Richard Lee's rebuildings at Sopwell Priory, Hertfordshire, at first making use of the original cloister (Lee I) and then abandoning it in favour of a more fashionable double-courtyard plan (Lee II) (Johnson)

it was some years later, in the 1550s, that Sir Richard, before turning his hand to other artillery works like the defences of Berwick-upon-Tweed, spent almost a decade of retirement in Hertfordshire, rebuilding Sopwell with material from St Albans and calling it now 'Lee's Place'. Whether then or, as would seem more likely, rather later in his long and active life, Sir Richard changed his mind about the plan of his new mansion, having begun with church as hall and cloister as courtyard, but ending by abandoning the claustral plan completely. This second scheme, on the evidence of the excavations at Sopwell, was never brought to fruition, neglected perhaps from 1575 on the death of its ambitious designer.[41]

In due course, rather naturally, such a failure as this would be taken as yet further evidence of the punishments supernaturally visited upon those guilty of the sacrilege of destruction, perhaps the best-known collection of horror stories on this theme being included in Sir Henry Spelman's *The History and Fate of Sacrilege*, a work of the seventeenth century.[42] However, there is little genuinely to suggest the fearfulness, 'long after the Dissolution', which Spelman thought he saw at the Norfolk houses he discussed, preventing any meddling with places long consecrated to God, nor were the 'many strange misfortunes and grievous accidents' of his guilty gentry families something which anybody, at the time, could predict. In the event, what distinguished the new owners of many of the former monastic houses was not the sensibility of their response to the past but the ruthless drive of their conversions. Religious buildings, of their nature, are difficult to adapt to a lay purpose, and the most usual solution of the converters was to demolish the church altogether, making use thereafter of the claustral buildings, as at Lacock Abbey in Wiltshire, or basing their reconstruction on a set of abbot's lodgings which, like those at Forde Abbey, might have been comparatively recently rebuilt.[43] But there were those, always, who were tempted by the drama of the buildings they had acquired to undertake more ambitious conversions, and of particular interest, in this connection, are the opposing solutions of Thomas Wriothesley and William Paulet at the abbeys of Titchfield and Netley, almost next door to each other in southern Hampshire. Wriothesley made his hall out of the former refectory at Titchfield, driving a pompous turreted gatehouse through the body of the original church nave, while, at Netley, Paulet reversed this plan, making his hall and kitchen out of what had been the church, and demolishing the monks' refectory on the far side of the cloister to make a suitable, centrally placed entrance to his court.[44] At both establishments, the fashionable Tudor mansion, with its characteristic courtyard plan, preserved exactly the claustral layout which centuries before had first suggested this particular design.

143   Sir William Sharington's re-use of the claustral buildings at Lacock Abbey, Wiltshire, later remodelled in the mid-eighteenth-century 'Gothick' style (Aerofilms)

144   The gatehouse at Thomas Wriothesley's new mansion at Titchfield Abbey, Hampshire, driven through the body of the former church (Kersting)

218

Overall, as was only to be expected, conversions everywhere were as individual as the men who commissioned them, showing strikingly little concern for what had been the original purpose of the buildings. Later in the century, for example, Sir Richard Grenville, Elizabeth's naval commander, made a manor-house of the church at Buckland Abbey, in Devon, which preserved in a most unusual fashion almost every detail of the original sacred building, even to the great tower over the crossing.[45] But others, as Wriothesley and Paulet very quickly showed, did not wait as long as this, and it was immediately after the suppression of Mottisfont Priory that their colleague William, Lord Sandys, devout believer though he was, set about a similar sacrilegious conversion of this small Hampshire house, demolishing the greater part of the original priory buildings while preserving the church, in nave and south transept alone, as the frame for his comparatively modest new mansion. Indeed, at the lower end of the scale of monastic wealth, diminutive houses like the Augustinian priories at Woodspring or at Stavordale, both in Somerset, might have no building other than the church itself which was really worth the trouble of converting. At Woodspring, the nave was floored over to make a farmhouse; at Stavordale, the nave and chancel became barn and dwellings. And Sampson Erdeswicke, the Elizabethan antiquary, had heard, he tells us, of another such conversion by 'a Lancashire man' of Calwich, an Augustinian cell in Staffordshire, his own county, where the new owner, heedless of tradition, had made 'a parlour of the chancel, a hall of the church and a kitchen of the steeple', by which he meant, of course, the tower.[46]

In a similar philistine spirit, others proceeded, without much pause, to make the best use of whatever they had fortuitously acquired. Thomas Bell, a Gloucester clothier, took on the Dominican friary as a site for his factory, re-using the church as a residence for himself,[47] and much the same purpose was found for the former claustral buildings of Malmesbury Abbey, the remains of one of the wealthiest Benedictine establishments being converted into a workshop for 'one Stumpe, an exceding riche clothier'.[48] Pressed to give the reasons why, having thought so well of the monks, he should have played a part of his own in their destruction, one of the despoilers of Roche replied, with an altogether commendable frankness, 'what should I do . . . might I not as well as others have some Profit of the Spoil of the Abbey? For I did see all would away; and therefore I did as others did.'[49]

Of course, *all* did as others did, and few thought any the worse of themselves because of it. But the processes of destruction, once started, were difficult to stop, and the good went out with the bad. From 1536, the fate of the monastic houses raised fears for the safety of the colleges and almshouses, the chantries and even the parish churches, and within ten years these too were under attack. When Mary came to the throne in 1553, bringing the reformers temporarily to a halt, the work of plunder, however acceptable the reasoning behind each one of its stages, had ended by offending almost everybody in turn, leaving all of them cumulatively bereft. It was said of Pontefract, soon after Mary's accession, that

> we had in that town one abbey, two colleges, a house of friars preachers, one ancress, one hermit, four chantry priests, one guild priest. . . . We have there left an unlearned vicar, which hireth two priests, for indeed he is not able to discharge the cure other ways, and I dare say the vicar's living is under forty marks.[50]

By such means, 'bodily and ghostly,' had the burgesses of Pontefract been deprived.

In the secular church, as in the monastic, change can have taken few altogether by surprise, nor were the lean emoluments of the post-Reformation vicar of Pontefract unknown in better days. We are in less doubt now than we used to be of the quality of the late-medieval clergy, but the recent studies that have cleared these misconceptions have pointed also, in every case, to a disastrously low level of clerical incomes in the final pre-reform decades, seriously endangering the work of the Church.[51] Non-residence among the clergy, with the merging of benefices and church closures, had widened the gap still further between a sophisticated career clergy on the one hand, promoted by reason of its mobility, and a depressed parish priesthood on the other, impoverished and immobile, unable to procure any preferment.[52] Afflicted at all levels by what has been described as the 'persistent harassment' of the crown,[53] the Church was divided within, ill-equipped to deflect its opponents. Those mergers and demolitions which, in earlier years, might have been promoted by the Church itself, accelerated greatly in the mid-sixteenth century on initiatives outside its control. From 1547, it was the corporation of York which undertook the suppression of what it judged the 'superfluous' parish churches of the city, to result in the disappearance of some seventeen churches out of an original total of forty.[54] In Lincoln, the church demolitions for which, in the 1530s, that city was already notorious, were hastened by the union of parishes sanctioned by the statute of 13 May 1549,[55] while at Stamford, prospering just as Lincoln itself was in decline, the twelve churches of the medieval town, north of the river, had nevertheless been reduced by 1548 to a total of no more than five.[56]

Some of these private urban 'dissolutions', already long overdue, would no doubt have occurred even without the Reformation. However, they were accompanied, too, by a plunder of church furnishings far exceeding the call of rationalization, to challenge many cherished beliefs. Certainly, the parish church after the 'Edwardian Reformation' – whitewashed, stripped of its fittings, and internally rearranged – was a very different place from its ornate and crowded precursor. And the changes here, because closer to the interests of the bulk of the population than the earlier fate of the religious communities, were ultimately to seem the more shocking. The devout women, formerly the prop of the Franciscans at Plymouth, who still 'gathered to Saynt Francis' there in 1549,[57] would have found many sympathizers among those who watched with growing concern the sacrilegious despoliation of the parish churches. At Southampton, it is plain, the more extreme teaching of the Edwardian reformers was received, at least by the leading burgesses, with undisguised distaste,[58] while the so-called 'Prayer Book Rebellion' of 1549, provoked in the West Country by the publication earlier that year of the first Act of Uniformity, although inflamed by contemporary economic distress, sought essentially a return to the faith.[59]

To some small degree, after 1553, the Marian Reaction halted the gathering in by the crown of what was left of the parish church plate, bringing to an end those collections which had started in earnest at the end of 1552, following the second and more austere Edwardian Act of Uniformity. But for many parishes, the damage had already been done, and there was nothing that Mary and her advisers could do to recover the lost church furnishings. Moreover, despite the genuine popular sympathy that the Reaction uncovered, especially in conservative areas like the north-west,[60] Mary's brief reign was no more than an interlude, underlining the weakness of the more extreme of the Protestant reformers, but unable to destroy the reform. Where the individual churches were concerned, the principal requirement of that reform had been for adequate provision, in buildings generally unsuited to such needs, for a genuinely corporate liturgical worship, bringing the priest and his flock together. To the Edwardian reformer, this had meant the taking down of the great screens which, in many late-medieval parish churches, had completed the separation of nave and chancel, the object being, in Bishop Hooper's words, that there should be no 'closures, imparting, and separations between the ministers and the people'.[61] It had required, too, the moving of the font from the west end of the church to a position nearer the altar, where the congregation might participate in baptisms; it had led to the reseating of the minister himself, in the nave rather than the chancel; and, most important, it had forced the replacement of the fixed stone altar of the traditional rite by a movable communion table, centrally placed in the choir, or chancel, where the communicants could gather about it.

In the fullness of time, under Elizabeth, many of the original certainties would fade, with the result that screens, albeit on a smaller scale, were frequently restored, fonts were moved back to their original positions, and a fixed stone altar, or communion table, reappeared at the east end of the chancel. However, with all this, the ideal of corporate worship persisted intact, preserved most particularly in a form of service now conducted invariably in the vernacular. To this way of thinking, the obscure symbolism of the medieval wall-painting might be not just unhelpful but even positively misleading. Whitewashed out, the grisly lessons of the medieval paintings were replaced by fundamental texts: the Creed, the Lord's Prayer, or the Ten Commandments, or selected sentences from the scriptures.[62] Over the chancel arch, where the great dooms of the later Middle Ages had customarily confronted the pre-Reformation congregations, there were now set the royal arms, perhaps accompanied, as at Tivetshall in Norfolk, by carefully chosen texts, reinforcing the lesson of authority in the Church, along with the essential elements of its teaching. Responding to the mood of their times, many

145   The royal arms of Elizabeth I at Tivetshall Church, in Norfolk; below the arms, the text includes the Ten Commandments with the names of those who 'caused this for to be done' (R.C.H.M.)

parish authorities, worried by a church dedication that reflected disgraced superstitions, changed it to something less offensive. Many dedications to St Mary survive, but for some this was the occasion for a switch to the Holy Trinity. St Thomas of Canterbury, conveniently, could become St Thomas the Apostle.[63]

In the churchwardens' accounts of the Holy Trinity, Chester, as in the many similar account-books that survive, the stops and starts of the English Reformation are neatly displayed, interspersed among the mass of routine transactions which underline the continuity of the parish. In 1542, following the order of Convocation that year that the lessons should be read in English, the churchwardens at Holy Trinity bought a bible, fixing it with a chain to a desk. Three years later, in good time for Easter, the church was whitewashed, while the first Act of Uniformity, in 1549, brought the dismantling of the medieval altars and their replacement by a new-style movable communion table. In 1551, the sale of church furnishings began, chiefly vestments, canopies, altar-cloths and copes, then to be followed the next year, more seriously, by the collection of church plate by the crown. The Marian Reaction, from 1553, was reflected immediately at Holy Trinity, Chester, in the painting and gilding of the Rood, the restoration of discredited images, and the purchase of office-books of the ancient and traditional rite. Through Mary's reign, former church goods were reassembled or new ones bought; there were repeated purchases of incense and candles; the altars were repaired and replaced. Yet, within months of Elizabeth's accession, all this was once again reversed. Following the Act of Supremacy of 1559 and the final break with Rome, the images at Holy Trinity were taken down again and the refurbished altars destroyed. During the next decade, in a succession of sales, the remaining church goods were sold off. In 1566, a painter was employed by the churchwardens to put up a table of the Ten Commandments and to write appropriate scriptures on the walls; there was further whitewashing; 'superstitious' painted glass was replaced by plain; and the Rood loft, after its many vicissitudes, was finally taken down in 1571, never again to be replaced.[64] One of the items purchased by the parish in 1566 was a poor-box, newly made for the purpose and presciently furnished with two strong locks, almost as expensive as itself. The transaction may serve us as a useful reminder that to many, at Chester as elsewhere, the circumstances of the Reformation, for all their excitement, continued less devotional than economic.

Indeed, perhaps the majority of the protests associated with contemporary religious changes, whether in the monasteries or out in the parishes, were essentially social and economic at root. There is much evidence, for example, that the Norfolk disturbances of 1536–7, although coloured by religion, were promoted more particularly by class grievance,[65] and the clear anti-gentry bias of Kett's Rebellion, in the same county just over a decade later, was the cause of much concern to the authorities. Yet Kett's Rebellion, of course, coincided with the more genuinely religious Prayer Book Rebellion in the West Country, and it is neither easy nor particularly useful to separate one source of grievance from another. Whether there was any truth in it or not, many contemporaries remembered the monks as soft landlords, attributing the more serious troubles of the times not to their real causes – population increase, epidemics and bad harvests, inflation, and the disastrous economic policies of Tudor governments – but to the unscrupulous rack-renting of greedy yeomanry and gentry, planting their feet in the faces of the poor. Rents, of course, had begun to rise already in the late fifteenth century, and monks were to figure prominently among those accused, from at least the 1520s, of extortionate increases in rents.[66] But rents, too, have their own built-in inertia, and by the time the really serious rent-hikes occurred, usually not before the 1570s and 1580s, this characteristic of the monks had been forgotten. What men saw was a redistribution of lands which, while it might in the short term benefit such lesser tenantry as the twenty Cumberland families who divided between them a single former grange of Holm Cultram,[67] in the long run favoured only the rich. It was a redistribution, moreover, which gathered such momentum as to take it well beyond the disposal of ex-monastic lands. The private land market, stagnant in its upper reaches throughout the fifteenth century, was stimulated after 1540 into unusual, perhaps excessive, activity by the flood of crown leases and sales.[68] And, in the meantime, a profoundly unsettling social mobility – upwards, downwards, and even horizontal – was both the consequence and itself a cause of change.[69]

The departure of the monks had left the landscape badly scarred. Yet this was not the only contemporary change transforming the face of rural England, nor was it even the most important. When the men of Landbeach rose in 1549, in what has been described as a miniature Kett's Rebellion, what provoked them was aggressive landlordism and a threat to their rights of common.[70] But although they, like so many others, looked back on what they recognized as gentler days, those times had vanished long before, having little to do with the monks. Back in the fifteenth century, the conversion of arable to pasture had been accomplished often more by default of tenants than despite them, and there would be men still in the early sixteenth century, as there had been quite commonly in the fifteenth, 'lever to departe the lordshipp' than agree to an increase in rents.[71] However, the return of agricultural prosperity in the late fifteenth century, with prices and rents both rising, had restored the initiative to the landlords again, and very soon there were those willing to take it. Enclosure, it has frequently been argued, was not the evil it was commonly held to be in the sixteenth century, being still less a major instrument of depopulation in Tudor England than it had been through the centuries before.[72] Nevertheless, enclosure everywhere was a demonstration of growing authority among the better-off landholders, significantly altering the existing social balance. There were those who held (wrongly, as it turned out) that the population of England was on the decline in the mid-sixteenth century: that the sheep were eating the men. What had happened in practice was that those very same men, long left to themselves, had become once again the legitimate prey of their landlords.

Few instances of landlord oppression are surely more striking than that well-documented expulsion of the villagers of Sellergarth, in Lancashire, begun in person by the abbot of Furness, just a few days before Christmas 1516, 'with more than 22 of his monks and people . . . in riotous manner assembled'.[73] But although the monks, with stories like this gathering about them, attracted their share of opprobrium, it is not to be doubted that, as landlords, they had usually been no worse than any others of their time, while frequently being very much better.[74] Under-renting, for example, characterized the Durham Priory estates before the Dissolution, continuing to do so even after the cathedral had taken over the priory lands.[75] And this, of course, with other examples of its kind, would have made the contrast with less scrupulous landowners all the more obvious and disheartening. In the Durham region, as elsewhere, it was not the great landowners like the Nevill earls of Westmorland, any more than it had been the Church, who stood in the van of the oppressors. Rather, it was the 'new' gentry and the coal-rich merchants of Newcastle who, as graziers, were the leading engrossers and depopulators.[76] At the start of the century, they had had their equivalents in such 'rising' gentry as the Spencers, first depopulators and then resettlers, in a new location, of the Warwickshire village of Wormleighton.[77] However, there are more convincing parallels, nearer their day, in the enclosing gentry of Yorkshire, with some 130 families actively engaged in the engrossing of lands through the decades on either side of 1600.[78] And there are many other instances, all over the country, of precisely these oppressions, not necessarily resulting in total depopulation, and quite frequently accomplished by agreement and with adequate compensation, but inevitably socially divisive.

Most immediately offensive was the emparking of common pasture, reducing land that had been the livelihood of village families to the merest plaything of the wealthy. There is no reason to think that emparking, more than other forms of

146   The alabaster memorial of Robert Gylbert (d. 1492), with his wife, Joan, and their seventeen children, at Youlgreave Church, Derbyshire (Hallam Ashley)

enclosure, was conducted with especial insensibility and violence. Indeed, it was seen by the aristocracy as a preparation for building which, though essential to the builder's purpose, might very well cost him dear in the considerable expense of resettling. Nevertheless, moral outrage and the growing value of agricultural land combined to reverse the movement towards any further emparking, and more land, before the end of the sixteenth century, was being taken back into cultivation from former parks than was currently being removed to enlarge them.[79] Undoubtedly more unsettling in the long term, however, harder to recognize and virtually impossible to reverse, was the steady engrossment of unwanted lands and the reclamation of waste, damaging the poor to all appearances but slightly, while of immediate advantage to the encloser. Even where, as in rural Sussex, the size of the average farming unit did not increase very markedly during the later sixteenth and early seventeenth century, there was continual activity on the part of the property-holders both to improve their inherited lands and to gather in what they could of the waste.[80] And the vigour of the Sussex improvers was matched elsewhere by those freeholders and better-off tenants in every county who, while spurred by the threat of uncontrolled inflation, were yet uniquely in the position to

226

take advantage of it. We need not see the sixteenth century as a period of agricultural advance to appreciate that there were many, in the yeoman and gentry classes, who thrived through its crises and reversals.[81] As always, there were others, like the Langholme squires of Conisholme in Lincolnshire, who had done well enough under the patronage systems of fifteenth-century England but who, under the Tudors, would exhibit downward mobility.[82] Nor is it clear that the many small freeholders who, for example, had owned so much of northern Buckinghamshire in the early sixteenth century,[83] continued to prosper as well a century later, by which time, certainly, their Cambridgeshire equivalents, the 20–30 acre farmers of townships like Orwell, Willingham and Chippenham, had begun to do very badly.[84] But, in an active land market, it was precisely the sufferings of the under-capitalized, whoever they might be, that gave their opportunity to the engrossers. Before the wealthier yeoman farmer himself came to grief in the agricultural vicissitudes of the later seventeenth century, he had never done as well.

It is impossible now to put a number to these more prosperous freeholders. However, the widely held contemporary belief in their importance, thought by all patriots to be the reason for England's success at arms, very probably included much truth, while we know it to be the case with the greater landowners, for whom the evidence certainly is better, that they multiplied appreciably under the Tudor

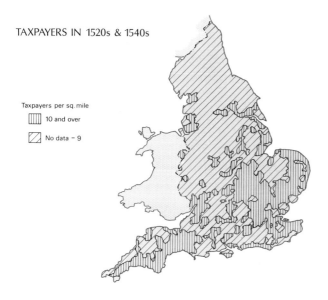

TAXPAYERS IN 1520s & 1540s

Taxpayers per sq. mile
|||| 10 and over
//// No data – 9

147 Degrees of prosperity in sixteenth-century England, as measured by the number of taxpayers (Sheail)

227

monarchy, perhaps doubling in number between the mid-fifteenth and the mid-seventeenth centuries.[85] Possession of freehold land, as it has been remarked of the small county of Rutland, was the first and most reliable indicator of social status in the sixteenth century. And the gathering-together of the bulk of this land into very few hands, being a phenomenon already apparent in the record of the Rutland 'Survey of Harness' of 1522, was a long-continuing process.[86]

In the measurement of wealth, the most obvious inequalities may show regionally, as well as between classes. Thus England, by the mid-sixteenth century, can be seen to have developed a wealth in its central and southern counties scarcely visible at all in the north-west,[87] while there were differences at least as profound as this between, for example, the well-off yeomen farmers of Leicestershire or Cambridgeshire and the overwhelming majority of their fellow parishioners in those counties, as many as 50 per cent of whom were listed as wage-earners and landless.[88] Inevitably, inflation widened the gulf still further, nor was it alone in doing so. As the population rose, which it was beginning to do from the 1520s and perhaps earlier, labour lost that bargaining edge it had enjoyed for almost two centuries. Demand, meanwhile, was forcing up prices, and the rich grew richer every day alongside the distraction of the poor.

What this meant, in practical terms, was immediately apparent to contemporaries. William Harrison wrote of the late 1570s,

> There are old men yet dwelling in the village where I remain, which have noted three things to be marvellously altered in England within their sound remembrance. . . . One is the multitude of chimneys lately erected. . . . The second is the great (although not general) amendment of lodging. . . . The third thing they tell of is the exchange of vessel, as of treen platters into pewter, and wooden spoons into silver or tin.

However, these same old men were very well aware of the cost of what they saw, for

> as they commend these, so . . . they speak also of three things that are grown to be very grievous unto them, to wit: the enhancing of rents . . . the daily oppression of copyholders, whose lords seek to bring their poor tenants almost into plain servitude and misery . . . (and) the third thing they talk of is usury, a trade brought in by the Jews, now perfectly practised almost by every Christian and so commonly that he is accounted but for a fool that doth lend his money for nothing.[89]

On one side of the coin, the brave new world of the 'Great Rebuilding'; on the other, the manifold oppressions that financed it.

Reasonably enough, critics of the Great Rebuilding hypothesis have found it hard to accept Professor Hoskins's comparatively narrow dating of this phenomenon, within the half-century beginning in 1575.[90] Certainly, the importance of the hall, always a crucial factor in these changes, had long been in decline, and a good many of the characteristics of the Great Rebuilding, as Professor Hoskins himself first defined them, had already had clear antecedents in the fifteenth century (above, pp. 199–200). By the early sixteenth century, the Rebuilding was anticipated quite commonly in such buildings as the Merton College farmhouse at Holywell, in Oxford, for which a contract, dated 1516, specified the provision of a ground-floor hall, of fireplaces in all the principal chambers, of many good windows and the refinement of two indoor privies.[91] And with the Great Rebuilding, on the Hoskins dating, still almost a generation away, there were those in mid-sixteenth-century England who recognized 'of late days' buildings 'far more excessive than at any time heretofore'.[92] Moreover, there were areas experiencing no major rebuildings in the new tradition before the eighteenth century at earliest, to which the Great Rebuilding, so far as we can judge, was scarcely relevant at all.[93] But although, at either end, the period of building activity must surely be accepted as much longer, there is no doubting the widespread appeal of improved housing standards, evident particularly from the late sixteenth century, nor would areas otherwise scarcely touched by innovation, like the economically backward north-west, entirely escape these influences. Gaythorn Hall, a remote farmhouse in the isolation of northern Westmorland, would be built to a near-symmetrical centralized plan with many Renaissance touches, remarkably modern in many of its characteristics yet constructed in the

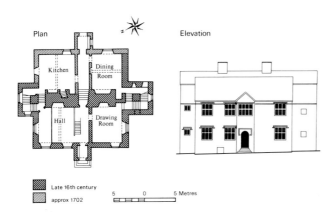

148   An unusually advanced centralized plan at Gaythorn Hall, Westmorland; late-sixteenth-century (Brunskill)

late sixteenth century.[94] And if the Great Rebuilding came more slowly to Wales, moving westwards across country from the borderlands, its usual manifestations – glazed windows, stairs, wainscoting, plasterwork, fireplaces, and floored-over halls – were all to be found in Welsh country houses of the seventeenth century, much as they had come to be accepted, some generations before, as normal requirements of the housing of the more prosperous south-east.[95]

Undoubtedly, the most important change in the vernacular building tradition was the abandonment of the long-familiar three-part house – the chamber, hall, and kitchen lined up in series on the medieval plan – in favour of a symmetrical two-part house, with its central chimney-bay and stair. Later, although not usually before the eighteenth century, the two-part house would develop naturally into the conventional 'double' house, of which Gaythorn Hall had already been an exceptionally early example, where the 'hall' had become no more than an entrance passage, and where there were sets of rooms, back and front, on either side of the door.[96] But the option of building entirely anew is rarely open to many, and the most common response to the new housing standards of Elizabethan England was, rather, the conversion of an existing older building to meet at least some of these needs. Many examples are known of these conversions, and there are more being recognized all the time,[97] although it is easy to see, too, the persistence of medieval traditions, both in planning and in architectural detail, through the length of the sixteenth century. Great houses, that is, like the Suffolk mansions of Giffords Hall and Redgrave Hall, built in the 1520s and late 1540s respectively, preserved important characteristics of the medieval plan, whether

149 Late-medieval survivals in the detailing of doors and windows at the 'Priory', Marcham, in Berkshire, the building being otherwise characteristically early-modern in plan (R.C.H.M.)

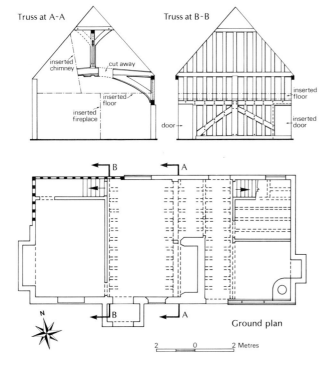

Truss at A-A

inserted chimney
cut away
inserted floor
inserted fireplace

Truss at B-B

inserted floor
inserted floor
door
inserted door

B   A

N

B   A

Ground plan

2   0   2 Metres

150   Blue Gates Farm, Bromley, a timber-built house of *c.* 1500, improved a hundred years later by the insertion of a chimney-stack and the chambering-over of the hall (Mercer)

internally in the hall, solar and kitchen arrangements, or in overall disposition, as in the grandiose courtyard layout of Giffords Hall, entered through a showy and expensive stone gatehouse.[98] Nor was the conservatism of country-bred craftsmen easy to shake, as it might show, for example, in the late-medieval detailing of the doors and windows at the so-called 'Priory' at Marcham, in Berkshire, a farmhouse built in the late sixteenth century which, in every other particular, is characteristically early-modern in plan.[99] In common with other buildings of its date, the Priory was planned entirely on two storeys, the same effect being achieved at older houses at this time by the flooring-over of their halls. Archaeologically, there has been recent useful evidence of just such a chambering-over of the hall at a small farmhouse at Caldecote, in Hertfordshire, completed only shortly before its late-sixteenth-century abandonment.[100] And it can be seen too, of course, at many surviving buildings, among them Middle Farm and Prince's Manor, Harwell, in Berkshire, or the farmhouse at Northend, Long Crendon, just across the Buckinghamshire border.[101] Conveniently, when the new floor was inserted at Middle Farm, chambering-over the former hall, the date 1589 was carved on a bracket of one of the great beams that supported it.

231

Inevitably, the insertion of the floor, at Middle Farm as elsewhere, required a redesign of heating arrangements in the modernized house, the usual solution being the replacement of the former central hearth by a large end-wall fireplace in a substantial chimney-stack intended to serve other chambers as well. There have been various explanations of this particular phenomenon of the chimney which, although known since the twelfth century, was yet the first thing that William Harrison's ancient villagers noted as 'marvellously altered' in their time. However, although it may well be true that the introduction of coal as a cheap domestic fuel, with the new popularity of brick as a convenient material for chimney-stack construction, each played its part in the change, essentially the demand for improved heating throughout the house derived from a movement in residential habits both older and more fundamental than this: from single- to many-chambered living. Towards the bottom of the social scale, a one-room labourer's cottage in the sixteenth century might come to be divided by a permanent partition. Higher up it, a house of two rooms might acquire a third, while five- and even seven-roomed houses, still most uncommon among the yeoman farmers of mid-sixteenth-century England, were to be quite unremarkable less than a century later.[102]

Exactly this contrast, between relative poverty and relative abundance, showed again, over the same period, in the quality of internal furnishings, now at last more measurable than before as the probate inventory became common. Naturally, such inventories were still only made of the goods of the wealthier deceased, being restricted, in effect, to precisely those people who were recognizably advancing in prosperity. Nevertheless, obvious differences in domestic standards have become apparent in this class in counties as distinct as Oxfordshire, Leicestershire and Shropshire, and these occurred, in many instances, within a generation or less.[103] In almost every case, that is, the transition would be complete by early in the seventeenth century, although for many the improvement had come rather earlier. Basically a product of increasing wealth, the rising demand for household goods may be seen as a natural reflection of the new prosperity. But the *proportion* of wealth invested in such goods also increased during this period, and it is this, of course, which is so striking. When, for example, the 1587 inventory of Richard Collins, an Oxfordshire farmer, is compared with another of 1553, being that of John Sims, a farmer of similar status in the same county, the proportions have dramatically changed. John Sims had lived in a one- or two-roomed farmhouse in which the household goods, totalled together, were valued at less than one-fortieth of his entire personal estate. In contrast, Richard Collins, as representative of his own day as John Sims himself

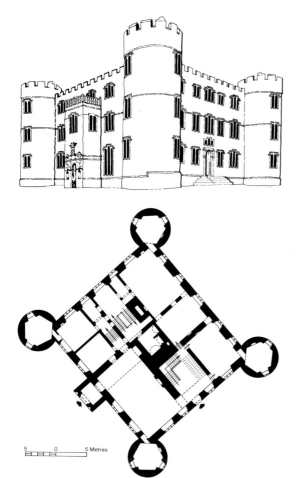

5   0   5 Metres

151   Rhiwperra, in Glamorgan, an early-
seventeenth-century imitation castle, very
much in the Renaissance manner
(R.C.H.M.)

had been, occupied a ten-roomed house which, with hall, parlour, kitchen, buttery
and dairy, had additionally five further chambers. Collins's household goods,
including a rich store of bed-linen and personal clothing, were valued at his death
at fully a third of his considerable total estate.[104]

The pressures that Richard Collins evidently felt to develop his comforts, as some
would have believed, out of all proportion to his means, were experienced even
more oppressively by the gentry. At just his time, an unprecedented inflation of
honours, embarked on by the crown for both political and financial purposes, had
begun to broaden the ranks of the armigerous gentry, opening fresh areas and
providing new incentives for indulgence in conspicuous waste.[105] Amongst the

233

wealthier, the more successful and the more ambitious, some responded by building themselves mock-castles in the Renaissance manner, like Walworth, County Durham (1600), or Rhiwperra, in Glamorgan (1626), to a style befitting their new status.[106] But even if the wealth were not yet there, the wish was certainly present. 'Every man almost is a builder', said William Harrison of the Englishmen of his time, so that in general 'how they set up, how they pull down, how they enlarge, how they restrain, how they add to, how they take from' was enough to keep 'their heads . . . never idle, their purses never shut, nor their books of account never made perfect.' And always the new buildings, whatever their purpose, were to be made more 'curious and excellent' than before.[107]

Indeed, this pursuit of the conceit – the more curious and ingenious, witty and cunning the better – was as much a part of sixteenth-century architectural practice as it was of contemporary cultivated writing and speech. In its most extreme form, it found expression in such fanciful follies as the Triangular Lodge, at Rushton in Northamptonshire, built by a Catholic convert, Sir Thomas

152 The Triangular Lodge at Rushton, Northamptonshire, built in 1593 for Sir Thomas Tresham as a neighbour-bating allegory on the Trinity (R.C.H.M.)

153   Sir Thomas Gorges's triangular plan at Longford Castle, in Wiltshire, built in the 1580s and perhaps again an allusion to the Trinity (Aerofilms)

Tresham, as a defiant allegory on the Trinity.[108] On a larger scale, it inspired Sir Thomas Gorges's Longford Castle, in Wiltshire, a work of the 1580s also in the form of a triangle, while prompting, too, that whole series of country houses, utterly characteristic of the period, designed on alphabet plans.[109] And yet it was responsible also for the readiness to experiment in the use of new materials which was one of the more attractive features of the architecture of Tudor England, being ultimately more influential than its extravagance. Among these experimental materials was terracotta, ideally suited for ornamental work in the new Renaissance style but only briefly in use in England, during the second quarter of the sixteenth century, on projects as large as Sir Richard Weston's Sutton Place, in Surrey, or as small as Old Hall Farm, Kneesall, in Nottinghamshire, put up originally as a hunting-lodge.[110] Of greater significance, though, was plaster, whether in chalk or the more durable stuccos, which would become one of the better-known artistic materials of the century. With the less usual slate, it was chosen, for example, as a principal decorative medium at Henry VIII's Nonsuch Palace, directly influenced by Francis I's almost contemporary work at Fontainebleau, near Paris, and itself a model for many of the more elaborate country-house constructions of its time.[111] Decorative plasterwork, within not more than a generation, had reached as far as the remoter parts of northern Yorkshire, and was used in a farmhouse that had once been a grange of the dissolved Cistercian community at Fountains Abbey, bringing at least a flavour of the English Renaissance to the parlour of a prosperous yeoman.[112]

Such influences, too, touched more traditional crafts, even those as old as tile-making. An inlaid floor-tile pavement in the English Renaissance style

235

154 Terracotta detailing at Sutton Place, in Surrey, completed for Sir Richard Weston in the early 1530s (Kersting)

survives still at Lacock Abbey, a former Augustinian nunnery, datable to about 1550. Soon tiles of this inlaid kind were replaced in the public favour by painted tiles, imported with other household luxuries from the Netherlands. At Lacock these final products of an ancient industry, known in Wiltshire since the thirteenth century with the Church as its most important customer, bore the initials of Sir William Sharington, purchaser and rebuilder of Lacock, himself high on the list of the brash new men who had brought down the industry's markets. On other tiles, also from Lacock, the W of William and the G of Grace, Sir William's third wife, are bound together in an Italianate frame by the love-knot which is so typically a Tudor conceit.[113]

Much of the building in Elizabethan England was undisguisedly competitive, the work of courtiers and other men of position who vied with each other, frequently on a scale they could barely afford, to put up palaces of ever greater refinement and magnificence. Such were the Howards of Audley End, the

236

155 Sophisticated brickwork with terracotta panels at Great Cressingham Manor, Norfolk, a house of the 1540s (Hallam Ashley)

0 ⟼ 10 Cm

156 An ornamental slate panel with guilloche carving, a familiar Renaissance motif, from Nonsuch Palace, in Surrey (Museum of London and the Nonsuch Excavation Committee)

237

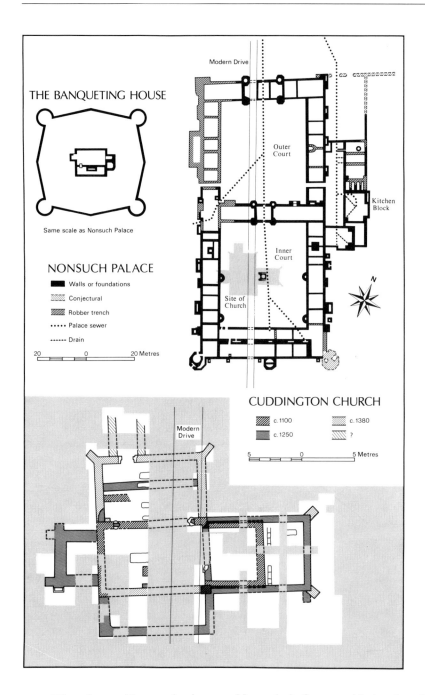

THE BANQUETING HOUSE

Same scale as Nonsuch Palace

NONSUCH PALACE

▬ Walls or foundations

▨ Conjectural

▨ Robber trench

••••• Palace sewer

•••••• Drain

20   0   20 Metres

Modern Drive

Outer Court

Kitchen Block

Inner Court

Site of Church

N

CUDDINGTON CHURCH

▨ c.1100   ▨ c.1380

▨ c.1250   ▨ ?

5   0   5 Metres

Modern Drive

157   The palace and banqueting house at Nonsuch, in Surrey, with the plan of Cuddington Church, demolished by the order of Henry VIII to make room for his extraordinary new buildings (Biddle)

158   A polychrome tin-glazed tile in the new pictorial tradition, being a mid-sixteenth-century Low Countries import or a slightly later English imitation (Museum of London)

159   Inlaid floor-tiles from Lacock Abbey, Wiltshire, showing the conversion of the old-established tile-making industry to the new Italianate motifs; the initials are those of Sir William Sharington, purchaser of Lacock from the Crown, and of Grace, Sir William's third wife (B.M.)

Sackvilles of Knole, and the Cecils of Burghley House and Hatfield, whose close partnership with the crown enabled them, with others of the peerage, to evade the worst pressures of taxation.[114] Nevertheless, the Great Rebuilding could not have become as general as it did had it not been for a genuine increase in disposable income, allowing cash accumulation among the gentry and the lesser nobility, as much as among the yeomanry and the peerage. To take just two examples, neither Sir Francis Willoughby, of Wollaton near Nottingham, nor Rowland Eyre, of Hassop in Derbyshire, were in any sense national figures, and the Eyres, it is certain, achieved what they did despite the higher aristocracy of their county, with whom they were in constant dispute. But for all the reverses that each family suffered, their success was far the more striking, and it included its measure of building. Both the Willoughbys and the Eyres had already prospered in the fifteenth century, but for neither was the opportunity as great in the earlier period

239

160   Wollaton Hall, in Nottinghamshire, built in the 1580s for Sir Francis Willoughby on the profits of the Wollaton coal-mines (R.C.H.M.)

as it was for Sir Francis and Rowland Eyre towards the end of the sixteenth century. Like others of their kind, they saw their chance and seized it when they could.[115]

To a very real degree, landowning families like the Willoughbys and the Eyres owed their latter-day prosperity to the onset of a consumer boom. Everywhere, a sharp increase in population had filled up the villages and the towns so that, for the first time in more than two centuries, landless squatters were found enclosing the waste, and even the village greens, at such settlements as Willingham and Orwell, in Cambridgeshire,[116] Myddle, in Shropshire,[117] and Solihull, in Warwickshire,[118] while multi-occupant tenements, as at Botolph Street in Norwich,[119] were crowding the back-lots in the towns. Of course, the speed of such increases varied, the 'fully 50 per cent' population rise between 1563 and 1603 at Wigston Magna, in Leicestershire, being nothing like matched at Chippenham, in Cambridgeshire,

240

a much poorer village, where the climb in the considerably longer period 1544–1664 was little more than 20 per cent.[120] And there were many regions, too, that would experience a population surge in the second quarter of the seventeenth century even more marked than it had been a couple of generations earlier.[121] But the markets that the Eyres found for their Derbyshire lead and that the Willoughbys had exploited already with their coal and their iron, later less successfully extended to ventures in woad and in glass, were just those that encouraged the entrepreneur in every branch of industry, for they seemed to promise unlimited expansion. In a uniquely favourable conjunction, the swelling demand for basic foodstuffs, which was everywhere forcing up agricultural prices and receipts, coincided with a strong spending instinct, transforming the market for luxuries. Sir Francis Willoughby's luckless venture in woad to supply the booming textile industry was inspired directly by the shortage of funds he had brought upon himself by his extravagance at Wollaton Hall. In the next generation, Sir Percival Willoughby, succeeding to an encumbered estate, tried his luck, with little more success, in the early-seventeenth-century market for glass.[122]

One of the professional glass-makers to whom Sir Percival Willoughby turned for the setting up of the Wollaton industry was Jacob Henzey, of the Lorrainer family which had already become known in the later sixteenth century for its prominent part in developing the new technology in England. Henzey came to Wollaton for its coal, following the patent of 1615 which had prohibited the use of timber as fuel in the industry. And it is clear that the over-heavy consumption of timber in glass-making, itself the ostensible reason for the granting of the 1615 monopoly, had been a chief cause of the spread of the industry, since the Lorrainers' arrival in the 1570s, over the face of woodland England. It had been the principal achievement of the glass-makers during this period that they had been able to hold down the price of their product while other costs had soared. And as glass windows, relatively, became cheaper, demand increased significantly, even in the remoter areas, permitting further reductions in price. However, local needs could scarcely be served, nor was the fuel easily available, unless the glass-makers moved into their chosen market regions, carrying their skills through the land. Beginning in the Sussex Weald, Lorrainer activity had reached an old glass-making centre at Abbots Bromley, in Staffordshire, by 1585 when Sir Richard Bagot, a local landowner with woodland to spare, entered into an agreement with that same Henzey family which later took its skills to Wollaton.[123] Clearly, what interested Sir Richard, and what developed the glass-house at Bagot's Park to a scale it had never reached before, was the new

161 A fifteenth-century glass-making scene (B.M., Add. 24, 189, f.16)

profitability of an ancient industry, able to capitalize on consumer preferences, coinciding with a markedly more sophisticated technology. Norman and Lorrainer glass-makers, many of whom had arrived in England as religious refugees from their homelands, were to place their mark on English glass-production within a very few years of their coming, at sites as widely dispersed as Knightons, in Surrey,[124] St Weonards, in Herefordshire,[125] and Bickerstaffe and Denton, in Lancashire,[126] as well as at such remote rural glass-houses as Hutton and Rosedale, both near Lastingham, up on the edge of the North York moors.[127] Transmitted to local craftsmen, theirs was the impetus which converted window glass from the luxury it remained in the late sixteenth century to the necessity it had become by the seventeenth. Meanwhile, in other industries, sustained demand through the reigns of the Tudors was to bring about closely comparable advances.

Among these, of course, was the textile industry, flourishing already in the

162 An English-made glass bowl with diamond-point floral engraving, perhaps a product of Verzelini's late-sixteenth-century London glasshouse (Museum of London)

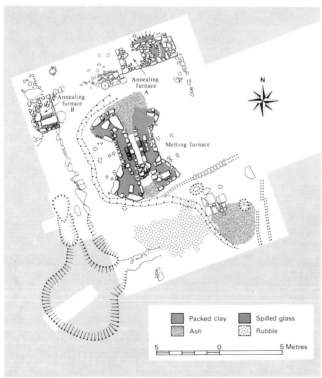

163 Plan of a recently excavated rural glasshouse at Rosedale, in Yorkshire, probably worked by immigrant glassmakers, bringing their skills to late-sixteenth-century England (Crossley and Aberg)

243

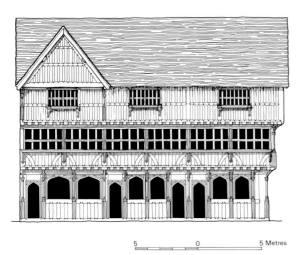

164 A town house at Worcester in the early sixteenth century, with shops on the ground floor and a possible first-floor weaving workshop, reconstructed from the original builder's sketch (Charles and Down)

early sixteenth century, but much advanced as Low Countries immigrants, in the 1560s and 1570s, brought the worsteds, or 'New Draperies', to England. Worsteds, indeed, were the making of many Elizabethan urban cloth industries, as they were, probably, of such rural workshops as the recently excavated Elmhirst establishment at the Yorkshire site at Houndhill, in Worsborough,[128] with its greater equivalents at Leeds and Halifax, in the same county. However, despite (and perhaps because of) the long continuance of the woollen cloth industry, it has left fewer traces in the archaeological record than that other highly important technological advance in early-modern England, the introduction and development of the blast-furnace in iron-working, beginning in the late fifteenth century.

Here, in particular, the capitalist landowner came into his own, for the fully developed blast-furnace, with its associated finery forge, was an expensive piece of capital equipment, further requiring resources in fuel which only the largest estates could provide. Continuing an aristocratic tradition at least as old as the mining interests of the Percy family, in north-east England, and of Humphrey, duke of Buckingham, in South Wales, both of the previous century,[129] the Sidneys of Penshurst Place, in Kent, operated furnaces and forges through the mid-sixteenth century on their Sussex estates at Panningridge and Robertsbridge, the latter at the site of a Cistercian monastery of that name, bought by Sir William Sidney in 1539, immediately following its suppression.[130] Just a few miles away, on the same Kent-Sussex border, the Darells, of Scotney Castle near Lamberhurst, had their long-lived furnace at Chingley in the Bewl Valley.[131]

Essentially, what had converted prominent Wealden landowners like the

Sidneys and the Darells into iron-masters was the opportunity they saw for vertical integration, where a single estate, adequately provided with ore, timber and water, permitted the mining, refining and working of the iron in a planned consecutive operation. However, the high profits obtainable through such integration, at least at the level that would keep a landowner personally involved, would obviously not continue if one of these conditions were missing, and in the iron industry, as in the glass, a persisting difficulty was the maintenance of an adequate supply of fuel. The failure of charcoal supplies can scarcely have been the principal reason, as we have recently been warned, for the rapid spread of the

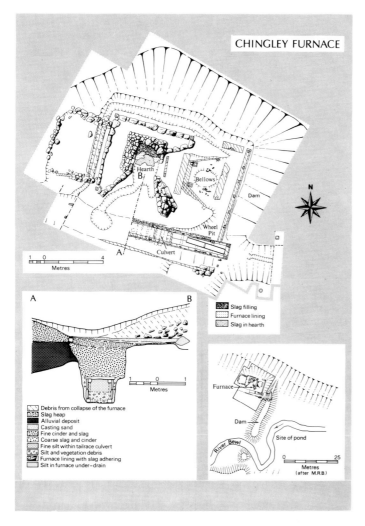

165   An iron-working furnace of the second half of the sixteenth century at Chingley, in the Bewl Valley (Crossley)

iron industry in sixteenth-century England, nor even for that levelling-off of productivity in the industry which, in the following century, was evidently less a consequence of chronic fuel shortage than of the inhibiting vagaries of demand.[132] Nevertheless, it was the rising cost of charcoal, as supplies on the estate were exhausted, that constituted an important factor in the decision of the Sidneys, in 1562–3, to close their Panningridge furnace,[133] while overall it was the declining profitability of such Wealden furnaces as Panningridge and Chingley, influenced also by demand, that persuaded the great landowners, comparatively quickly, to withdraw from direct participation in the running of the industry in favour of professional iron-masters. To these, without the resources of family capital or the surplus of timber which on many estates had made experiments in iron and glass first possible, the benefits of the new methods, whatever the technical advantage, had carefully to be weighed against their cost. Much depended on the size of the market in each case. The old-style bloomeries at Rockley Smithies and Muncaster Head, in Yorkshire and Cumberland respectively, continuing well into the seventeenth century, are unlikely to have stayed that way for lack of expertise.[134] In effect, the new technology which had taken the charcoal blast-furnace by 1564 already as far as Shifnal, in eastern Shropshire,[135] was not everywhere equally acceptable.

When the blast-furnace came to Rockley Smithies, as it did only as late as 1652, its background was the developing secondary metal industry of nearby Sheffield with, beyond that, the greatly enlarged market for consumer goods which the growth of population had created. A hundred years earlier, to the dismay of contemporaries, the demand for such goods had been met by imports, 'inestimable treasure' being expended, according to one view, on such trivial inessentials as

> glasses as well looking as drinking as to glass windows, dials, tables, cards, balls, puppets, penhorns, inkhorns, toothpicks, gloves, knives, daggers, owches (buckles), brooches, aglets (tags), buttons of silk and silver, earthen pots, pins, points, hawks' bells, paper both white and brown, and a thousand like things that might either be clean spared or else made within the realm sufficient for us.[136]

But the strengthening home market transformed English industry much as Sir Thomas Smith, in 1549, had advised it. With the 'making of glasses, making of swords, daggers, knives, and all tools of iron and steel' which he had urged,[137] came other home-based industries on a more than purely local scale, initially

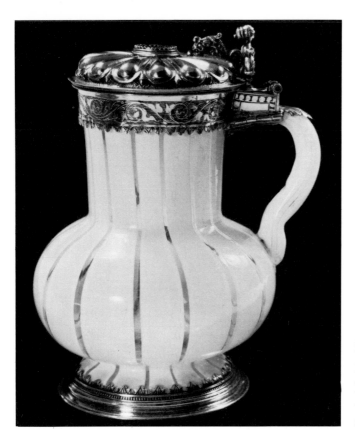

166 Domestic extravagance in the mid-sixteenth century: a tankard in milk-white Venetian-style glass with English silver-gilt mounts, originally the property of Sir William Parr, uncle of Henry VIII's sixth queen (Glanville and Museum of London)

imitative but increasingly able to stand up to the pressure of overseas competition. Old-established English crafts like alabaster-carving, originally sustained before the Reformation by the continuing demand for church images, might dwindle away in the sixteenth century as the images themselves lost favour.[138] Yet the pewterers, practising another ancient craft which had done especially well in the later Middle Ages, profited most particularly from the consumer boom of the reigns of Elizabeth and James I,[139] as did other long-time craftsmen like the potters. Still, through the later sixteenth century and into the seventeenth century as well, the market in finer pottery wares continued to be dominated by the tin glazes, or 'delfts', of the Netherlands, the maiolicas of Italy, the lustres of Spain, and the ubiquitous stoneware beer-mugs of the Rhineland.[140] But these imports themselves generated a demand for some cheaper local substitute, and even while the market, for example, in Rhineland stonewares continued sufficiently attractive

247

167 A stoneware tankard, imported from the Rhineland, with a similar vessel in earthenware (right), probably from a Surrey kiln (Museum of London)

to deserve a monopoly of its own,[141] some acceptable home-produced alternatives were emerging. Farnham-ware jugs and beer-mugs, in use at the London Inns of Court from the mid-sixteenth century at latest, had been modelled very obviously on the Rhineland prototypes with which both the potters and their customers were familiar.[142] Before the end of the century, Hampshire potters had begun to make their own versions of these German beer-pots for local sale, with frying-pans and pipkins after the Netherlands manner, and with handsome high-standing chafing-dishes based on contemporary French imports from the Saintonge.[143] Aided by protective trading legislation, the Southwark delfts and Fulham stonewares of seventeenth-century London were almost totally to defeat the competition of the pots on which originally they had been modelled.

Not every industry, in early-modern England, achieved the same success. And while advances, certainly, were made, with the result that English industry, significantly behind its continental rivals in 1500, had caught up and even improved upon its competitors not more than two centuries later, a genuinely innovatory technology, for all that, continued to develop only slowly.

248

England in 1700, that is, was scarcely less a 'pre-industrialized' society than it had been in 1485, on the accession of Henry Tudor,[144] this technological conservatism being precisely the reason why it is so difficult to accept the *political* date of 1485 as meaningful to the archaeology of the period. Admittedly, the closing-down of the Middle Ages, in England as elsewhere, was not merely a matter of economics, for it included a confrontation between Church and state which cast many preconceptions to the winds. Moreover that confrontation, it could very well be argued, had a good deal to do with politics. Nevertheless, the assault on the Church, once begun, had the economy behind to drive it, while in almost every way it was the so-called 'commercial revolution' of Elizabeth's reign which did most to make the break with the past.

To many, of course, the transition was painful. And at no time was this more likely to be the case than in those difficult years of the mid-sixteenth century when the ills of the currency, the repeated harvest failures, and the heavy mortalities of influenza epidemics caused William Humberston so pessimistically to write of the fate of the Staffordshire boroughs. In the old days, he said in 1559, men had known their station; they had stuck to the crafts they had been brought up in, and they had prospered deservedly as a result –

> And by this meanes the good Townes were buylded inhabyted and maynetened, whiche nowe are decayed and depopulated, the markettes plentyfull, with all kinde of provicions and victualls, whiche nowe are unfurnisshed and the countrye replenysshed with gentlemen and husbondes (husbandmen), whiche nowe are inhabyted with marchauntes and men of occupacion (tradesmen), so that no man is contented with his owne estate, whiche hathe brought all thynges to suche extremytie, as they have not bene of many yeres before.[145]

But Staffordshire, like the rest of the country, picked up again in the bounteous years from the 1570s through to the early 1590s, and it was then, before the return of famine and disease in the final years of the century, that new habits of consumption were established.

Almost certainly, the social upheaval in Elizabethan England was not as severe as William Humberston, in his own day, had judged it. Technological conservatism was matched, and probably exceeded, by conservatism of manners and of social relationships in general. Nevertheless, the comfortable domestic standards attained by many property-owners before the end of the sixteenth century, if they did rather little to extinguish invidious social distinctions, at

249

least contributed noticeably to their blurring. A full century (and sometimes more) after 1485, there were men all over England shaking off, at last, the traditional life-style of their forebears. There would be, of course, reversals, and few who survived the mortalities of the early 1600s would have considered this a time of hope. But nothing that could happen after Elizabeth's reign would bring about a return to the old ways. Indeed, of the comforts that a man has once enjoyed, he will not very readily let go.

Abbreviations

Agric. Hist. Rev.	*Agricultural History Review*
Antiq.	Antiquarian, antiquaries
Antiq. J.	*Antiquaries Journal*
Arch.	Archaeology, archaeological
Arch. J.	*Archaeological Journal*
Archit.	Architecture, architectural
Assoc.	Association
B.M.	British Museum
Bodleian	Bodleian Library, Oxford
Bul.	Bulletin
Bul. Inst. Hist. Res.	*Bulletin of the Institute of Historical Research*
C.B.A.	Council for British Archaeology
Coll.	Collections
E.H.R.	*English Historical Review*
Ec.H.R.	*Economic History Review*
Hist.	History, historic, historical
H.M.S.O.	Her Majesty's Stationery Office
Inst.	Institute
J.	Journal
J. Brit. Arch. Assoc.	*Journal of the British Archaeological Association*
King's Works	*The History of the King's Works* (general editor: H. M. Colvin)
Med. Arch.	*Medieval Archaeology*
Mag.	Magazine
Nat.	Natural
Post-Med. Arch.	*Post-Medieval Archaeology*
Proc.	Proceedings
R.C.H.M.	Royal Commission on Historical Monuments
Rev.	Review
Soc.	Society
Trans.	Transactions
T.R.H.S.	*Transactions of the Royal Historical Society*
V.C.H.	*Victoria History of the Counties of England*

Notes and References

Chapter 1 The Anglo-Norman Settlement

1 The circumstances and objectives of the survey are discussed by Sally Harvey, 'Domesday Book and Anglo-Norman governance', *T.R.H.S.*, 5th series, 25 (1975), pp. 175–93.

2 Reginald Lennard, *Rural England 1086–1135*, 1959, p. 393.

3 H. C. Darby (ed.), *A New Historical Geography of England*, 1973, pp. 43–4.

4 W. G. Hoskins, *Provincial England*, 1965, pp. 51–2.

5 Lennard, op. cit., pp. 269–70.

6 Alan Rogers, 'Parish boundaries and urban history: two case studies', *J. Brit. Arch. Assoc.*, 3rd series, 35 (1972), p. 47.

7 Lennard, op. cit., pp. 218–19, 230–1.

8 Darby, op. cit., pp. 55–7, 58.

9 Guy Beresford, *The Medieval Clay-land Village: Excavations at Goltho and Barton Blount*, 1975, pp. 7–8; also *Med. Arch.*, 18 (1974), pp. 210–11, and *Current Archaeology*, 56 (1976), pp. 262–70; for Sulgrave, see *Med. Arch.*, 17 (1973), p. 147.

10 For a recent firm restatement of this view, see R. Allen Brown, *English Castles*, 1976 (3rd revised edn), pp. 37, 39, 49–51.

11 For Orderic Vitalis, born in 1075 and here described as 'the most gifted of all the Anglo-Norman historians, with the exception of William of Malmesbury', see Antonia Gransden, *Historical Writing in England c. 550 to c. 1307*, 1974, pp. 136, 151–65.

12 William of Poitiers, quoted in *King's Works*, i:20.

13 Ibid., i:21.

14 Brian K. Davison, 'Castle Neroche: an abandoned Norman fortress in South So-merset', *Somerset Arch. and Nat. Hist.*, 116 (1972), pp. 20–1.

15 A. D. Saunders, 'Excavations at Launceston Castle 1965–69: interim report', *Cornish Archaeology*, 9 (1970), p. 91; also *Arch. J.*, 130 (1973), pp. 251–4.

16 P. V. Addyman, 'Excavations at Ludgershall Castle, Wiltshire, England (1964–1972)', *Chateau Gaillard VI*, 1973, p. 8.

17 Brian K. Davison, 'Three eleventh-century earthworks in England: their excavation and implications', *Chateau Gaillard II*, 1967, pp. 40–2. Other sites discussed here are Castle Neroche and Sulgrave. A somewhat similar re-use of part of an Iron-Age fort, within which a late-eleventh-century motte was sited, has been noted also at Thetford, in Norfolk (*Med. Arch.*, 8 (1964), p. 257).

18 Martin Biddle, 'Excavations at Winchester, 1971: tenth and final interim report', *Antiq. J.*, 55 (1975), pp. 104–9.

19 *Med. Arch.*, 8 (1964), p. 257; *King's Works*, ii:750.

20 The evidence is discussed by Derek Renn, *Norman Castles in Britain*, 1973, pp. 31–2; see also *King's Works*, i:24.

21 E. M. Jope, 'Late Saxon pits under Oxford castle mound: excavations in 1952', *Oxoniensia*, 17–18 (1952–3), pp. 77–81.

22 Lennard, op. cit., pp. 30–2. For a useful recent discussion of the military settlement of the Sussex rapes and of Battle Abbey's part in this, see Eleanor Searle, *Lordship and Community. Battle Abbey and its Banlieu 1066–1538*, 1974, pp. 48–68; and see also John Le Patourel, *The Norman Empire*, 1976, pp. 307–11.

23 John Le Patourel, 'The Norman conquest

of Yorkshire', *Northern History*, 6 (1971), pp. 14–15, 18–19.

24 W. E. Wightman, 'The significance of "waste" in the Yorkshire Domesday', *Northern History*, 10 (1975), pp. 55–71.

25 Jonathan Coad, personal communication. As the excavations at Castle Acre are still unfinished, these conclusions are subject to revision.

26 Philip Barker and James Lawson, 'A pre-Norman field system at Hen Domen, Montgomery', *Med. Arch.*, 15 (1971), pp. 58–72.

27 Peter Wade-Martins, 'The origins of rural settlement in East Anglia', in P. J. Fowler, (ed.), *Recent Work in Rural Archaeology*, 1975, pp. 147–9.

28 J. C. Holt, 'Politics and property in early medieval England', *Past and Present*, 57 (1972), p. 25.

29 *King's Works*, i:33–4.

30 D. J. Cathcart King, 'The field archaeology of mottes in England and Wales: eine kurze übersicht', *Chateau Gaillard V*, 1972, p. 107.

31 Leslie Alcock, *Dinas Powys*, 1963, pp. 54–5. For the origins of the ring-work, see D. J. Cathcart King and Leslie Alcock, 'Ring-works of England and Wales', *Chateau Gaillard III*, 1969, pp. 90–127; in the same volume, Brian Davison develops his controversial theory about the late arrival of the classic motte-and-bailey plan ('Early earthwork castles: a new model', ibid., pp. 37–47).

32 Leslie Alcock, 'Castle Tower, Penmaen: a Norman ring-work in Glamorgan', *Antiq. J.*, 46 (1966), p. 178; for Aldingham, see *Med. Arch.*, 13 (1969), p. 258; for Burton, see Stephen Moorhouse, 'Excavations at Burton-in-Lonsdale: a reconsideration', *Yorkshire Arch. J.*, 43 (1971), pp. 85–98.

33 *Med. Arch.*, 11 (1967), p. 285 (Bramber); ibid., 2 (1958), p. 195 (Duffield).

34 Brian Hope-Taylor, 'The excavation of a motte at Abinger in Surrey', *Arch. J.*, 107 (1950), pp. 15–43.

35 Jonathan Coad, personal communication.

36 Martin Biddle, 'The excavation of a motte and bailey castle at Therfield, Hertfordshire', *J. Brit. Arch. Assoc.*, 3rd series, 27 (1964), pp. 53–91.

37 Christopher Taylor, *Fieldwork in Medieval Archaeology*, 1974, pp. 130–2.

38 *Med. Arch.*, 5 (1961), p. 319.

39 Ibid., 5 (1961), p. 318; 6–7 (1962–3), p. 322; 8 (1964), p. 255.

40 T. C. M. and A. Brewster, 'Tote Copse Castle, Aldingbourne, Sussex', *Sussex Arch. Coll.*, 107 (1969), pp. 141–79.

41 E. M. Jope and R. I. Threlfall, 'The twelfth-century castle at Ascot Doilly, Oxfordshire: its history and excavation', *Antiq. J.*, 39 (1959), pp. 219–73.

42 M. W. Thompson, 'Recent excavations in the keep of Farnham Castle, Surrey', *Med. Arch.*, 4 (1960), pp. 81–94, summarized in the same author's 'Excavations in Farnham Castle keep, Surrey, England, 1958–60', *Chateau Gaillard II*, 1967, pp. 100–5. For a first attempt at a classification of such below-ground works, see Dr Thompson's 'Motte substructures', *Med. Arch.*, 5 (1961), pp. 305–6.

43 *King's Works*, i:29–32; R. Allen Brown, 'The Norman Conquest and the genesis of English castles', *Chateau Gaillard III*, 1969, pp. 12–13. For a useful additional comment on Norman 'imperialism' in building, see John Le Patourel, op. cit. (1976), pp. 351–3.

44 *King's Works*, i:38–9. Other castles of its type and period are those at Winchester, Rochester, Corfe, Wareham and, perhaps, Portchester.

45 David Knowles, *The Monastic Order in England*, 1966 (2nd edn), pp. 120–1.

46 Richard Gem, 'A recession in English architecture during the early eleventh century, and its effect on the development of the Romanesque style', *J. Brit. Arch. Assoc.*, 3rd series, 38 (1975), pp. 48–9.

47 N. Drinkwater, 'Hereford Cathedral: the bishop's chapel of St Katherine and St Mary Magdalene', *Trans. Woolhope Naturalists' Field Club*, 35 (1955–7), pp. 256–60.

48 J. T. Smith, 'The Norman structure of Leominster Priory church', *Trans. Ancient Monuments Soc.*, new series, 11 (1963), pp. 97–108.

49 George Zarnecki, '1066 and architectural sculpture', *Proc. British Academy*, 52 (1966), pp. 97–8.

50 Francis Wormald, *English Drawings of the Tenth and Eleventh Centuries*, 1952, pp. 53–8.

51 E. M. Jope, 'The tinning of iron spurs: a continuous practice from the tenth to the seventeenth century', *Oxoniensia*, 21 (1956), pp. 35–42.

52 C. R. Dodwell, *The Canterbury School of Illumination 1066–1200*, 1954, pp. 24–6.

53 R. W. Southern, *Saint Anselm and his Biographer*, 1963, pp. 246–8.

54 Martin Biddle, 'The archaeology of Winchester', *Scientific American*, 230:5 (1974), pp. 41–2.

55 *King's Works*, i:28–9, ii:806–7.

56 Quoted by B. Dodwell, 'The foundation of Norwich Cathedral', *T.R.H.S.*, 5th series, 7 (1957), p. 9.

57 Ibid., pp. 4–6.

58 Quoted by H. E. J. Cowdrey, *The Cluniacs and the Gregorian Reform*, 1970, p. 190.

59 Knowles, op. cit., p. 151; for the foundation narrative of Lewes Priory, see William Dugdale, *Monasticon Anglicanum* (eds J. Caley, H. Ellis and B. Bandinel), 1846, v:12–13.

60 J. C. Dickinson, 'English regular canons and the Continent in the twelfth century', *T.R.H.S.*, 5th series, 1 (1951), pp. 74–5; for the foundation narrative, see William Dugdale, op. cit., vi:i:344–8. Oliver de Merlemond was on his way home from a pilgrimage to Santiago when he stopped at the abbey of St Victor, being inspired by what he saw there to set about a Victorine foundation of his own.

61 Marcel Aubert, *L'Architecture Cistercienne en France*, 1947, i:97–8.

62 For discussions of the withdrawal from St Mary's, in each case making the point that it was not a consequence of disorder or of laxity at that house, see Denis Bethell, 'The foundation of Fountains Abbey and the state of St Mary's York in 1132', *J. Ecclesiastical History*, 17 (1966), pp. 11–27, and L. G. D. Baker, 'The foundation of Fountains Abbey', *Northern History*, 4 (1969), pp. 29–43.

63 R. Gilyard-Beer, 'Fountains Abbey: the early buildings, 1132–50', *Arch. J.*, 125 (1968), pp. 313–19.

64 Ibid., p. 315.

65 R. Gilyard-Beer, 'Rufford Abbey, Nottinghamshire', *Med. Arch.*, 9 (1965), pp. 161–3. For Westminster, see *King's Works*, i:47.

66 *Med. Arch.*, 6–7 (1962–3), pp. 316–17.

67 Brian Philp, *Excavations at Faversham, 1965*, 1968, pp. 35–6.

68 Knowles, op. cit., p. 136.

69 For the twelfth-century buildings at Minster-in-Thanet, a dependency of St Augustine's, Canterbury, and at Swanborough, a demesne manor of the Cluniacs of Lewes Priory, see my own *The Monastic Grange in Medieval England*, 1969, pp. 18–22, 217–19, 237–8. Comments on the manorial plan of the lesser houses may be found in Knowles, op. cit., p. 135; also in W. A. Pantin, 'Minchery Farm, Littlemore', *Oxoniensia*, 35 (1970), pp. 25–6.

70 J. C. Dickinson, 'The buildings of the English Austin canons after the dissolution of the monasteries', *J. Brit. Arch. Assoc.*, 31 (1968), p. 73.

71 H. Mayr-Harting, 'Functions of a twelfth-century recluse', *History*, 60 (1975), pp. 345, 349.

72 Ibid., pp. 344, 346–7.

73 Warwick and Kirsty Rodwell, 'Excavations at Rivenhall Church, Essex. An interim report', *Antiq. J.*, 53 (1973), pp. 219–31.

74 For church dedications, the standard work remains Francis Bond's *Dedications and Patron Saints of English Churches. Ecclesiastical symbolism, saints and their emblems*, 1914; for churches in Domesday, see Lennard, op. cit., pp. 288–94.

75 Christopher Brooke and Gillian Keir, *London 800–1216: the Shaping of a City*, 1975, pp. 122–48.

76 G. H. Tupling, 'The pre-Reformation parishes and chapelries of Lancashire', *Trans. Lancashire and Cheshire Antiquarian Soc.*, 67 (1957), pp. 1–16; S. A. Jeavons, 'The pattern of ecclesiastical building in Staffordshire during the Norman period', *Trans. Lichfield and South Staffordshire Arch. and Hist. Soc.*, 4 (1962–3), pp. 5–22; Dorothy Sylvester, 'Parish and township in Cheshire and north-east Wales', *J. Chester Arch. Soc.*, 54 (1967), pp. 23–35.

77 B. R. Kemp, 'Hereditary benefices in the medieval English church: a Herefordshire example', *Bul. Inst. Hist. Res.*, 43 (1970) pp. 1–15; Colin Morris, 'Letheringsett: the early history of a parish church', ibid., 44 (1971), pp. 116–20.

78 The North Petherwin transaction, noted as

displaying a 'touch of cynical humour in this plan of making one abbey contribute to the building of another, while the credit of the benefaction goes to a third party', took place in 1171 (H. P. R. Finberg, *West-Country Historical Studies*, 1969, pp. 97–8).

79 M. Brett, *The English Church under Henry I*, 1975, pp. 230–1.

80 Brian R. Kemp, 'The churches of Berkeley Hernesse', *Trans. Bristol and Gloucestershire Arch. Soc.*, 87 (1968), pp. 96–110; also Arthur Sabin, 'St Augustine's Abbey and the Berkeley churches', ibid., 89 (1970), pp. 90–8.

81 Edward Miller, 'Some twelfth-century documents concerning St Peter's church at Babraham', *Proc. Cambridge Antiquarian Soc.*, 59 (1966), pp. 113–23.

82 Rodwell, op. cit., pp. 225–7.

83 *Current Archaeology*, 49 (1975), p. 45; *Med. Arch.*, 2 (1958), p. 206; ibid., 17 (1973), pp. 159–60.

84 For London, see Peter R. V. Marsden, 'Archaeological finds in the city of London, 1963–4', *Trans. London and Middlesex Arch. Soc.*, 21 (1967), pp. 217–8, and 'Archaeological finds in the city of London, 1965–6', ibid., 22 (1968), pp. 14–16; for Norwich, see A. Carter and J. P. Roberts, 'Excavations in Norwich – 1972. The Norwich Survey – second interim report', *Norfolk Archaeology*, 35 (1973), pp. 455–7; for Winchester, see Barry Cunliffe, *Winchester Excavations 1949–1960*, 1964, pp. 43–4, and Martin Biddle, 'Excavations at Winchester, 1970. Ninth interim report', *Antiq. J.*, 52 (1972), pp. 104–7. For notes on Thetford, Barpham and Irthlingborough, see *Med. Arch.*, 15 (1971), pp. 130–1, 1 (1956), p. 155, and 10 (1966), pp. 187–9; also A. Barr-Hamilton, 'The excavation of Barpham Church site, Upper Barpham, Angmering, Sussex', *Sussex Arch. Coll.*, 99 (1961), pp. 38–65.

85 For Thurleigh and St Mary-le-Port, Bristol, see notes in *Med. Arch.*, 16 (1972), p. 177, and 8 (1964), pp. 249, 251. The results of the excavations at St Nicholas, Angmering, are summarized by Owen Bedwin in Peter Drewett's 'Rescue archaeology in Sussex, 1974', *Bull. Inst. Archaeology*, 12 (1975), pp. 46–9.

86 Frances Arnold-Forster, *Studies in Church Dedications or England's Patron Saints*, 3 vols, 1899, and Bond, op. cit. For recent local studies, see C. L. S. Linnell, *Norfolk Church Dedications*, St Anthony's Hall Publications 21, 1962; also R. V. H. Burne, 'Church dedications in Dorset', *Proc. Dorset Nat. Hist. and Arch. Soc.*, 90 (1968), pp. 269–81, and William Addison, 'Parish church dedications in Essex', *Trans Essex Arch. Soc.*, 2 (1966–70), pp. 34–46.

Chapter 2 Economic Growth

1 Robin E. Glasscock (ed.), *The Lay Subsidy of 1334*, British Academy Records of Social and Economic History, new series, 11, 1975.

2 For a discussion of these, see my own *The English Medieval Town*, 1976, in particular chapter 5 and the references given there.

3 D. M. Palliser, 'The boroughs of medieval Staffordshire', *North Staffordshire J. Field Studies*, 12 (1972), pp. 65–6.

4 W. G. Hoskins and H. P. R. Finberg, *Devonshire Studies*, 1952, p. 172.

5 Useful studies of market creations in individual counties have been made by Bryan E. Coates, 'The origin and distribution of markets and fairs in medieval Derbyshire', *Derbyshire Arch. J.*, 85 (1965), pp. 92–111, and by D. M. Palliser and A. C. Pinnock, 'The markets of medieval Staffordshire', *North Staffordshire J. Field Studies*, 11 (1971), pp. 49–59.

6 J. B. Harley, 'The settlement geography of early medieval Warwickshire', *Trans. and Papers Inst. British Geographers*, 34 (1964), pp. 126–7.

7 Jim Gould, 'The medieval burgesses of Tamworth: their liberties, courts and markets', *Trans. South Staffordshire Arch. and Hist. Soc.*, 13 (1971–2), p. 21.

8 Maurice Beresford, *New Towns of the Middle Ages: Town Plantation in England, Wales and Gascony*, 1967.

9 A recent example, though with proper cautions expressed, is Lawrence Butler's 'The evolution of towns: planted towns after 1066', in M. W. Barley (ed.), *The Plans and Topography of Medieval Towns in England and Wales*, CBA Research Report 14, 1975, pp. 32–48.

10 Maurice Beresford, 'The six new towns of

the bishops of Winchester, 1200–55', *Med. Arch.*, 3 (1959), pp. 187–215.

11 Joseph Hillaby, 'The boroughs of the bishops of Hereford in the late 13th century, with particular reference to Ledbury', *Trans. Woolhope Naturalists' Field Club*, 40 (1970–2), pp. 10–35.

12 E. M. Carus-Wilson, 'The first half-century of the borough of Stratford-upon-Avon', *Ec.H.R.*, 2nd series, 18 (1965), pp. 46–63.

13 *Current Archaeology*, 41 (1973), p. 176; *Med. Arch.*, 17 (1973), p. 167.

14 C. J. Bond, 'Deserted medieval villages in Warwickshire: a review of the field evidence', *Trans. Birmingham and Warwickshire Arch. Soc.*, 86 (1974), pp. 92–4.

15 Alison Ravetz and Gillian Spencer, 'Excavation of the Battle Ditches, Saffron Walden, Essex, 1959', *Trans. Essex Arch. Soc.*, 1 (1961–5), pp. 141–56.

16 N. H. Field, 'The Leaze, Wimborne; an excavation in a deserted medieval quarter of the town', *Proc. Dorset Nat. Hist. and Arch. Soc.*, 94 (1972), pp. 49–62.

17 *Med. Arch.*, 8 (1964), pp. 264–5.

18 Ibid., 10 (1966), p. 158.

19 Colin Platt and Richard Coleman-Smith, *Excavations in Medieval Southampton 1953–1969*, 1975, i:238–9.

20 Ibid., i:32–5; for the Wimborne evidence, see Field, op. cit., p. 59.

21 *Med. Arch.*, 18 (1974), p. 202 (Northampton); for Norwich, see A. Carter, J. P. Roberts and Helena Sutermeister, 'Excavations in Norwich – 1973. The Norwich Survey – third interim report', *Norfolk Archaeology*, 36 (1974), pp. 43–4. Other recent evidence, of a building burnt down in *c.* 1400, has come from Hythe, in Kent (*Med. Arch.*, 19 (1975), p. 245).

22 For a summary of this evidence, with full references, see Platt, op. cit. (1976), pp. 58–60.

23 Helen Parker, 'A medieval wharf in Thoresby College courtyard, King's Lynn', *Med. Arch.*, 9 (1965), pp. 94–104.

24 *Med. Arch.*, 19 (1975), pp. 247–8.

25 Hilary L. Turner, *Town Defences in England and Wales; an Architectural and Documentary Study, A.D. 900–1500*, 1971, passim.

26 Christina Colyer, 'Excavations at Lincoln,

1970–1972: the western defences of the lower town. An interim report', *Antiq. J.*, 55 (1975), pp. 260–6.

27 K. J. Barton, 'The excavation of a medieval bastion at St Nicholas's Almshouses, King Street, Bristol', *Med. Arch.*, 8 (1964), pp. 184–212.

28 M. W. Barley, 'Excavation of the borough ditch, Slaughterhouse Lane, Newark, 1961', *Trans. Thoroton Soc.*, 65 (1961), pp. 12–13; Barry Cunliffe, 'The Winchester city wall', *Proc. Hampshire Field Club and Arch. Soc.*, 22 (1961–3). pp. 69–70.

29 M. W. Ponsford, 'Nottingham town wall: Park Row excavations', *Trans. Thoroton Soc.*, 75 (1971), p. 9.

30 Terence Paul Smith, 'The medieval town defences of King's Lynn', *J. Brit. Arch. Assoc.*, 3rd series, 33 (1970), pp. 57–88.

31 Eileen Gooder, *Coventry's Town Wall*, Coventry and North Warwickshire History Pamphlets, 4 (1971: revised edn).

32 R. H. Britnell, *Colchester and the countryside in the fourteenth century. A search for interdependence between urban and rural economy*, Cambridge Ph.D. thesis, 1970, pp. 127–34.

33 J. R. Ravensdale, *Liable to Floods. Village Landscape on the Edge of the Fens A.D. 450–1850*, 1974, pp. 126–31, 145–6.

34 J. A. Alexander, 'Clopton: the life-cycle of a Cambridgeshire village', in Lionel M. Munby (ed.), *East Anglian Studies*, 1968, p. 57.

35 Ibid., p. 60.

36 Warren O. Ault, 'Village by-laws by common consent', *Speculum*, 29 (1954), pp. 385–6.

37 J. Ambrose Raftis, *Tenure and Mobility. Studies in the Social History of the Mediaeval English Village*, 1964, p. 207.

38 R. B. Dobson, *Durham Priory 1400–1450*, 1973, p. 275; Brian K. Roberts, 'Village plans in County Durham: a preliminary statement', *Med. Arch.*, 16 (1972), pp. 33–56.

39 Sölve Göransson, 'Regular open-field pattern in England and Scandinavian *solskifte*', *Geografiska Annaler*, 43 (1961), pp. 80–104; Pamela Allerston, 'English village development. Findings from the Pickering district of North Yorkshire', *Trans. Inst. British Geographers*, 51 (1970),

pp. 95–109; Brian K. Roberts, op. et loc. cit.; June A. Sheppard, 'Metrological analysis of regular village plans in Yorkshire', *Agric. Hist. Rev.*, 22 (1974), pp. 118–35.

40 H. S. A. Fox, 'The chronology of enclosure and economic development in medieval Devon', *Ec.H.R.*, 2nd series, 28 (1975), pp. 183–4.

41 D. Roden and A. R. H. Baker, 'Field systems of the Chiltern Hills and of parts of Kent from the late thirteenth to the early seventeenth century', *Trans. Inst. British Geographers*, 38 (1966), pp. 73–88.

42 For a useful recent summary, reviewing the arguments of Thirsk, Titow and others, see Alan R. H. Baker and Robin A. Butlin, 'Conclusion: problems and perspectives', published in their *Studies of Field Systems in the British Isles*, 1973, pp. 619–56.

43 Christopher Taylor, *Fieldwork in Medieval Archaeology*, 1974, p. 63.

44 Martin Biddle, 'The deserted medieval village of Seacourt, Berkshire', *Oxoniensia*, 26–7 (1961–2), pp. 118–20.

45 Ravensdale, op. cit., pp. 122–3.

46 Guy Beresford, *The Medieval Clay-land Village: Excavations at Goltho and Barton Blount*, 1975, pp. 37–40.

47 For interim notes on the excavations at these sites, see *Med. Arch.*, 8 (1964), pp. 282–5, 9 (1965), pp. 210–12, 11 (1967), pp. 305–6, 12 (1968), pp. 199–200. The interpretation of turf as the building material on these sites has recently been questioned by Henrietta and Trevor Miles, 'Pilton, North Devon. Excavations within a medieval village', *Proc. Devon Arch. Soc.*, 33 (1975), pp. 292–3.

48 Guy Beresford, op. cit., pp. 24–7, 40–3.

49 For Faxton, see *Med. Arch.*, 11 (1967), pp. 307–9, 12 (1968), p. 203, 13 (1969), p. 279; for Wythemail, see D. Gillian Hurst and John G. Hurst, 'Excavations at the medieval village of Wythemail, Northamptonshire', ibid., 13 (1969), p. 180.

50 Biddle, op. cit., p. 120.

51 E. W. Holden, 'Excavations at the deserted medieval village of Hangleton, part I', *Sussex Arch. Coll.*, 101 (1963), p. 93; John G. Hurst and D. Gillian Hurst, 'Excavations at the deserted medieval village of Hangleton, part II', ibid., 102 (1964), pp. 118–9.

52 R. H. Hilton and P. A. Rahtz, 'Upton, Gloucestershire, 1959–1964', *Trans. Bristol and Gloucestershire Arch. Soc.*, 85 (1966), pp. 92–110; Philip Rahtz, 'Upton, Gloucestershire, 1964–1968', ibid., 88 (1969), pp. 75–98.

53 Michael G. Jarrett, 'The deserted village of West Whelpington, Northumberland: second report', *Archaeologia Aeliana*, 4th series, 48 (1970), pp. 244–6.

54 For a useful summary of the evidence up till 1968, see Maurice Beresford and John G. Hurst (eds), *Deserted Medieval Villages, Studies*, 1971, pp. 93–6.

55 Jayne Woodhouse, *Barrow Mead, Bath, 1964 Excavation*, British Arch. Reports 28, 1976, p. 22; Guy Beresford, op. cit., pp. 27–31, 40–3.

56 Maurice Beresford and John G. Hurst, op. cit., p. 175.

57 Biddle, op. cit., p. 121.

58 Guy Beresford, op. cit., pp. 12–13.

59 Maurice Beresford and John G. Hurst, op. cit., pp. 141–3.

60 Biddle, op. cit., pp. 72, 185.

61 Guy Beresford, op. cit., pp. 79–96.

62 For the comparable sixteenth-century evidence, see Alan Everitt, 'Social mobility in early modern England', *Past and Present*, 33 (1966), pp. 57–8.

63 J. B. Harley, 'Population trends and agricultural developments from the Warwickshire hundred rolls of 1279', *Ec.H.R.*, 2nd series, 11 (1958–9), pp. 8–18, and the same author's 'The settlement geography of early medieval Warwickshire', *Trans. and Papers Inst. British Geographers*, 34 (1964), pp. 115–30.

64 J. Z. Titow, *English Rural Society 1200–1350*, 1969, pp. 35–6.

65 P. F. Brandon, 'Medieval clearances in the East Sussex Weald', *Trans. Inst. British Geographers*, 48 (1969), pp. 141, 149.

66 Edmund King, *Peterborough Abbey 1086–1310. A Study in the Land Market*, 1973, pp. 70–87.

67 C. C. Taylor, 'The pattern of medieval settlement in the Forest of Blackmoor', *Proc. Dorset Nat. Hist. and Arch. Soc.*, 87 (1965), pp. 252–4, and the same author's 'Whiteparish. A study of the development of a forest-edge parish', *Wiltshire Arch. and Nat. Hist. Mag.*, 62 (1967), pp. 79–102.

68 H. E. Hallam, *Settlement and Society. A Study of the Early Agrarian History of South Lincolnshire*, 1965, p. 200; and see also H. C. Darby, *The Medieval Fenland*, 1974 (2nd edit.), chapter 4.

69 Hallam, op. cit., p. 201.

70 B. K. Roberts, 'A study of medieval colonization in the Forest of Arden, Warwickshire', *Agric. Hist. Rev.*, 16 (1968), p. 107.

71 *Med. Arch.*, 8 (1964), pp. 282–5.

72 Catherine D. Lineham, 'Deserted sites and rabbit warrens on Dartmoor, Devon', *Med. Arch.*, 10 (1966), pp. 113–44.

73 Aileen Fox, 'A monastic homestead on Dean Moor, S. Devon', *Med. Arch.*, 2 (1958), pp. 141–57.

74 H. C. Bowen and P. J. Fowler, 'The archaeology of Fyfield and Overton Downs, Wilts', *Wiltshire Arch. and Nat. Hist. Mag.*, 58 (1961–3), pp. 109–12; also P. J. Fowler, 'The archaeology of Fyfield and Overton Downs, Wilts', ibid., pp. 342–8.

75 *Med. Arch.*, 8 (1964), pp. 286, 288.

76 R. A. C. Lowndes, 'A medieval site at Millhouse, in the Lune Valley', *Trans. Cumberland and Westmorland Antiq. and Arch. Soc.*, 67 (1967), pp. 35–50.

77 A. J. F. Dulley, 'The level and port of Pevensey in the Middle Ages', *Sussex Arch. Coll.*, 104 (1966), pp. 30–2 and fig. 2. For an account of the Battle Abbey estate at Barnhorn, described as a 'favourite abbatial residence', see Eleanor Searle, *Lordship and Community*, 1974, pp. 254–5.

78 *Med. Arch.*, 9 (1965), p. 213.

79 R. A. L. Smith, *Canterbury Cathedral Priory. A Study in Monastic Administration*, 1943, chapter 11; H. E. Hallam, 'Goll Grange. A grange of Spalding Priory', *Reports and Papers Lincolnshire Archit. and Arch. Soc.*, 5 (1953–4), pp. 1–18; Colin Platt, *The Monastic Grange in Medieval England*, 1969, pp. 63–5.

80 C. C. Taylor, 'Strip lynchets', *Antiquity*, 40 (1966), pp. 277–83; also G. Whittington, 'The distribution of strip lynchets', *Trans. and Papers Inst. British Geographers*, 31 (1962), pp. 115–30.

81 P. D. A. Harvey, 'The English inflation of 1180–1220', *Past and Present*, 61 (1973), pp. 3–30, and the same author's 'The English trade in wool and cloth, 1150–1250: some problems and suggestions', in *Produzione, Commercio e Consumo dei Panni di Lana*, Florence, 1976, pp. 369–75.

82 For price rises in the first years of the thirteenth century, following a period of prolonged price stability in the twelfth century, see D. L. Farmer, 'Some price fluctuations in Angevin England', *Ec.H.R.*, 2nd series, 9 (1956–7), pp. 34–43. The economic and social explanations for the change-over to demesne farming are discussed by Clyve G. Reed and Terry L. Anderson, 'An economic explanation of English agricultural organization in the twelfth and thirteenth centuries', ibid., 26 (1973), pp. 134–7, and by Edward Miller, 'Farming of manors and direct management', being a rejoinder in the same volume (pp. 138–40). Both papers refer to Edward Miller's 'England in the twelfth and thirteenth centuries: an economic contrast?', ibid., 24 (1971), pp. 1–14.

83 F. R. H. Du Boulay, *The Lordship of Canterbury: an Essay on Medieval Society*, 1966, pp. 204–5.

84 For the progress of the conversion to demesne farming during John's reign, see P. D. A. Harvey, 'The Pipe Rolls and the adoption of demesne farming in England', *Ec.H.R.*, 2nd series, 27 (1974), pp. 345–59. For useful cautions on the extent and profitability of thirteenth-century demesne farming even at Canterbury, see Du Boulay, op. cit., p. 206. At Ely, the bishop preferred to keep his revenues in large part in the form of rents (Edward Miller, *The Abbey and Bishopric of Ely*, 1951, pp. 77–80), as did the small Leicestershire abbey of Owston (R. H. Hilton, *The Economic Development of some Leicestershire Estates in the 14th and 15th Centuries*, 1947, p. 117).

85 L. M. Cantor, 'The medieval parks of Leicestershire', *Trans. Leicestershire Arch. and Hist. Soc.*, 46 (1970–1), pp. 9–24.

86 Ibid., pp. 15–17 and fig. 2. Similar massive earthworks at some Hampshire parks are described by O. G. S. Crawford, *Archaeology in the Field*, 1953, pp. 189–97.

87 L. M. Cantor, 'The medieval deer-parks of North Staffordshire: I', *North Staffordshire J. Field Studies*, 2 (1962), p. 73. The second part of this paper was published later in the

same journal (4 (1964), pp. 61–6), there being other useful studies of parks, also by Professor Cantor, in *Proc. Dorset Nat. Hist. and Arch. Soc.*, 83 (1961), pp. 109–16 (with follow-up papers in succeeding issues of the same journal), in *Trans. and Proc. Birmingham Arch. Soc.*, 80 (1962), pp. 1–9 (for south Staffordshire), and again in *North Staffordshire J. Field Studies*, 3 (1963), pp. 37–58 (for the parks of the earls of Stafford at Madeley).

88 The judgment is John Hatcher's in his *Rural Economy and Society in the Duchy of Cornwall 1300–1500*, 1970, p. 184, where he argues that the dukes of Cornwall, after the fourteenth century, made very little use of their parks, sustaining a net loss on them for many years before the decision was taken to depark.

89 The two barns are lovingly described and illustrated by Walter Horn and Ernest Born, *The Barns of the Abbey of Beaulieu at its Granges of Great Coxwell and Beaulieu-St. Leonard's*, 1965.

90 *Med. Arch.*, 19 (1975), pp. 250–1.

91 *Archaeological Excavations 1974*, pp. 85–6.

92 *Archaeological Excavations 1972*, pp. 87–8.

93 T. C. M. Brewster, 'An excavation at Weaverthorpe Manor, East Riding, 1960', *Yorkshire Arch. J.*, 44 (1972), pp. 114–33, and Glyn Coppack, 'Low Caythorpe, East Yorkshire – the manor site', ibid., 46 (1974), pp. 34–41.

94 *Archaeological Excavations 1974*, p. 82. Other examples, still more recently published, are Bradwell Bury, in Buckinghamshire, and Quinton, in Northamptonshire (*Med. Arch.*, 20 (1976), pp. 193–5, 196).

95 Dorothea Oschinsky, *Walter of Henley and other Treatises on Estate Management and Accounting*, 1971, p. 407.

96 For a useful general discussion of the type, recently republished in the Royal Archaeological Institute's *Medieval Domestic Architecture* (1975), see J. T. Smith, 'Medieval aisled halls and their derivatives', *Arch. J.*, 112 (1955), pp. 76–94.

97 C. F. Tebbutt, Granville T. Rudd and Stephen Moorhouse, 'Excavation of a moated site at Ellington, Huntingdonshire', *Proc. Cambridge Antiquarian Soc.*, 63 (1971), pp. 31–46.

98 For Goltho, see *Current Archaeology*, 56 (1976), pp. 262–70, and the interim notes in *Archaeological Excavations 1971*, pp. 31–2, *1972*, pp. 91–2, and for a still earlier version of the single-aisled hall, contemporary with the ring-work and datable to about 1100, *Archaeological Excavations 1973*, pp. 86–7. For Faccombe, see *Med. Arch.*, 18 (1974), p. 209.

99 Described, with a plan, by Margaret Wood, *Norman Domestic Architecture*, 1974, pp. 44–6, being a revised edition of her original paper in *Arch. J.*, 92 (1935).

100 For first-floor halls dated to the late thirteenth century, see Ann Dornier, 'Donington le Heath', *Trans. Leicestershire Arch. and Hist. Soc.*, 47 (1971–2), pp. 22–42, and the excavated manor-house at Holyoaks, also in Leicestershire (*Med. Arch.*, 17 (1973), p. 175). Ecclesiastical variants on the plan are discussed by S. E. Rigold, 'Two camerae of the military orders. Strood Temple, Kent, and Harefield, Middlesex', *Arch. J.*, 122 (1965), pp. 86–121.

101 P. Smith, *Houses of the Welsh Countryside*, 1975, pp. 21–35, 38–9.

102 Lesley L. Ketteringham, *Alsted: Excavation of a Thirteenth-Fourteenth Century Sub-Manor House with its Ironworks in Netherne Wood, Merstham, Surrey*, Research Volume of the Surrey Arch. Soc. 2 (1976), pp. 15, 17 and 31.

103 N. W. Alcock and M. W. Barley, 'Medieval roofs with base-crucks and short principals', *Antiq. J.*, 52 (1972), pp. 134–9.

104 J. M. Fletcher and P. S. Spokes, 'The origin and development of crown-post roofs', *Med. Arch.*, 8 (1964), in particular pp. 168–81 where the link between the contemporary building boom and the development of new roofing styles is again usefully emphasized.

105 For an important recent discussion of cruck origins in England, summarizing much of the earlier debate, see J. T. Smith, 'Cruck distributions: an interpretation of some recent maps', *Vernacular Archit.*, 6 (1975), pp. 3–18. For the descent down the social scale, see, for example, John Fletcher's 'Crucks in the West Berkshire and Oxford region', *Oxoniensia*, 33 (1968), p. 76.

106 The literature on this subject is already large and is increasing year by year under the influence of energetic bodies like the

Vernacular Architecture Group. Good summary guides, though both will need updating, are J. T. Smith's 'Medieval roofs: a classification', *Arch. J.*, 115 (1958), pp. 111–49, and 'Timber-framed building in England: its development and regional differences', ibid., 122 (1965), pp. 133–58. A useful classification of British roof-types was recently published by R. A. Cordingley, following discussion with other members of the Vernacular Architecture Group including J. T. Smith (*Trans. Ancient Monuments Soc.*, new series, 9 (1961), pp. 73–129).

107 *Current Archaeology*, 49 (1975), pp. 41–2.

108 Guy Beresford, op. cit., p. 9.

109 D. Gillian Hurst and John G. Hurst, 'Excavation of two moated sites: Milton, Hampshire, and Ashwell, Hertfordshire', *J. Brit. Arch. Assoc.*, 3rd series, 30 (1967), pp. 52, 68; J. G. Hurst, 'The kitchen area of Northolt Manor, Middlesex', 5 (1961), pp. 213–14.

110 Ann Dornier, 'Kent's Moat, Sheldon, Birmingham', *Trans. and Proc. Birmingham Arch. Soc.*, 82 (1965), pp. 45–57.

111 E. Clive Rouse and Audrey Baker, 'The wall-paintings at Longthorpe Tower, near Peterborough, Northants', *Archaeologia*, 96 (1955), pp. 1–57.

112 G. C. Dunning, 'Attached ventilator finial', in Ketteringham, op. cit., pp. 51–5.

113 G. C. Dunning, 'A pottery louver from Great Easton, Essex', *Med. Arch.*, 10 (1966), pp. 74–80.

114 G. C. Dunning, 'Medieval chimney-pots', in *Studies in Building History. Essays in Recognition of the Work of B.H. St J. O'Neil*, ed. E. M. Jope, 1961, pp. 78–93. Dr Dunning's many works on this and related subjects are now conveniently listed in Vera I. Evison, H. Hodges and J. G. Hurst (eds), *Medieval Pottery from Excavations. Studies Presented to Gerald Clough Dunning*, 1974, pp. 17–32.

115 *Archaeological Excavations 1963*, p. 14.

116 *Archaeological Excavations 1972*, pp. 87–8.

117 Adrian Oswald, 'Excavation of a thirteenth-century wooden building at Weoley Castle, Birmingham, 1960–1', *Med. Arch.*, 6–7 (1962–3), pp. 109–34; J. T. Smith, 'The structure of the timber kitchen at Weoley Castle, Birmingham', ibid., 9 (1965), pp. 82–93.

118 P. J. Tester and J. E. L. Caiger, 'Medieval buildings in the Joyden's Wood square earthwork', *Archaeologia Cantiana*, 72 (1958), pp. 18–39.

119 P. A. Rahtz, *Excavations at King John's Hunting Lodge, Writtle, Essex, 1955–57*, 1969, pp. 20–2.

120 Guy Beresford, 'The medieval manor of Penhallam, Jacobstow, Cornwall', *Med. Arch.*, 18 (1974), pp. 90–145.

121 P. Mayes, personal communication; also *Current Archaeology*, 9 (1968), pp. 232–7.

122 Colin Platt, *The Monastic Grange in Medieval England*, 1969, p. 80.

123 P. D. A. Harvey, *A Medieval Oxfordshire Village. Cuxham 1240 to 1400*, 1965, pp. 75–7. The argument for manorial servants living outside the court, being set up instead on neighbouring tenements of their own, is put by M. M. Postan in *The Famulus. The Estate Labourer in the XIIth and XIIIth Centuries*, Ec.H.R. supplements 2, 1954, in particular pp. 14–15. On Cistercian granges there is some evidence of adjoining peasant communities, presumably set up for grange servants (Platt, op. cit., pp. 86–91).

124 P. J. Huggins, 'Monastic grange and outer close excavations, Waltham Abbey, Essex, 1970–1972', *Essex Arch. and Hist.*, 3rd series, 4 (1972), pp. 30–127, and P. J. and R. M. Huggins, 'Excavation of monastic forge and Saxo-Norman enclosure, Waltham Abbey, Essex, 1972–73', ibid., 5 (1973), pp. 127–84.

125 For a good example of this plan, still unexcavated, see Melsonby, a grange of Jervaulx (Platt, op. cit., p. 216 and plate 11).

126 L. N. Parkes and P. V. Webster, 'Merthyrgeryn: a grange of Tintern', *Archaeologia Cambrensis*, 123 (1974), pp. 140–54; M. W. Thompson, 'Trial excavations at Ropsley Grange, near Grantham, Lincolnshire', *Reports and Papers Lincolnshire Archit. and Arch. Soc.*, 6 (1955–6), pp. 17–23.

127 Eleanor Searle, *Lordship and Community*, 1974, pp. 147–58.

128 Sandra Raban, 'Mortmain in medieval England', *Past and Present*, 62 (1974), p. 26.

129 R. M. Haines, 'The appropriation of Longdon Church to Westminster Abbey', *Trans.*

Worcestershire Arch. Soc., new series, 38 (1961), pp. 39–52.

130 John R. H. Moorman, *Church Life in England in the Thirteenth Century*, 1945, pp. 302–13.

131 C. Vincent Bellamy, *Pontefract Priory Excavations 1957–1961*, Thoresby Society Publications, 49 (1962–4), pp. xv, 9–12.

132 Barbara Harbottle and Peter Salway, 'Excavations at Newminster Abbey, Northumberland, 1961–1963', *Archaeologia Aeliana*, 4th series, 42 (1964), pp. 149–51.

133 Patrick Greene, 'Norton Priory', *Current Archaeology*, 43 (1974), pp. 246–50; David Baker, 'Excavations at Elstow Abbey, Bedfordshire' (1st–3rd interim reports), *Bedfordshire Arch. J.*, 3 (1966), pp. 22–30; 4 (1969), pp. 27–41; 6 (1971), pp. 55–64.

134 Eileen Power, *Medieval English Nunneries c. 1275 to 1535*, 1922, pp. 212–14.

135 David Knowles, *The Religious Orders in England*, 1948, ii:31–8.

136 L. F. Salzman, *Building in England down to 1540. A Documentary History*, 1967 (2nd edn), pp. 424–5.

137 Knowles, op. cit., ii:35–6.

138 For a lead *ampulla* of St Egwin and St Edwin, probably associated with a cult deliberately fostered by Evesham Abbey as early as 1200, see B. W. Spencer, 'An ampulla of St Egwin and St Edwin', *Antiq. J.*, 51 (1971), pp. 316–18. For pilgrim souvenirs found at Southampton, and for a general discussion of the cult of St Thomas, see B. W. Spencer, 'The *ampullae* from Cuckoo Lane', in Colin Platt and Richard Coleman-Smith, *Excavations in Medieval Southampton, 1953–1969*, 1975, ii:242–9. For a recent addition to the literature on pilgrim badges, in which the profitability of the pilgrim-badge industry receives full stress, see Esther Cohen's 'In haec signa: pilgrim-badge trade in southern France', *J. Medieval History*, 2 (1976), pp. 193–214.

139 *King's Works*, i:157.

140 H. M. Colvin (ed.), *Building Accounts of King Henry III*, 1971, p. 191.

141 Ibid., p. 193.

142 *King's Works*, i:252.

143 Ibid., i:253, being a revision of this part of the complete text as published in John Brownbill (ed.), *The Ledger Book of Vale Royal Abbey*, Lancashire and Cheshire Record Society, 68 (1914), pp. 161–3.

144 *King's Works*, i:256. Excavations at the east end of the church have revealed the elaborate *chevet* of chapels attributed to the programme of works financed by the Black Prince (F. H. Thompson, 'Excavations at the Cistercian abbey of Vale Royal, Cheshire, 1958', *Antiq. J.*, 42 (1962), pp. 183–207).

145 Aubrey Gwynn, *The English Austin Friars in the Time of Wyclif*, 1940, p. 21.

146 Ibid., pp. 15–16.

147 *King's Works*, i:157.

148 Colin Platt, *Medieval Southampton*, 1973, p. 64.

149 S. E. Rigold, 'Two Kentish Carmelite houses – Aylesford and Sandwich', *Archaeologia Cantiana*, 80 (1965), pp. 1–28.

150 The quotation is from John of Saxony, a contemporary of Dominic and later Master General of the order, reprinted by Rosalind B. Brooke, *The Coming of the Friars*, 1975, p. 170.

151 C. Woodfield, 'The Whitefriars, Coventry', *Arch.*, 3 (1973), p. 34). also notes in *Med. Arch.*, 5 (1961), p. 314, 6–7 (1962–3), p. 317, 8 (1964), p. 245, and 11 (1967), pp. 278–9. For the chief characteristics of friary churches, see A. R. Martin, *Franciscan Architecture in England*, 1937, in particular pp. 16–21.

152 The dimensions of the church were recorded in a survey of 1553–4 (David S. Neal, 'Excavations at the palace and priory at Kings Langley, 1970', *Hertfordshire Arch.*, 3 (1973), p. 34).

153 Knowles, op. cit., in particular i:130–5, 163–7, 194–204. For the location of the friaries and some details of their size and wealth, see David Knowles and R. Neville Hadcock, *Medieval Religious Houses. England and Wales*, 1953, pp. 180–208.

154 Martin, op. cit., p. 11.

155 Quoted by J. H. E. Bennett, 'The Black Friars of Chester', *J. Chester and North Wales Archit. Arch. and Hist. Soc.*, 39 (1952), p. 31.

156 *Archaeological Excavations 1972*, p. 97 (Northampton); *Med. Arch.*, 15 (1971), p. 138 (Chelmsford), and 18 (1974), pp. 189 (Bristol), 192 (Newcastle).

157 Platt, *op. cit.*, (1973), p. 66 and footnote 49.

158 Colin Morris, 'From synod to consistory:

the bishops' courts in England, 1150–1250', *J. Ecclesiastical History*, 22 (1971), p. 117.

159 Rosalind M. T. Hill, *The Labourer in the Vineyard. The Visitations of Archbishop Melton in the Archdeaconry of Richmond*, Borthwick Papers 35, 1968; to be read with David Robinson's *Beneficed Clergy in Cleveland and the East Riding 1306–1340*, Borthwick Papers 37, 1969.

160 H. G. Ramm, 'The tombs of Archbishops Walter de Gray (1216–55) and Godfrey de Ludham (1258–65) in York Minster, and their contents', *Archaeologia*, 103 (1971), pp. 101–47.

161 L. A. S. Butler, 'Minor medieval monumental sculpture in the East Midlands', *Arch. J.*, 121 (1964), pp. 111–53; also the same author's 'Medieval cross-slabs in Nottinghamshire', *Trans. Thoroton Soc.*, 56 (1952), pp. 25–40, and 'Medieval gravestones of Cambridgeshire, Huntingdonshire and the Soke of Peterborough', *Proc. Cambridge Antiquarian Soc.*, 50 (1956), pp. 89–100.

162 J. R. Earnshaw, 'Medieval grave slabs from the Bridlington district', *Yorkshire Arch. J.*, 42 (1967–70), pp. 333–44.

163 W. G. Hoskins, *The Midland Peasant. The Economic and Social History of a Leicestershire Village*, 1957, p. 61 and footnote 2.

164 Ibid., pp. 80–1.

165 See above, p. 255 (note 85), for full references.

166 For a general discussion of the introduction and spread of such pavements in England, see Elizabeth S. Eames, 'Decorated tile pavements in English medieval houses', J. G. N. Renaud (ed.), *Rotterdam Papers II*, 1975, pp. 5–15.

167 J. M. Bailey, 'Decorated 14th-century tiles at Northill Church, Bedfordshire', *Med. Arch.*, 19 (1975), pp. 209–13.

168 Laurence Keen, 'A fourteenth-century tile pavement at Meesden, Hertfordshire', *Hertfordshire Arch.*, 2 (1970), pp. 75–81.

169 Ethel Carleton Williams, 'Mural paintings of St Catherine in England', *J. Brit. Arch. Assoc.*, 3rd series, 19 (1956), pp. 20–33.

170 E. Clive Rouse, 'Wall paintings in the church of St Pega, Peakirk, Northamptonshire', *Arch. J.*, 110 (1953), pp. 141–2. Other St Christophers are discussed and catalogued by E. T. Long, 'Mediaeval wall paintings in Oxfordshire churches', *Oxoniensia*, 37 (1972), pp. 86–107.

171 E. Clive Rouse and Audrey Baker, 'Wall paintings in Stoke Orchard Church, Gloucestershire, with particular reference to the cycle of the life of St James the Great', *Arch. J.*, 123 (1966), pp. 79–119.

172 *King's Works*, i:86, ii:1014–17.

173 Elizabeth S. Eames, 'Medieval pseudo-mosaic tiles', *J. Brit. Arch. Assoc.*, 3rd series, 38 (1975), p. 81.

174 *King's Works*, i:142.

175 Ibid., i:149–50.

176 Elizabeth S. Eames, 'A thirteenth-century tiled pavement from the king's chapel, Clarendon Palace', *J. Brit. Arch. Assoc.*, 3rd series, 26 (1963), pp. 40–50, and the same author's 'A tile pavement from the queen's chamber, Clarendon Palace, dated 1250–2', ibid., 20–1 (1957–8), pp. 105–6.

177 Elizabeth Eames, 'The royal apartments at Clarendon Palace in the reign of Henry III', *J. Brit. Arch. Assoc.*, 3rd series, 28 (1965), pp. 64–5; also *King's Works*, i:128–30.

178 P. V. Addyman, 'Excavations at Ludgershall Castle, Wiltshire, England (1964–1972)', *Chateau Gaillard VI*, 1973, pp. 7–11; *King's Works*, ii:729–31.

179 John Webb (ed.), *A Roll of the Household Expenses of Richard de Swinfield, Bishop of Hereford, during part of the years 1289 and 1290*, 2 vols, Camden Society, 1854–5, i:cxix–cxxiii, ii:31–4.

180 Helen E. O'Neil, 'Prestbury Moat, a manor house of the bishops of Hereford in Gloucestershire', *Trans. Bristol and Gloucestershire Arch. Soc.*, 75 (1956), pp. 5–34.

181 C. A. Ralegh Radford, 'Acton Burnell Castle', in E. J. Jope (ed.), *Studies in Building History*, 1961, pp. 94–103.

182 R. Allen Brown, 'Framlingham Castle and Bigod 1154–1216', *Proc. Suffolk Inst. Arch.*, 25 (1949–52), pp. 127–48. For a useful general discussion of castle-policy under the Angevins, see the same author's 'Royal castle-building in England, 1154–1216', *E.H.R.*, 70 (1955), pp. 353–98, later supplemented by 'A list of castles, 1154–1216', ibid., 74 (1959), pp. 249–80.

183 For a brief note, with plan, on Conisborough, see M. W. Thompson, 'Conisborough Castle', *Arch. J.*, 125 (1968),

pp. 327–8.

184 *King's Works*, i:75.

185 Ibid., i:117–18, ii:634.

186 Ibid., i:118.

187 S. E. Rigold, 'Eynsford Castle and its excavation', *Archaeologia Cantiana*, 86 (1971), pp. 124–5, 127.

188 A. J. Taylor, 'Chepstow Castle', *Arch. J.*, 122 (1965), pp. 226, 228–9; P. A. Faulkner, 'Domestic planning from the twelfth to the fourteenth centuries', ibid., 115 (1958), p. 176.

189 *King's Works*, ii:682–5. Recent work on the water defences of Kenilworth is reported by M. W. Thompson in *Med. Arch.*, 13 (1969), pp. 218–20, and *Arch. J.*, 128 (1971), pp. 204–7. There was some evidence of the siege of 1266 detected during recent excavations at Kenilworth (Philip Rahtz, 'Kenilworth Castle, 1960', *Trans. and Proc. Birmingham Arch. Soc.*, 81 (1966), pp. 64–6).

190 In the Sir John Rhys lecture for 1944, published as 'Edward I's castle-building in Wales', *Proc. British Academy*, 32 (1946), pp. 15–81. For the later work, see especially A. J. Taylor, 'Castle-building in Wales in the later thirteenth century: the prelude to construction', in E. M. Jope (ed.), *Studies in Building History*, 1961, pp. 104–33; also the same author's chapter in *King's Works*, i:293–408.

191 *King's Works*, i:395–408.

Chapter 3 Set-back

1 E. Stone, 'Profit-and-loss accountancy at Norwich Cathedral Priory', *T.R.H.S.*, 5th series, 12 (1962), pp. 34–5.

2 For the partitioning of villein tenements at this period, see Barbara Dodwell, 'Holdings and inheritance in medieval East Anglia', *Ec.H.R.*, 2nd series, 20 (1967), p. 64.

3 H. E. Hallam, 'Population density in medieval fenland', *Ec.H.R.*, 2nd series, 14 (1961–2), p. 78.

4 H. E. Hallam, 'Some thirteenth-century censuses', *Ec.H.R.*, 2nd series, 10 (1957–8), pp. 340–61, and the same author's 'Further observations on the Spalding serf lists', ibid., 16 (1963–4), pp. 338–50.

5 Edwin Brezette Dewindt, *Land and People in Holywell-cum-Needingworth*, 1972, pp. 56–7; J. Z. Titow, *English Rural Society 1200–1350*, 1969, pp. 78–9.

6 Philip Rahtz, 'Upton, Gloucestershire, 1964–1968. Second report', *Trans. Bristol and Gloucestershire Arch. Soc.*, 88 (1969), pp. 75, 98–103.

7 Ibid., pp. 95–6.

8 J. F. R. Walmsley, 'The peasantry of Burton Abbey in the thirteenth century', *North Staffordshire J. Field Studies*, 12 (1972), p. 55.

9 Edward Miller, *The Abbey and Bishopric of Ely*, 1951, pp. 144–6; Edmund King, *Peterborough Abbey 1086–1310*, 1973, pp. 119–22.

10 M. M. Postan, 'Village livestock in the thirteenth century', *Ec.H.R.*, 2nd series, 15 (1962–3), pp. 219–49.

11 For this argument, based on some evidence from Essex, see R. H. Britnell, 'Agricultural technology and the margin of cultivation in the fourteenth century', *Ec.H.R.*, 2nd series, 30 (1977), pp. 53–66.

12 J. Z. Titow, *Winchester Yields. A Study in Medieval Agricultural Productivity*, 1972, pp. 20–4.

13 P. D. A. Harvey, *A Medieval Oxfordshire Village. Cuxham, 1240 to 1400*, 1965, pp. 57–8.

14 Titow, op. cit. (1972), pp. 32–3.

15 Ibid., p. 24, and the same author's 'Evidence of weather in the account rolls of the bishopric of Winchester 1209–1350', *Ec.H.R.*, 2nd series, 12 (1959–60), pp. 360–407.

16 H. H. Lamb, 'The early medieval warm epoch and its sequel', *Palaeogeography, Palaeoclimatology, Palaeoecology*, 1 (1965), pp. 13–37, and the same author's *The Changing Climate*, 1966, chapters 1 and 7.

17 S. J. Johnsen, W. Dansgaard, H. B. Clausen and C. C. Langway, 'Climatic oscillations 1200–2000 AD', *Nature*, 227 (1970), pp. 482–3.

18 *Med. Arch.*, 17 (1973), p. 153, and Patrick Greene, personal communication.

19 H. H. Lamb, op. cit. (1966), pp. 188–92.

20 J. R. Ravensdale, *Liable to Floods*, 1974, pp. 8–9.

21 Guy Beresford, *The Medieval Clay-land Village*, 1975, pp. 50–52; D. Gillian Hurst and John G. Hurst, 'Excavations at the

medieval village of Wythemail, Northamptonshire', *Med. Arch.*, 13 (1969), pp. 181–2. And see also Maurice Beresford and John G. Hurst (eds), *Deserted Medieval Villages*, 1971, pp. 121–2. For a useful recent comment on the relative importance of weather and other economic factors in the desertion of Barton Blount, see Susan M. Wright, 'Barton Blount: climatic or economic change?', *Med. Arch.*, 20 (1976), pp. 148–52.

22 P. A. Rahtz, 'Holworth, medieval village excavation 1958', *Proc. Dorset Nat. Hist. and Arch. Soc.*, 81 (1959), pp. 136–7.

23 Philip Rahtz and Susan Hirst, *Bordesley Abbey*, British Arch. Reports 23, 1976, pp. 56, 70–3; Eric C. Klingelhöfer, *Broadfield Deserted Medieval Village*, British Arch. Reports 2, 1974, pp. 36–7.

24 Ian Kershaw, 'The Great Famine and agrarian crisis in England 1315–1322', *Past and Present*, 59 (1973), pp. 18–19.

25 Alan R. H. Baker, 'Some evidence of a reduction in the acreage of cultivated lands in Sussex during the early fourteenth century', *Sussex Arch. Coll.*, 104 (1966), pp. 1–5.

26 R. A. L. Smith, *Canterbury Cathedral Priory*, 1943, p. 156.

27 Alan R. H. Baker, 'Evidence in the "Nonarum Inquisitiones" of contracting arable lands in England during the early fourteenth century', *Ec.H.R.*, 2nd series, 19 (1966), p. 527.

28 Colin Platt, *The Monastic Grange in Medieval England*, 1969, p. 65.

29 P. F. Brandon, 'Agriculture and the effects of floods and weather at Barnhorne, Sussex, during the Late Middle Ages', *Sussex Arch. Coll.*, 109 (1971), pp. 82–5.

30 The continuing debate is usefully summarized by Kershaw, op. cit. (1973).

31 Ibid., p. 29.

32 The original argument as set down by M. M. Postan and J. Z. Titow, 'Heriots and prices on Winchester manors', *Ec.H.R.*, 2nd series, 11 (1958–9), pp. 392–417, has been extended by Dr Titow in 'Some evidence of the thirteenth-century population increase', ibid., 14 (1961–2), pp. 218–24, and 'Some differences between manors and their effects on the condition of the peasant in the thirteenth century',

Agric. Hist. Rev., 10 (1962), pp. 1–13. For a critical comment, see Barbara Harvey's 'The population trend in England between 1300 and 1348', *T.R.H.S.*, 5th series, 16 (1966), pp. 23–42, and G. Ohlin, 'No safety in numbers: some pitfalls of historical statistics', in Roderick Floud (ed.), *Essays in Quantitative Economic History*, 1974, pp. 73–7. Dr Titow's answer to Miss Harvey was published in his *English Rural Society*, 1969, pp. 73–8.

33 John Hatcher, 'Non-manorialism in medieval Cornwall', *Agric. Hist. Rev.*, 18 (1970), pp. 1–16, and the same author's *Rural Economy and Society in the Duchy of Cornwall 1300–1500*, 1970, passim.

34 H. E. Hallam, 'Population density in medieval fenland', *Ec.H.R.*, 2nd series, 14 (1961–2), pp. 78–9.

35 D. G. Watts, 'A model for the early fourteenth century', *Ec.H.R.*, 2nd series, 20 (1967), p. 547.

36 Marjorie Morgan, *The English Lands of the Abbey of Bec*, 1968 (revised edn), pp. 103, 112–3.

37 Edward Miller, *The Abbey and Bishopric of Ely*, 1951, pp. 105–6, 111.

38 David Roden, 'Field systems in Ibstone, a township of the south-west Chilterns, during the later Middle Ages', *Records of Buckinghamshire*, 18 (1966–70), p. 52.

39 Ian Keil, 'Farming on the Dorset estates of Glastonbury Abbey in the early fourteenth century', *Proc. Dorset Nat. Hist. and Arch. Soc.*, 87 (1965), pp. 234–50; J. A. Raftis, *Assart Data and Land Values. Two Studies in the East Midlands 1200–1350*, 1974, pp. 97–109.

40 Alan R. H. Baker, 'Evidence in the "Nonarum Inquisitiones" of contracting arable lands in England during the early fourteenth century', *Ec.H.R.*, 2nd series, 19 (1966), pp. 518–32.

41 P. J. Fowler, 'The archaeology of Fyfield and Overton Downs, Wilts (second interim report)', *Wiltshire Arch. and Nat. Hist. Mag.*, 58 (1961–3), pp. 342–8.

42 For this general thesis, forcibly expressed, see J. R. Maddicott, *The English Peasantry and the Demands of the Crown 1294–1341*, *Past and Present*, supplement 1, 1975, passim.

43 N. J. Mayhew and D. R. Walker, 'Croc-

kards and pollards: imitation and the problem of fineness in a silver coinage', in N. J. Mayhew (ed.), *Edwardian Monetary Affairs (1279–1344)*, British Arch. Reports 36, 1977, pp. 125–46.

44 For the mould from York, see the note in the York Archaeological Trust's bulletin *Interim*, 2:2:12; for the Boston token, see Stephen Moorhouse, 'Finds from excavations in the refectory at the Dominican Friary, Boston', *Lincolnshire Hist. and Arch.*, 7 (1972), p. 44 and fig. 8; for the Dublin tokens, see Michael Dolley and W. A. Seaby, 'A find of thirteenth-century pewter tokens from the National Museum excavations at Winetavern Street, Dublin', *Numismatic Circular*, 1972, pp. 446–8. The general circumstances of the Dublin site are discussed by Breandán Ó Ríordáin, 'Excavations at High Street and Winetavern Street, Dublin', *Med. Arch.*, 15 (1971), pp. 73–85.

45 R. H. M. Dolley, 'The 1955 Dover treasure trove', *Archaeologia Cantiana*, 69 (1955), pp. 62–8, and the same author's 'The Dover hoard. The first English hoard with groats of Edward I', *British Numismatic J.*, 28 (1955–7), pp. 147–68.

46 Mavis Mate, 'High prices in early fourteenth-century England: causes and consequences', *Ec.H.R.*, 2nd series, 28 (1975), p. 9. For a lucid exposition of the financial policies of Edward I, generally favourable to that king and his advisers, see the same author's 'Monetary policies in England, 1272–1307', *British Numismatic J.*, 41 (1972), pp. 34–79; also Michael Prestwich, 'Edward I's monetary policies and their consequences', *Ec.H.R.*, 2nd series, 22 (1969), pp. 406–16, concluding 'on this question of the currency, there is no doubt that he (Edward) and his advisers adopted sound and sensible methods' (p. 416).

47 D. L. Farmer, 'Some grain price movements in thirteenth-century England', *Ec.H.R.*, 2nd series, 10 (1957–8), pp. 207–20, and the same author's 'Some livestock price movements in thirteenth-century England', ibid., 22 (1969), pp. 1–16.

48 N. J. Mayhew, 'Numismatic evidence and falling prices in the fourteenth century',

Ec.H.R., 2nd series, 27 (1974), pp. 1–15.

49 Mayhew, op. cit., pp. 13–14. For silver production, see C. C. Patterson, 'Silver stocks and losses in ancient and medieval times', *Ec.H.R.*, 2nd series, 25 (1972), pp. 229–30.

50 Maddicott, op. cit., pp. 45–67. Taxation in the half-century after 1294 is again usefully discussed by Edward Miller, 'War, taxation and the English economy in the late thirteenth and early fourteenth centuries', in J. M. Winter (ed.), *War and Economic Development*, 1975, pp. 11–31.

51 See, for example, H. A. Hanley and C. W. Chalklin, 'The Kent lay subsidy of 1334/5', in F. R. H. Du Boulay (ed.), *Kent Records. Documents Illustrative of Medieval Kentish Society*, Kent Archaeological Society Records Series, 18 (1964), pp. 67–70; also R. E. Glasscock, 'The distribution of lay wealth in Kent, Surrey, and Sussex, in the early fourteenth century', *Archaeologia Cantiana*, 80 (1965), pp. 61–8.

52 Robin E. Glasscock (ed.), *The Lay Subsidy of 1334*, British Academy Records of Social and Economic History, new series, 11 (1975), pp. xxviii–xxix.

53 R. E. Glasscock, 'England circa 1334', in H. C. Darby (ed.), *A New Historical Geography of England*, 1973, pp. 183–5.

54 Hanley and Chalklin, op. cit., p. 62.

55 Margaret Curtis, 'The London lay subsidy of 1332', in George Unwin (ed.), *Finance and Trade under Edward III*, 1918 (reprinted 1962), pp. 44, 48.

56 *V.C.H. City of York*, p. 109.

57 Colin Platt, *The English Medieval Town*, 1976, p. 111.

58 P. D. A. Harvey, *A Medieval Oxfordshire Village*, 1965, p. 133.

59 W. G. Hoskins, *The Midland Peasant. The Economic and Social History of a Leicestershire Village*, 1957, pp. 71–2.

60 Harvey, op. et loc. cit.

61 J. A. Raftis, 'Social structures in five East Midland villages. A study of possibilities in the use of court roll data', *Ec.H.R.*, 2nd series, 18 (1965), pp. 83–100. See also his detailed study of a single manor *Warboys. Two Hundred Years in the Life of an English Mediaeval Village*, 1974, passim.

62 Edmund King, *Peterborough Abbey 1086–1310. A Study in the Land Market*,

1973, pp. 116–17.

63 Alan R. H. Baker, 'Some fields and farms in medieval Kent', *Archaeologia Cantiana*, 80 (1965), p. 171.

64 E. M. Halcrow, 'The decline of demesne farming on the estates of Durham Cathedral Priory', *Ec.H.R.*, 2nd series, 7 (1954–5), p. 350.

65 Edward Miller, *The Abbey and Bishopric of Ely*, 1951, pp. 150–1.

66 Harvey, op. cit., pp. 115–19.

67 Marjorie Morgan, *The English Lands of the Abbey of Bec*, 1968 (revised edn), p. 110.

68 R. H. Hilton, *The English Peasantry in the Later Middle Ages*, 1975, pp. 154–5.

69 Edwin Brezette Dewindt, *Land and People in Holywell-cum-Needingworth*, 1972, pp. 98–100.

70 R. H. Hilton and P. A. Rahtz, 'Upton, Gloucestershire, 1959–1964', *Trans. Bristol and Gloucestershire Arch. Soc.*, 85 (1966), pp. 111–13; also P. A. Rahtz, 'Upton, Gloucestershire, 1964–1968. Second report', ibid., 88 (1969), p. 103.

71 *Med. Arch.*, 9 (1965), p. 214 (Thuxton); ibid., 13 (1969), p. 279, *Current Archaeology*, 2 (1967), pp. 48–50, and 16 (1969), pp. 144–7 (Faxton); D. Gillian Hurst and John G. Hurst, 'Excavations at the medieval village of Wythemail, Northamptonshire', *Med. Arch.*, 13 (1969), pp. 167–203.

72 David Algar and John Musty, 'Gomeldon', *Current Archaeology*, 14 (1969), pp. 87–91; *Med. Arch.*, 10 (1966), pp. 214–16, 11 (1967), pp. 312, 314, 12 (1968), pp. 203–5, 13 (1969), pp. 281–3.

73 Maurice Beresford and John G. Hurst (eds), *Deserted Medieval Villages*, 1971, pp. 107, 111–12.

74 R. H. Hilton, 'Peasant movements in England before 1381', *Ec.H.R.*, 2nd series, 2 (1949–50), pp. 131–2.

75 Morgan, op. cit., p. 110.

76 J. F. R. Walmsley, 'The peasantry of Burton Abbey in the thirteenth century', *North Staffordshire J. Field Studies*, 12 (1972), pp. 50–1.

77 Alfred N. May, 'An index of thirteenth-century peasant impoverishment? Manor court fines', *Ec.H.R.*, 2nd series, 26 (1973), pp. 389–91. For a critical comment on this paper, not affecting this particular point, see J. B. Post, 'Manorial amercements and

peasant poverty', ibid., 28 (1975), pp. 304–11.

78 Harvey, op. cit., pp. 128–9 (Cuxham); Morgan, op. cit., p. 107 (Ogbourne).

79 Gabrielle Lambrick, 'Abingdon and the riots of 1327', *Oxoniensia*, 29–30 (1964–5), pp. 129–41.

80 Alan Cameron, 'William de Amyas and the community of Nottingham, 1308–50', *Trans. Thoroton Soc.*, 75 (1971), pp. 74–5.

81 Ralph B. Pugh, 'Some reflections of a medieval criminologist', *Proc. British Academy*, 59 (1973), pp. 83–4. For a very striking recent demonstration of the coincidence of crime waves with periods of dearth and high grain prices, see the graph in Dr Barbara Hanawalt's *Crime in East Anglia in the Fourteenth Century. Norfolk Gaol Delivery Rolls, 1307–1316*, Norfolk Record Society, 44 (1976), p. 15. Taken over three counties, the coincidence, while not as close, is still very striking (Barbara A. Hanawalt, 'Economic influences on the pattern of crime in England, 1300–1348', *American Journal of Legal History*, 18 (1974), p. 290).

82 M. T. Clanchy, 'Law, government, and society in medieval England', *History*, 59 (1974), p. 78.

83 From 'The Outlaw's Song of Trailbaston' (Isabel S. T. Aspin (ed.), *Anglo-Norman Political Songs*, 1953, p. 74), quoted in an adapted version by E. L. G. Stones, 'The Folvilles of Ashby-Folville, Leicestershire, and their associates in crime, 1326–1347', *T.R.H.S.*, 5th series, 7 (1957), p. 133.

84 J. G. Bellamy, 'The Coterel gang: an anatomy of a band of fourteenth-century criminals', *E.H.R.*, 79 (1964), p. 703, and the same author's useful chapter on 'The Criminal Bands' in his *Crime and Public Order in England in the Later Middle Ages*, 1973, pp. 69–88. See also P. H. W. Booth, 'Taxation and public order: Cheshire in 1353', *Northern History*, 12 (1976), pp. 16–31.

85 Bellamy, op. cit. (1973), pp. 77–9.

86 Ibid., p. 79.

87 H. E. Jean Le Patourel, *The Moated Sites of Yorkshire*, 1973, p. 19. The concentration in dating between 1250 and c. 1320 had been suggested already, a decade earlier, by F. V. Emery, 'Moated settlements in Eng-

land', *Geography*, 47 (1962), p. 384.

88 Emery, op. cit., pp. 385–6; B. K. Roberts, 'Moated sites in Midland England', *Trans. and Proc. Birmingham Arch. Soc.*, 80 (1962), pp. 26–37, and the same author's 'A study of medieval colonization in the Forest of Arden, Warwickshire', *Agric. Hist. Rev.*, 16 (1968), p. 109.

89 N. Denholm-Young, *The Country Gentry in the Fourteenth Century*, 1969, pp. 34–8.

90 Roberts, op. cit. (1962), p. 33.

91 C. C. Taylor, 'Medieval moats in Cambridgeshire', in P. J. Fowler (ed.), *Archaeology and the Landscape*, 1972, pp. 246–7.

92 D. Gillian Hurst and John G. Hurst, 'Excavation of two moated sites: Milton, Hampshire, and Ashwell, Hertfordshire', *J. Brit. Arch. Assoc.*, 3rd series, 30 (1967), pp. 48–86.

93 *Med. Arch.*, 12 (1968), pp. 195–6, 13 (1969), pp. 273–4, 14 (1970), p. 194, 16 (1972), pp. 195–6, and David Martin, personal communication.

94 For the same conclusion, based on the historical evidence, see Daniel Williams, 'Fortified manor houses', *Trans. Leicestershire Arch. and Hist. Soc.*, 50 (1974–5), pp. 1–16.

95 J. G. Hurst, 'The kitchen area of Northolt Manor, Middlesex', *Med. Arch.*, 5 (1961), p. 239, and Hurst and Hurst, op. cit., pp. 83–4.

96 Colin Platt, *The Monastic Grange in Medieval England*, 1969, p. 73; Stuart and Susan Wrathmell, 'Excavations at the moat site, Walsall, Staffs. 1972–74', *Trans. South Staffordshire Arch. and Hist. Soc.*, 16 (1974–5), pp. 19–53.

97 Adrian Oswald and G. S. Taylor, 'Durrance Moat, Upton Warren, Worcestershire', *Trans. and Proc. Birmingham Arch. Soc.*, 79 (1960–1), pp. 61–75. For other late moats, see N. P. Bridgewater, 'The manor of Tretire', *Trans. Woolhope Naturalists' Field Club*, 39 (1967–9), pp. 447–55; M. W. Thompson, 'Excavation of a medieval moat at Moat Hill, Anlaby, near Hull', *Yorkshire Arch. J.*, 39 (1956–8), pp. 67–85; J. B. Whitwell, 'Excavations on the site of a moated medieval manor-house in the parish of Saxilby, Lincolnshire', *J. Brit. Arch. Assoc.*, 3rd series, 32 (1969), pp. 128–43; Edward A. Martin, 'The excavation of a

moat at Exning', *East Anglian Archaeology*, 1 (1975), pp. 24–38. For other sites of this period, see the remarks in C. F. Tebbutt, Granville T. Rudd and Stephen Moorhouse, 'Excavation of a moated site at Ellington, Huntingdonshire', *Proc. Cambridge Antiquarian Soc.*, 63 (1971), pp. 46–9.

98 Adrian Oswald, 'Excavations at Shareshill, Staffs. 1959', *Trans. and Proc. Birmingham Arch. Soc.*, 77 (1959), p. 47; the report includes a discussion of other West Midlands sites similarly refortified at this date (pp. 47, 49).

99 Adrian Oswald, 'Interim report on excavations at Weoley Castle, 1955–60', *Trans. and Proc. Birmingham Arch. Soc.*, 78 (1962), pp. 61–85.

100 The original contract for this work has survived and has been published by L. F. Salzman, *Building in England down to 1540*, 1967, pp. 422–4; see also *King's Works*, ii:930–1.

101 H. E. Hallam, *Settlement and Society. A Study of the Early Agrarian History of South Lincolnshire*, 1965, p. 222.

102 Ibid., p. 217 and passim.

103 Jean Birrell, 'Peasant craftsmen in the medieval forest', *Agric. Hist. Rev.*, 17 (1969), pp. 91–107.

104 For a stimulating debate on the degree of specialization in the contemporary extractive industries, see John Hatcher, 'A diversified economy: later medieval Cornwall', *Ec.H.R.*, 2nd series, 22 (1969), pp. 208–27; Ian Blanchard, 'The miner and the agricultural community in late medieval England', *Agric. Hist. Rev.*, 20 (1972), pp. 93–106; John Hatcher, 'Myths, miners, and agricultural communities', ibid., 22 (1974), pp. 54–61; and Ian Blanchard, 'Rejoinder: stannator fabulosus', ibid., pp. 62–74.

105 Colin Platt, *The English Medieval Town*, 1976, pp. 112–13.

106 Eric S. Wood, 'A medieval glasshouse at Blunden's Wood, Hambledon, Surrey', *Surrey Arch. Coll.*, 62 (1965), pp. 54–79.

107 *Archaeological Excavations 1969*, p. 30; *Med. Arch.*, 14 (1970), p. 208, 17 (1973), p. 188.

108 J. H. Money, 'Medieval iron-workings in Minepit Wood, Rotherfield, Sussex', *Med. Arch.*, 15 (1971), pp. 86–111.

109 See, for example, E. M. Carus-Wilson,

Medieval Merchant Venturers, 1967 (2nd edn), chs 4 and 5, and some criticism of the general thesis in Edward Miller, 'The fortunes of the English textile industry during the thirteenth century', *Ec.H.R.*, 2nd series, 18 (1965), pp. 64–82. The first building of a fulling mill in Taunton in 1218–19, followed by the reduction of receipts at the mill as others were built in the area, is discussed by T. J. Hunt, 'Some notes on the cloth trade in Taunton in the thirteenth century', *Proc. Somersetshire Arch. and Nat. Hist. Soc.*, 101–2 (1956/7), pp. 89–107.

110 J. B. Blake, 'The medieval coal trade of North East England: some fourteenth-century evidence', *Northern History*, 2 (1967), pp. 1–26.

111 L. A. S. Butler, 'Medieval gravestones of Cambridgeshire, Huntingdonshire and the Soke of Peterborough', *Proc. Cambridge Antiquarian Soc.*, 50 (1956), pp. 89–100.

112 *Med. Arch.*, 17 (1973), p. 166.

113 M. L. Ryder, 'The animal remains from Petergate, York, 1957–8', *Yorkshire Arch. J.*, 42 (1967–70), pp. 418–28; Peter Wenham, 'Excavations in Low Petergate, York, 1957–58', ibid., 44 (1972), pp. 65–113.

114 Sheppard Frere, 'Canterbury excavations, summer 1946. The Rose Lane sites', *Archaeologia Cantiana*, 68 (1954), pp. 127–8, 139–40; B. W. Spencer, 'A scallop-shell ampulla from Caistor and comparable pilgrim souvenirs', *Lincolnshire Hist. and Arch.*, 6 (1971), pp. 59–66.

115 J. Ambrose Raftis, *Warboys. Two Hundred Years in the Life of an English Mediaeval Village*, 1974, p. 235.

116 Elizabeth S. Eames, 'A thirteenth-century tile kiln site at North Grange, Meaux, Beverley, Yorkshire', *Med. Arch.*, 5 (1961), pp. 137–68; ibid., 9 (1965), p. 181 (Haverholme), and 17 (1973), p. 153 (Norton).

117 J. S. Gardner and Elizabeth Eames, 'A tile kiln at Chertsey Abbey', *J. Brit. Arch. Assoc.*, 3rd series, 17 (1954), pp. 24–42; Elizabeth S. Eames, *Medieval Tiles. A Handbook*, 1968, pp. 7–10.

118 T. G. Manby, 'Medieval pottery kilns at Upper Heaton, West Yorkshire', *Arch. J.*, 121 (1964), pp. 108–10.

119 Kenneth James Barton, 'A medieval pottery kiln at Ham Green, Bristol', *Trans.*

Bristol and Gloucestershire Arch. Soc., 82 (1963), pp. 115–19.

120 G. C. Dunning, 'The trade in medieval pottery around the North Sea', in J. G. N. Renaud (ed.), *Rotterdam Papers*, 1968, pp. 41–2. For the very similar distribution of bearded face-jugs, see Dunning, op. cit., pp. 38–41, and H. E. Jean Le Patourel, 'Hallgarth, Doncaster, and the incidence of face-jugs with beards', *Med. Arch.*, 10 (1966), pp. 160–4.

121 H. E. Jean Le Patourel, 'Documentary evidence and the medieval pottery industry', *Med. Arch.*, 12 (1968), p. 122.

122 John M. Steane and Geoffrey F. Bryant, 'Excavations at the deserted medieval settlement at Lyveden. Fourth report', *J. Northampton Museums and Art Gallery*, 12 (1975), pp. 17–44 (area J), 152–7 (bone report); for the earlier evidence, see in particular G. F. Bryant and J. M. Steane, 'Excavations at the deserted medieval settlement at Lyveden. A third interim report', ibid., 9 (1971), p. 43.

123 John Musty, D. J. Algar and P. F. Ewence, 'The medieval pottery kilns at Laverstock, near Salisbury, Wiltshire', *Archaeologia*, 102 (1969), pp. 83–150.

124 *Med. Arch.*, 16 (1972), p. 205, 17 (1973), p. 184, 18 (1974), p. 220.

125 Ibid., 12 (1968), pp. 208–10, 13 (1969), p. 287, 14 (1970), p. 205, 16 (1972), pp. 207–8.

126 Ibid., 3 (1959), p. 325, 4 (1960), p. 163, 6–7 (1962–3), p. 348, 8 (1964), p. 296, 9 (1965), p. 217, 17 (1973), pp. 184–5.

127 Ibid., 15 (1971), p. 176, 16 (1972), p. 206.

128 Musty, Algar and Ewence, op. cit., p. 85.

129 Le Patourel, op. cit., pp. 112–13; also John Musty, 'Medieval pottery kilns', in Vera I. Evison, H. Hodges and J. G. Hurst (eds), *Medieval Pottery from Excavations*, 1974, pp. 58–9.

130 Alec Down and Margaret Rule, *Chichester Excavations I*, 1971, pp. 157–64, being the discussion by K. J. Barton of the products of the excavated kiln. For other urban or suburban pottery industries, see Aileen Fox and G. C. Dunning, 'A medieval pottery kiln in Exeter', *Antiq. J.*, 37 (1957), pp. 42–53; also *Current Archaeology*, 33 (1972), p. 277 (Doncaster), *Med. Arch.*, 8 (1964), pp. 294–6 (Stamford), and Brian

Philp, 'A medieval kiln site at Tyler Hill, Canterbury', *Kent Arch. Rev.*, 36 (1974), pp. 175–81.

131 N. H. Field and John Musty, 'A thirteenth-century kiln at Hermitage, Dorset', *Proc. Dorset Nat. Hist. and Arch. Soc.*, 88 (1966), pp. 161–75.

132 *Med. Arch.*, 12 (1968), pp. 208–10.

133 Ibid., 11 (1967), pp. 316–18.

134 Eames, op. cit. (1968), pp. 16–21; Jane A. Wight, *Mediaeval Floor Tiles. Their Design and Distribution in Britain*, 1975, pp. 65, 70, 124–35.

135 Platt, op. cit. (1976), p. 146; and see also John Harvey, *Mediaeval Craftsmen*, 1975, p. 141, with other examples of tile-works set up either in or next to towns (pp. 139–40).

136 P. Mayes, 'A medieval tile kiln at Boston, Lincolnshire', *J. Brit. Arch. Assoc.*, 3rd series, 28 (1965), pp. 86–106.

137 P. J. Drury and G. D. Pratt, 'A late 13th and early 14th-century tile factory at Danbury, Essex', *Med. Arch.*, 19 (1975), pp. 92–164.

138 For useful discussions of the Scarborough and Worcester industries, see J. G. Rutter, *Medieval Pottery in the Scarborough Museum, 13th and 14th Centuries*, Scarborough and District Archaeological Society, Research Report 3, 1961, and K. J. Barton, 'The medieval pottery of the city of Worcester', *Trans. Worcestershire Arch. Soc.*, 3rd series, 1 (1965–7), pp. 29–44.

139 Brian Spencer, 'A face-jug from the site of the Old Bailey, London', *Antiq. J.*, 49 (1969), p. 388 and plate XCII.

140 Graham Webster and G. C. Dunning, 'A medieval pottery kiln at Audlem, Cheshire', *Med. Arch.*, 4 (1960), pp. 109–25; C. V. Bellamy and H. E. Jean Le Patourel, 'Four medieval pottery-kilns on Woodhouse Farm, Winksley, near Ripon, W. Riding of Yorkshire', ibid., 14 (1970), pp. 104–25. At Winksley, the influence on vessel forms is suggested to be Continental rather than the more usually accepted Midland, although this depends on an inconclusive archaeomagnetic date.

141 D. C. Mynard, 'Medieval pottery from Dartford', *Archaeologia Cantiana*, 88 (1973), pp. 195–8.

142 Guildhall Museum, 'Archaeological finds from the City of London 1965–6', *Trans.*

London and Middlesex Arch. Soc., 22:1 (1968), p. 13.

143 Colin Platt and Richard Coleman-Smith, *Excavations in Medieval Southampton, 1953–1969*, 1975, i:293–4, ii:26.

144 *Med. Arch.*, 16 (1972), p. 189. The identification of the men with the pits will never, of course, be certain, though there seems little point in avoiding the use of their names. For details of the career of William de Amyas, see Alan Cameron, 'William de Amyas and the community of Nottingham, 1308–50', *Trans. Thoroton Soc.*, 75 (1971), pp. 68–78; and for a biographical note on Richard of Southwick, see Colin Platt, *Medieval Southampton*, 1973, pp. 258–9.

145 Rutter, op. cit., p. 8.

146 Guy Beresford, *The Medieval Clay-land Village*, 1975, pp. 55–77.

147 Barbara Green, G. C. Dunning and Peter Wade-Martins, 'Some recent finds of imported pottery', *Norfolk Archaeology*, 34 (1966–9), pp. 403–5.

148 J. G. Hurst in *The Times*, archaeological report, 12.9.75. For Stonar, see *Archaeological Excavations 1970*, pp. 30–1; for Southampton, see Platt and Coleman-Smith, op. cit., ii:16–183 (The Pottery).

149 Dorothea Oschinsky, *Walter of Henley and Other Treatises on Estate Management and Accounting*, 1971, pp. 398–9.

Chapter 4   After the Black Death

1 V. Pritchard, *English Medieval Graffiti*, 1967, pp. 181–2.

2 A. R. Bridbury, 'The Black Death', *Ec.H.R.*, 2nd series, 26 (1973), p. 591.

3 For a recent gathering together of the statistics, see Alan R. H. Baker, 'Changes in the later Middle Ages', in H. C. Darby (ed.), *A New Historical Geography of England*, 1973, pp. 187–90. These are discussed again, with some striking new evidence of plague recurrence in the fifteenth century taken from the Christ Church, Canterbury, obituary lists, by John Hatcher, *Plague, Population and the English Economy 1348–1530*, 1977.

4 P. D. A. Harvey, *A Medieval Oxfordshire Village*, 1965, pp. 78–9, 85, 135–7.

5 David Roden, 'Field systems in Ibstone, a

township of the south-west Chilterns, during the later Middle Ages', *Records of Buckinghamshire*, 18 (1966–70), p. 52,

6 Eleanor Searle, *Lordship and Community*, 1974, pp. 258, 262.

7 R. B. Dobson, *Durham Priory 1400–1450*, 1973, p. 270.

8 Bridbury, op. cit., p. 584.

9 For example, on the Devon manors of the earls of Devon (K. Ugawa, 'The economic development of some Devon manors in the thirteenth century', *Report and Trans. Devonshire Assoc.*, 94 (1962), pp. 613–4) and on at least one of the Merton College estates (R. H. Hilton, 'Kibworth Harcourt. A Merton College manor in the thirteenth and fourteenth centuries', in W. G. Hoskins (ed.), *Studies in Leicestershire Agrarian History*, 1949, p. 32).

10 R. R. Davies, 'Baronial accounts, incomes, and arrears in the later Middle Ages', *Ec.H.R.*, 2nd series, 21 (1968), in particular p. 218.

11 R. A. L. Smith, *Canterbury Cathedral Priory*, 1943, pp. 191–3.

12 Ibid., p. 200.

13 F. R. H. Du Boulay, 'Late-continued demesne farming at Otford', *Archaeologia Cantiana*, 73 (1959), pp. 116–24.

14 Judith A. Brent, 'Alciston Manor in the later Middle Ages', *Sussex Arch. Coll.*, 106 (1968), p. 101; and see also P. F. Brandon, 'Arable farming in a Sussex scarp-foot parish during the Late Middle Ages', ibid., 100 (1962), pp. 60–72.

15 G. S. Haslop, 'The abbot of Selby's financial statement for the year ending Michaelmas 1338', *Yorkshire Arch. J.*, 44 (1972), pp. 166–7.

16 W. F. Mumford, 'The manor of Oxted, 1360–1420', *Surrey Arch. Coll.*, 63 (1966), pp. 66–94. Oxted continued to be farmed in demesne until well into the fifteenth century, but already in 1370 the grange and oxhouse were ruinous and several parcels of the demesne had been leased out to local peasant farmers.

17 D. G. Watts, 'A model for the early fourteenth century', *Ec.H.R.*, 2nd series, 20 (1967), p. 547.

18 P. F. Brandon, 'Cereal yields on the Sussex estates of Battle Abbey during the later Middle Ages', *Ec.H.R.*, 2nd series, 25 (1972), pp. 403–20; for the leasing of the Battle demesnes, see Searle, op. cit., pp. 324–37.

19 John Hatcher, *Rural Economy and Society in the Duchy of Cornwall 1300–1500*, 1970, pp. 157–8.

20 Dobson, op. cit., p. 272 (Durham); Barbara Harvey, 'The leasing of the abbot of Westminster's demesnes in the later Middle Ages', *Ec.H.R.*, 2nd series, 22 (1969), pp. 17–27; J. Ambrose Raftis, *The Estates of Ramsey Abbey*, 1957, pp. 289–91; R. H. Hilton, *The Economic Development of some Leicestershire Estates in the 14th and 15th Centuries*, 1947, pp. 88–94 (Leicester); Ian Kershaw, *Bolton Priory*, 1973, p. 181.

21 J. M. Wagstaff, 'The economy of Dieulacres Abbey, 1214–1539', *North Staffordshire J. Field Studies*, 10 (1970), pp. 93–5.

22 P. J. Huggins, 'Monastic grange and outer close excavations, Waltham Abbey, Essex, 1970–1972', *Essex Arch. and Hist.*, 3rd series, 4 (1972), pp. 91–2.

23 *Archaeological Excavations 1973*, p. 85.

24 Glyn Coppack, 'The deserted medieval village of Keighton', *Trans. Thoroton Soc.*, 75 (1971), pp. 41–58.

25 Philip Rahtz, 'Upton, Gloucestershire, 1964–1968. Second report', *Trans. Bristol and Gloucestershire Arch. Soc.*, 88 (1969), p. 95; Jayne Woodhouse, *Barrow Mead, Bath, 1964 Excavation*, British Arch. Reports 28, 1976, p. 25.

26 K. J. Allison, M. W. Beresford and J. G. Hurst, *The Deserted Villages of Oxfordshire*, 1965, p. 27.

27 Maurice Beresford and John G. Hurst (eds), *Deserted Medieval Villages*, 1971, pp. 12–14.

28 R. H. Hilton and P. A. Rahtz, 'Upton, Gloucestershire, 1959–1964', *Trans. Bristol and Gloucestershire Arch. Soc.*, 85 (1966), pp. 84–5.

29 Christopher Dyer, 'The deserted medieval village of Woollashill, Worcestershire', *Trans. Worcestershire Arch. Soc.*, 3rd series, 1 (1965–7), pp. 55–61.

30 J. R. Ravensdale, *Liable to Floods*, 1974, pp. 134, 160.

31 Elizabeth M. Elvey, 'The abbot of Missenden's estates in Chalfont St Peter', *Records of Buckinghamshire*, 17 (1961–5),

p. 33; Margaret Spufford, *A Cambridge-shire Community. Chippenham from Settlement to Enclosure*, 1965, p. 36.

32 J. Ambrose Raftis, *Tenure and Mobility*, 1964, p. 192.

33 T. H. Lloyd, 'Some documentary sidelights on the deserted Oxfordshire village of Brookend', *Oxoniensia*, 29–30 (1964–5), pp. 125–6.

34 N. W. Alcock, 'The medieval cottages of Bishops Clyst, Devon', *Med. Arch.*, 9 (1965), pp. 146–53, and see also the same author's 'An East Devon manor in the later Middle Ages. Part II: leasing the demesne. 1423–1525; 1525–1650', *Report and Trans. Devonshire Assoc.*, 105 (1973), pp. 158–9, 173–5; for the urban artisan terraces, see my own *The English Medieval Town*, 1976, pp. 66–8.

35 K. Rutherford Davis, *The Deserted Medieval Villages of Hertfordshire*, 1973; Allison, Beresford and Hurst, op. cit. (1965, Oxfordshire); K. J. Allison, 'The lost villages of Norfolk', *Norfolk Archaeology*, 31 (1955–7), pp. 116–62; M. W. Beresford and J. G. Hurst, 'Introduction to a first list of deserted medieval village sites in Berkshire', *Berkshire Arch. J.*, 60 (1962), pp. 92–7; K. J. Allison, M. W. Beresford and J. G. Hurst, *The Deserted Villages of Northamptonshire*, 1966.

36 C. C. Taylor, 'Whiteparish. A study of the development of a forest-edge parish', *Wiltshire Arch. and Nat. Hist. Mag.*, 62 (1967), pp. 92–4.

37 Hatcher, op. cit., pp. 125–6, 132–3, 140.

38 Lloyd, op. cit., pp. 125–6.

39 P. D. A. Harvey, op. cit., p. 140.

40 B. W. Spencer, 'A fourteenth-century wooden effigy from Much Marcle, Herefordshire', *Antiq. J.*, 53 (1973), pp. 266–7.

41 Mumford, op. cit., p. 72.

42 Barbara Harvey, op. cit., p. 20.

43 Hilton, op. cit., p. 105.

44 F. R. H. Du Boulay, *The Lordship of Canterbury*, 1966, p. 232; Dobson, op. cit., p. 282 (Durham).

45 L. A. S. Butler, 'Hambleton Moat, Scredington, Lincolnshire', *J. Brit. Arch. Assoc.*, 3rd series, 26 (1963), pp. 62–3.

46 Guy Beresford, *The Medieval Clay-land Village*, 1975, pp. 40–3. For another good example of a late-medieval long-house of a

more sophisticated form, see the house at Riplingham, Yorkshire (*Med. Arch.*, 11 (1967), pp. 313–14).

47 *Archaeological Excavations 1973*, p. 85.

48 Rosamond Jane Faith, 'Peasant families and inheritance customs in medieval England', *Agric. Hist. Rev.*, 14 (1966), p. 89.

49 R. H. Hilton, *The English Peasantry in the Later Middle Ages*, 1975, p. 173.

50 Ambrose Raftis, op. cit. (1964), p. 209.

51 J. Ambrose Raftis, *Warboys. Two Hundred Years in the Life of an English Mediaeval Village*, 1974, pp. 216–17; Edwin Brezette Dewindt, *Land and People in Holywell-cum-Needingworth*, 1972, pp. 263–4.

52 Dewindt, op. cit., pp. 271–3.

53 M. Mollat and P. Wolff, *The Popular Revolutions of the Late Middle Ages*, 1973, pp. 138–210; and see also Rodney Hilton, *Bond Men made Free. Medieval Peasant Movements and the English Rising of 1381*, 1973, in particular ch. 3.

54 R. H. Hilton, *The English Peasantry in the Later Middle Ages*, 1975, pp. 61–3.

55 Bridbury, op. cit., p. 585.

Chapter 5 Stability at a Reduced level: the Church

1 For a discussion and listing of such purposes, see J. G. Davies, *The Secular Use of Church Buildings*, 1968.

2 J. F. Williams, 'The Black Book of Swaffham', *Norfolk Archaeology*, 33 (1962–5), p. 252.

3 T. F. Reddaway, 'The London Goldsmiths, *circa* 1500', *T.R.H.S.*, 5th series, 12 (1962), p. 57.

4 J. T. Rosenthal, 'The Yorkshire chantry certificates of 1546: an analysis', *Northern History*, 9 (1974), pp. 30–1.

5 N. P. Tanner, *Popular religion in Norwich with special reference to the evidence of wills, 1370–1532*, Oxford D. Phil. thesis, 1973, pp. 16, 206, 246–54.

6 J. A. F. Thomson, 'Piety and charity in late medieval London', *J. Ecclesiastical History*, 16 (1965), p. 193.

7 W. O. Ault, 'Manor court and parish church in fifteenth-century England: a study of village by-laws', *Speculum*, 42 (1967), pp. 53–67.

8 K. B. McFarlane, *The Nobility of Later*

Medieval England, 1973, p. 95.

9 For some recent studies of these workmen and their styles, see Cora J. Ough, 'Local style in church architecture in the Stour Valley', *Nottingham Medieval Studies*, 4 (1960), pp. 81–104, and the work of Dr Eileen Roberts, 'Thomas Wolvey, mason', *Arch. J.*, 129 (1972), pp. 119–44, and 'Totternhoe stone and flint in Hertfordshire churches', *Med. Arch.*, 18 (1974), pp. 66–89; also, for the later thirteenth and early fourteenth century, see Richard Keith Morris, *Decorated architecture in Herefordshire. A study of its sources, workshops, and influence*, London Ph.D. thesis, 1972.

10 L. F. Salzman, *Building in England down to 1540*, 1967, pp. 547–9.

11 Ibid., pp. 487–90.

12 *Current Archaeology*, 49 (1975), pp. 44–5.

13 Owen Bedwin, 'The excavation of the Church of Saint Nicholas, Angmering, West Sussex', *Bull. Inst. Archaeology*, 12 (1975), pp. 46–9.

14 Warwick Rodwell, 'The archaeological investigation of Hadstock Church, Essex. An interim report', *Antiq. J.*, 56 (1976), p. 65.

15 Salzman, op. cit., pp. 490–1.

16 Ibid., p. 503.

17 E. Clive Rouse, 'Bradwell Abbey and the Chapel of St Mary', *Milton Keynes J.*, 2 (1973), pp. 34–8; Dennis C. Mynard, 'Excavations at Bradwell Priory', ibid., 3 (1974), pp. 31–66.

18 D. U. Seth Smith and G. M. A. Cunnington (eds), 'An inventory of gifts to the Chapel of the Holy Sepulchre that was at Edington', *Wiltshire Arch. and Nat. Hist. Mag.*, 55 (1953–4), pp. 161–4.

19 Brian S. Smith, 'Little Waltham church goods, c. 1400', *Trans. Essex Arch. Soc.*, I (1961–5), pp. 111–13; for the church goods of St Mary-at-Hill, see Henry Littlehales (ed.), *The Medieval Records of a London City Church*, 2 vols, Early English Text Society, 125 (1904) and 128 (1905).

20 E. Clive Rouse, 'Wall paintings in the church of St Pega, Peakirk, Northamptonshire', *Arch. J.*, 110 (1953), pp. 144–7. For a useful general treatment of the links between folk religion and church art, see M. D. Anderson, *History and Imagery in British Churches*, 1971.

21 E. Clive Rouse, 'The Penn Doom', *Records of Buckinghamshire*, 17 (1961–5), pp. 95–103, and the same author's 'Wallpaintings in St Andrew's Church, Pickworth, Lincolnshire', *J. Brit. Arch. Assoc.*, 3rd series, 13 (1950), pp. 25–8.

22 Wilfrid Puddephat, 'The mural paintings of the Dance of Death in the guild chapel of Stratford-upon-Avon', *Trans. and Proc. Birmingham Arch. Soc.*, 76 (1958), pp. 29–35.

23 E. A. Gee, 'The painted glass of All Saints' Church, North Street, York', *Archaeologia*, 102 (1969), pp. 158–62 and plate XXIII.

24 Richard Marks, 'Henry Williams and his "Ymage of Deth" roundel at Stanford on Avon, Northamptonshire', *Antiq. J.*, 54 (1974), pp. 272–4 and plate LIV.

25 Norman Davis (ed.), *Paston Letters and Papers of the Fifteenth Century*, 1971, in particular pp. xliv–l. For a useful discussion of magnate foundations of this kind, see Joel T. Rosenthal, *The Purchase of Paradise*, 1972, chapter 4 (New Foundations).

26 For the foundation details of this hospital, see A. Hamilton Thompson, *The History of the Hospital and the New College of the Annunciation of St Mary in the Newarke, Leicester*, 1937.

27 These and some other examples are given by McFarlane, op. cit., p. 95.

28 David Josephson, 'In search of the historical Taverner', *Tempo*, 101 (1972), p. 41.

29 Recent excavations by the gatehouse at Tattershall are briefly reported in *Med. Arch.*, 12 (1968), pp. 168–9. For the castle and church at Tattershall, with a note on the college foundation, see *Arch. J.*, 131 (1974), pp. 317–22.

30 Hamilton Thompson, op. cit., p. 18.

31 Henry Hurst, 'Excavations at Gloucester, 1971–1973: second interim report', *Antiq. J.*, 54 (1974), pp. 41–6; A. C. Harrison, 'Excavations on the site of St Mary's Hospital, Strood', *Archaeologia Cantiana*, 84 (1969), pp. 139–60. For useful discussions of hospital plans, see Walter H. Godfrey, 'Some medieval hospitals of East Kent', *Arch. J.*, 86 (1929), pp. 99–110; S. E. Rigold, 'Two Kentish hospitals reexamined: S. Mary, Ospringe, and SS. Stephen and Thomas, New Romney', *Archaeologia Cantiana*, 79 (1964), pp. 31–69;

and especially Rotha Mary Clay, *The Mediaeval Hospitals of England*, 1909, pp. 112–25.

32 K. Jane Evans, 'The Maison Dieu, Arundel', *Sussex Arch. Coll.*, 107 (1969), pp. 65–78.

33 Denys Spittle, 'Browne's Hospital, Stamford', *Arch. J.*, 131 (1974), pp. 351–2.

34 *King's Works*, iii:196–206.

35 Quoted by Clay, op. cit., p. 120.

36 Salzman, op. cit., pp. 544–5.

37 Mackenzie E. C. Walcott, 'Inventories of St Mary's Hospital or Maison Dieu, Dover (etc.)', *Archaeologia Cantiana*, 7 (1868), pp. 273–80.

38 Hamilton Thompson, op. cit., pp. 180–5.

39 Francis W. Steer, 'The statutes of Saffron Walden almshouses', *Trans. Essex Arch. Soc.*, 25:2 (1958), pp. 166–7.

40 David Knowles, *The Religious Orders in England*, 1959, iii:13.

41 Ibid., p. 14.

42 Colin Platt, *Medieval Southampton*, 1973, p. 206.

43 Deirdre Le Faye, 'Selborne Priory, 1233–1486', *Proc. Hampshire Field Club and Arch. Soc.*, 30 (1973), p. 67.

44 Marjorie Morgan, *The English Lands of the Abbey of Bec*, 1968, p. 124.

45 C. F. Tebbutt, 'St Neots Priory', *Proc. Cambridge Antiquarian Soc.*, 59 (1966), p. 38.

46 Morgan, op. cit., pp. 124–6.

47 The point is made by K. B. McFarlane, *Lancastrian Kings and Lollard Knights*, 1972, pp. 190–1, contradicting the view of Professor David Knowles (op. cit., iii:164–5).

48 Morgan, op. cit., pp. 132–3.

49 Ibid., p. 124.

50 Eleanor Searle, *Lordship and Community*, 1974, p. 264.

51 David Owen, *Kirkstall Abbey Excavations 1950–1954*, Thoresby Society Publications, 43 (1955), pp. 73–5.

52 Eileen Power, *Medieval English Nunneries c. 1275 to 1535*, 1922, p. 216.

53 Ibid., p. 216.

54 R. B. Dobson, *Durham Priory 1400–1450*, 1973, pp. 303–4.

55 S. D. T. Spittle, 'Denney Abbey', *Arch. J.*, 124 (1967), pp. 232–4. The Minoresses had themselves moved from a short-lived foundation at Waterbeach, established in 1293–4 and abandoned for Denney between 1342 and 1351 (Mary D. Cra'ster, 'Waterbeach Abbey', *Proc. Cambridge Antiquarian Soc.*, 59 (1966), pp. 75–94).

56 Morgan, op. cit., p. 125.

57 Marjorie Morgan, 'Inventories of three small alien priories', *J. Brit. Arch. Assoc.*, 4th series, 3 (1939), pp. 141–9; A. J. Taylor, 'The alien priory of Minster Lovell', *Oxoniensia*, 2 (1937), pp. 103–17.

58 Stanley E. West, 'The excavation of Walton Priory', *Proc. Suffolk Inst. Arch.*, 33 (1975), pp. 131–52.

59 *Med. Arch.*, 14 (1970), p. 189; 15 (1971), pp. 161–2; 16 (1972), p. 193; and Dennis Mynard, personal communication.

60 *Med. Arch.*, 10 (1966), pp. 202–4, and Christine Mahany, personal communication.

61 Stephen Moorhouse, 'Medieval distilling-apparatus of glass and pottery', *Med. Arch.*, 16 (1972), pp. 79–121. For the important Stamford group, see the note in *Med. Arch.*, 15 (1971), p. 139.

62 The information on Mount Grace derives from a lecture delivered by Mr Laurence Keen at the Society for Medieval Archaeology's annual conference at York in April 1976. For the Tavistock printing press, see H. P. R. Finberg, *Tavistock Abbey. A Study in the Social and Economic History of Devon*, 1951 (reprinted 1969), pp. 290–3.

63 Andrew Gray, 'A Carthusian *Carta Visitationis* of the fifteenth century', *Bul. Inst. Hist. Res.*, 40 (1967), pp. 91–101.

64 Finberg, op. cit., pp. 186–7, 191.

65 Constance M. Fraser, 'The north-east coal trade until 1421', *Trans. Archit. and Arch. Soc. Durham and Northumberland*, 11 (1953–65), pp. 211–12.

66 Dobson, op. cit., pp. 156–62.

67 Ian Keil, 'Impropriator and benefice in the later Middle Ages', *Wiltshire Arch. and Nat. Hist. Mag.*, 58 (1961–3), pp. 351–61.

68 Ian Keil, 'A landlord in medieval Bristol', *Trans. Bristol and Gloucestershire Arch. Soc.*, 84 (1965), pp. 44–52, and the same author's 'London and Glastonbury Abbey in the later Middle Ages', *Trans. London and Middlesex Arch. Soc.*, 21 (1967), pp. 173–7.

69 L. F. Salzman, *Building in England down to 1540*, 1967, pp. 441-4, 446-8.

70 A. M. Erskine and D. Portman, 'The history of an Exeter tenement (229 High Street)', *Report and Trans. Devonshire Assoc.*, 92 (1960), pp. 142-57.

71 *Med. Arch.*, 12 (1968), p. 197.

72 Charles Green and A. B. Whittingham, 'Excavations at Walsingham Priory, Norfolk, 1961', *Arch. J.*, 125 (1968), pp. 261-6, 274-7.

73 R. A. L. Smith, *Canterbury Cathedral Priory*, 1943, p. 194.

74 L. R. Shelby, 'The role of the master mason in mediaeval English building', *Speculum*, 39 (1964), p. 391.

75 Dobson, op. cit., pp. 294-5.

76 Salzman, op. cit., pp. 473-7.

77 Power, op. cit., pp. 316-7.

78 David Owen, C. Vincent Bellamy and C. M. Mitchell, *Kirkstall Abbey Excavations 1955-1959*, Thoresby Society Publications, 48 (1959), pp. 1-11; for the kitchen, see Owen, op. cit. (1955), pp. 73-5.

79 David Knowles and J. K. St Joseph, *Monastic Sites from the Air*, 1952, pp. xxvi, 100-1.

80 Ibid., pp. 142-3, and R. Gilyard-Beere, *Cleeve Abbey* (H.M.S.O. guide), 1960.

81 D. H. S. Cranage, 'The monastery of St Milburge at Much Wenlock', *Archaeologia*, 72 (1922), pp. 118-28.

82 P. A. Faulkner, 'Ely: the monastic buildings south of the cloister', *Arch. J.*, 124 (1967), pp. 216-21; *Med. Arch.*, 5 (1961), pp. 314-5 (Rievaulx); P. A. Faulkner, 'A model of Castle Acre Priory', ibid., 6-7 (1962-3), pp. 300-3; David A. Hinton, 'Bicester Priory', *Oxoniensia*, 33 (1968), p. 37; *CBA Calendar of Excavations, Summaries 1975* (Bayham).

83 A. R. Myers (ed.), *English Historical Documents 1327-1485*, 1969, pp. 1146-50.

84 Power, op. cit., p. 320.

85 David Knowles, *The Religious Orders in England*, 1955, ii:182-4.

86 G. H. Rooke, 'Dom William Ingram and his account-book, 1504-1533', *J. Ecclesiastical History*, 7 (1956), pp. 36-7.

87 Mackenzie E. C. Walcott, 'Inventories of St Mary's Hospital or Maison Dieu, Dover (etc.)', *Archaeologia Cantiana*, 7 (1868), pp. 296-7.

88 W. A. Pantin, 'Minchery Farm, Littlemore', *Oxoniensia*, 35 (1970), pp. 19-26.

89 C. R. Peers, 'Finchale Priory', *Archaeologia Aeliana*, 4th series, 4 (1927), pp. 193-220.

Chapter 6 Conspicuous Waste

1 Owen Ashmore, 'The Whalley Abbey bursars' account for 1520', *Trans. Hist. Soc. Lancashire and Cheshire*, 114 (1962), pp. 51-2.

2 Eleanor Searle, *Lordship and Community*, 1974, p. 264.

3 R. B. Dobson, *Durham Priory 1400-1450*, 1973, pp. 290-1.

4 For these families, see especially J. M. W. Bean, *The Estates of the Percy Family 1416-1537*, 1958; J. R. Lander, 'Marriage and politics in the fifteenth century: the Nevilles and the Wydevilles', *Bul. Inst. Hist. Res.*, 36 (1963), pp. 119-52; J. T. Driver, 'The Mainwarings of Over Peover: a Cheshire family in the fifteenth and early sixteenth centuries', *J. Chester Arch. Soc.*, 57 (1970-1), pp. 27-40; A. Cameron, 'Sir Henry Willoughby of Wollaton', *Trans. Thoroton Soc.*, 74 (1970), pp. 10-21; J. Taylor, 'The Plumpton letters, 1416-1552', *Northern History*, 10 (1975), pp. 72-87.

5 Lander, op. cit., p. 120.

6 K. B. McFarlane, *The Nobility of Later Medieval England*, 1973, pp. 92-3.

7 The point, in criticism of McFarlane, is made by A. R. Bridbury, *Economic Growth. England in the Later Middle Ages*, 1975 (2nd edn), pp. xxii-xxiii.

8 Bean, op. cit., p. 105.

9 R. I. Jack (ed.), *The Grey of Ruthin Valor*, 1965, p. 57.

10 L. S. Woodger, *Henry Bourgchier, earl of Essex, and his family (1408-83)*, Oxford D. Phil. thesis, 1974, p. 237.

11 Ibid., pp. 241-2.

12 For the siege of Caister, after Fastolf's death, see John H. Harvey, *William Worcestre Itineraries*, 1969, pp. 187-91, and Norman Davis, *Paston Letters and Papers of the Fifteenth Century*, 1971, pp. 340-7, 398-409, 541-8. For Raglan, see Anthony Emery, 'The development of Raglan Castle and keeps in late medieval England', *Arch. J.*, 132 (1975), pp. 151-86. The troubles at

Tattershall are discussed by Roger Virgoe, 'William Tailboys and Lord Cromwell: crime and politics in Lancastrian England', *Bul. John Rylands Library*, 55 (1972–3), pp. 459–82, and R. L. Storey, 'Lincolnshire and the Wars of the Roses', *Nottingham Medieval Studies*, 14 (1970), pp. 77–8.

13 K. B. McFarlane, 'The investment of Sir John Fastolf's profits of war', *T.R.H.S.*, 5th series, 7 (1957), p. 104.

14 Terence Paul Smith, 'Rye House, Hertfordshire, and aspects of early brickwork in England', *Arch. J.*, 132 (1975), pp. 111–50.

15 A. D. K. Hawkyard, *Some late-medieval fortified manor houses; a study of the building works of Sir John Fastolf, Ralph, Lord Cromwell, and Edward Stafford, third duke of Buckingham*, Keele M. A. thesis, 1969, pp. 13–14.

16 Ibid., pp. 35–6, 37–8.

17 McFarlane, op. cit. (1957), passim.

18 H. D. Barnes and W. Douglas Simpson, 'Caister Castle', *Antiq. J.*, 32 (1952), pp. 35–51.

19 W. Douglas Simpson (ed.), *The Building Accounts of Tattershall Castle 1434–1472*, Lincoln Record Society, 55 (1960), pp. xx–xxiii.

20 For local brick production, see Douglas Simpson, op. cit., p. 44 (Tattershall), and S. E. Glendenning's note on the Caister bricks in H. D. Barnes and W. Douglas Simpson, 'The building accounts of Caister Castle A.D. 1432–1435', *Norfolk Archaeology*, 30 (1947–52), pp. 186–8.

21 Smith, op. cit., passim.

22 Sir Charles Peers, *Kirby Muxloe Castle, Leicestershire* (H.M.S.O. guide), 1957, pp. 12–13. For such brick-building in general, see also Jane A. Wight, *Brick Building in England from the Middle Ages to 1550*, 1972, pp. 116–35.

23 *King's Works*, i:246–7; Michael Thompson, 'The construction of the manor at South Wingfield, Derbyshire', in G. de G. Sieveking, I. H. Longworth and K. E. Wilson (eds), *Problems in Economic and Social Archaeology*, 1976, pp. 417–38.

24 For a useful account of the building up of the archbishop's interests at Knole, see F. R. H. Du Boulay, 'The assembling of an estate: Knole in Sevenoaks, c. 1275 to

c. 1525', *Archaeologia Cantiana*, 89 (1974), pp. 1–10.

25 Martin Biddle, Lawrence Barfield and Alan Millard, 'The excavation of the Manor of the More, Rickmansworth, Hertfordshire', *Arch. J.*, 116 (1959), in particular pp. 150–4.

26 James Orchard Halliwell (ed.), *A Chronicle of the First Thirteen Years of the Reign of King Edward the Fourth, by John Warkworth, D.D.*, Camden Society, 1839, p. 25.

27 The inventory, as presented by Thomas Amyot in a communication to the Society of Antiquaries of London, was later published in *Archaeologia*, 21 (1827), pp. 232–80.

28 Halliwell, op. cit., p. 26.

29 McFarlane, op. cit. (1957), pp. 108–9.

30 John Cherry, 'The Dunstable swan jewel', *J. Brit. Arch. Assoc.*, 32 (1969), pp. 38–53.

31 Joan Evans, E. T. Leeds and Anthony Thompson, 'A hoard of gold rings and silver groats found near Thame, Oxfordshire', *Antiq. J.*, 21 (1941), pp. 197–202, recently redated by John Cherry (*Archaeologia*, 104 (1973), pp. 320–1).

32 John Cherry, 'The medieval jewellery from the Fishpool, Nottinghamshire, hoard', *Archaeologia*, 104 (1973), pp. 307–21.

33 Barbara Ross, *The accounts of the Talbot household at Blakemere in the county of Shropshire, 1394–1425*, Australian National University M.A. thesis, 1970, pp. 76, 100. I owe this reference to my colleague Mr T. B. Pugh.

34 Ibid., p. 99.

35 Ibid., p. 80.

36 C. D. Ross, 'The household accounts of Elizabeth Berkeley, Countess of Warwick, 1420–1', *Trans. Bristol and Gloucestershire Arch. Soc.*, 70 (1951), pp. 81–105.

37 Eleanor Searle and Barbara Ross (eds), *The Cellarers' Rolls of Battle Abbey 1275–1513*, Sussex Record Society, 65 (1967), p. 22; Ian Keil, 'London and Glastonbury Abbey in the Later Middle Ages', *Trans. London and Middlesex Arch. Soc.*, 21 (1967), pp. 173–7.

38 For the Canterbury evidence, see F. R. H. Du Boulay, 'The Pagham estates of the archbishops of Canterbury during the fifteenth century', *History*, 38 (1953), p. 207.

39 Searle and Ross, op. cit., p. 18.

40 M. L. Ryder, 'The animal remains found at

Kirkstall Abbey', *Agric. Hist. Rev.*, 7 (1959), pp. 1–5, and the same author's report on the bones from Kirkstall, published in David E. Owen, C. V. Bellamy and C. M. Mitchell, *Kirkstall Abbey Excavations 1955–1959*, Thoresby Society Publications, 48 (1959), pp. 41–54, 67–77, 98–100.

41 Searle and Ross, op. cit., p. 19.

42 Ryder, op. cit., p. 3.

43 P. L. Drewett, 'Excavations at Hadleigh Castle, Essex, 1971–1972', *J. Brit. Arch. Assoc.*, 3rd series, 38 (1975), p. 148.

44 Ibid., pp. 149–50.

45 P. A. Rahtz, *Excavations at King John's Hunting Lodge, Writtle, Essex, 1955–57*, 1969, pp. 114–15.

46 M. L. Ryder, 'Animal remains from Wharram Percy', *Yorkshire Arch. J.*, 46 (1974), p. 50; Colin Platt and Richard Coleman-Smith, *Excavations in Medieval Southampton 1953–1969*, 1975, i:332–43.

47 Ryder, op. cit. (1974), p. 50, and the same author's 'The animal remains from Petergate, York, 1957–58', *Yorkshire Arch. J.*, 42 (1967–70), p. 419.

48 R. H. Hilton and P. A. Rahtz, 'Upton, Gloucestershire, 1959–1964', *Trans. Bristol and Gloucestershire Arch. Soc.*, 85 (1966), pp. 139–43.

49 Platt and Coleman-Smith, op. cit., i:33, 342–4.

50 K. L. Wood-Legh (ed.), *A Small Household of the XVth Century, being the Account Book of Munden's Chantry, Bridport*, 1956, pp. xxiv–xxv.

51 C. D. Ross, op. cit., p. 101.

52 J. M. Steane, 'The medieval fishponds of Northamptonshire', *Northamptonshire Past and Present*, 4 (1966–9), p. 304.

53 C. F. Hickling, 'Prior More's fishponds', *Med. Arch.*, 15 (1971), pp. 118–23.

54 Quoted by Margaret Wade Labarge, *A Baronial Household of the Thirteenth Century*, 1965, p. 81.

55 A. J. F. Dulley, 'The early history of the Rye fishing industry', *Sussex Arch. Coll.*, 107 (1969), p. 54.

56 Peter Heath, 'North Sea fishing in the fifteenth century: the Scarborough fleet', *Northern History*, 3 (1968), pp. 61–2.

57 Thomas Wright (ed.), *Alexandri Neckam. De Naturis Rerum*, Rolls Series, 34 (1863),

p. lxi. The translation used here is Thomas Wright's own abbreviated version of Neckam's passage on gardens; for the full Latin text, see pp. 274–5.

58 T. J. Hunt and Ian Keil, 'Two medieval gardens', *Proc. Somersetshire Arch. and Nat. Hist. Soc.*, 104 (1959/60), pp. 91–101.

59 Wood-Legh, op. cit., pp. xxv–xxvii.

60 Platt and Coleman-Smith, op. cit., i:344–6.

61 *Med. Arch.*, 14 (1970), p. 183.

62 Breandán Ó Ríordáin, 'Excavations at High Street and Winetavern Street, Dublin', *Med. Arch.*, 15 (1971), p. 77.

63 Wright, op. cit., pp. lxi, 274–5.

64 D. Gay Wilson, 'Plant foods and poisons from mediaeval Chester', *J. Chester Arch. Soc.*, 58 (1975), pp. 55–67.

65 Platt and Coleman-Smith, op. cit., i-32–3.

66 Colin Platt, *The English Medieval Town*, 1976, pp. 48–50.

67 *Med. Arch.*, 18 (1974), pp. 198, 205.

68 Tim Tatton-Brown, 'Excavations at the Custom House site, City of London, 1973', *Trans. London and Middlesex Arch. Soc.*, 25 (1974), pp. 117–219, and the same author's 'Excavations at the Custom House site, City of London, 1973 – part 2', ibid., 26 (1975), pp. 103–70. For the Seal House and Trig Lane excavations, as reported by John Schofield and Mark Harrison respectively, see *Current Archaeology*, 49 (1975), pp. 54–9.

69 A. J. F. Dulley, 'Excavations at Pevensey, Sussex, 1962–6', *Med. Arch.*, 11 (1967), pp. 209–32; Helen Parker, 'A medieval wharf in Thoresby College courtyard, King's Lynn', ibid., 9 (1965), pp. 94–104; *Archaeological Excavations 1972*, pp. 80–1 (Harwich); ibid. *1973*, p. 86 (Lincoln); ibid. *1970*, p. 77 (Portsmouth), and Elizabeth Lewis, personal communication.

70 L. F. Salzman, *Building in England down to 1540*, 1967, pp. 434–5, 501–3. Salzman also publishes a contract, dated 1389, for the construction of a stone wharf at the Tower of London, financed by the king (pp. 469–70).

71 Caroline M. Barron, *The Medieval Guildhall of London*, 1974, passim.

72 Margaret Statham, 'The Guildhall, Bury St Edmunds', *Proc. Suffolk Inst. Arch.*, 31 (1967–9), pp. 120–31. A contract for the rebuilding of Canterbury Guildhall in 1438

has been printed by Salzman, op. cit., (pp. 510–12). This and two other public halls, at Fordwich and Milton Regis, are discussed by S. E. Rigold, 'Two types of court hall', *Archaeologia Cantiana*, 83 (1968), pp. 1–22.

73 Colin Platt, *Medieval Southampton*, 1973, in particular chs 12 and 14.

74 For examples of such internal garderobes at Southampton, see Platt and Coleman-Smith, op. cit., i:101 (111 High Street), 111 (11 and 13 St Michael's Square), 274–5 (Winkle Street); for the Exeter examples, see D. Portman, *Exeter Houses 1400–1700*, 1966, pp. 15–16, 63–4, 82–3.

75 A. Carter, J. P. Roberts and Helena Sutermeister, 'Excavations in Norwich – 1973. The Norwich Survey – third interim report', *Norfolk Archaeology*, 36 (1974), pp. 39–71.

76 John H. Harvey, 'Great Milton, Oxfordshire; and Thorncroft, Surrey. The building accounts for two manor-houses of the late fifteenth century', *J. Brit. Arch. Assoc.*, 3rd series, 18 (1955), pp. 42–56; the Great Milton contracts of 1474 are published also by Salzman, op. cit., pp. 599–600.

77 S. R. Jones and J. T. Smith, 'Manor Farm, Wasperton: an early fourteenth-century timber-framed house', *Trans. and Proc. Birmingham Arch. Soc.*, 76 (1958), pp. 19–28.

78 Guy Beresford, 'The Old Manor, Askett', *Records of Buckinghamshire*, 18 (1966–70), pp. 343–66.

79 Margaret Wood, 'Ashbury Manor, Berkshire', *Trans. Newbury District Field Club*, 11:3 (1965), pp. 5–11.

80 N. W. Alcock and Michael Laithwaite, 'Medieval houses in Devon and their modernization', *Med. Arch*, 17 (1973), pp. 100–25; Eric R. Swain, 'Divided and galleried hall-houses', ibid., 12 (1968), pp. 127–45.

81 Eric Mercer, *English Vernacular Houses. A study of traditional farmhouses and cottages*, 1975, pp. 13, 178.

82 M. W. Barley, *The English Farmhouse and Cottage*, 1961, pp. 33–4.

83 J. T. Smith, 'The evolution of the English peasant house to the late seventeenth century: the evidence of buildings', *J. Brit. Arch. Assoc.*, 33 (1970), p. 146.

84 F. R. H. Du Boulay, *The Lordship of Canterbury*, 1966, pp. 218–37, and the same author's 'Who were farming the English demesnes at the end of the Middle Ages?', *Ec.H.R.*, 2nd series, 17 (1964–5), pp. 443–55. For a recently excavated example of the possibly post-plague decay of a manorial dovecote, presumably because it had become surplus, see the excavations at Clapham, Bedfordshire (*Med. Arch.*, 20 (1976), p. 193).

85 S. E. Rigold, 'Yardhurst, Daniel's Water', *Arch. J.*, 126 (1969), pp. 267–8.

86 Frank Atkinson and R. W. McDowall, 'Aisled houses in the Halifax area', *Antiq. J.*, 47 (1967), pp. 77–94; also Mercer, op. cit., pp. 14–16. For the discussion of a similar gentry house in the area, see T. G. Manby, 'Lees Hall, Thornhill, a medieval timber-framed building in the West Riding of Yorkshire', *Yorkshire Arch. J.*, 43 (1971), pp. 112–27.

87 Barbara Hutton, 'Timber-framed houses in the Vale of York', *Med. Arch.*, 17 (1973), pp. 87–99. For a recent map of these northern aisled halls, together with other previously known examples in the south and the west, see Kathleen Sandall, 'Aisled halls in England and Wales', *Vernacular Archit.*, 6 (1975), pp. 19–27.

88 Smith, op. cit., p. 132; and see also Mercer, op. cit., pp. 17–19.

Chapter 7 Reorientation under the Tudors

1 D. M. Metcalf, *Coins of Henry VII*, Sylloge of Coins of the British Isles 23, 1976, pp. xvi–xvii, xxxvii.

2 *King's Works*, ii:793–804.

3 B. H. St J. O'Neil, 'Dartmouth Castle and other defences of Dartmouth Haven', *Archaeologia*, 85 (1936), p. 143.

4 John Gough Nichols (ed.), *The Chronicle of Calais*, Camden Society, 35 (1846), pp. 125–9. I am most grateful to John Kenyon for bringing this passage to my attention.

5 G. de Boer, 'The two earliest maps of Hull', *Post-Med. Arch.*, 7 (1973), pp. 79–87. The excavation of the central fort in the defensive line, built to Henry's order on this

occasion, has been reported briefly in the same journal (5 (1971), pp. 198–201).

6 Martin Biddle, 'Nonsuch Palace 1959–60: an interim report', *Surrey Arch. Coll.*, 58 (1961), pp. 11–13.

7 H. S. Ames, 'A note on the results of recent excavations at Camber Castle, Sussex', *Post-Med. Arch.*, 9 (1975), pp. 233–6.

8 Victor T. C. Smith, 'The artillery defences at Gravesend', *Archaeologia Cantiana*, 89 (1974), pp. 141–68.

9 T. J. Miles, and A. D. Saunders, 'King Charles's Castle, Tresco, Scilly', *Post-Med. Arch.*, 4 (1970), pp. 1–30. For the Portsmouth defences, see A. D. Saunders, 'Hampshire coastal defence since the introduction of artillery, with a description of Fort Wallington', *Arch. J.*, 123 (1966), pp. 141–2.

10 Iain MacIvor, 'The Elizabethan fortifications of Berwick-upon-Tweed', *Antiq. J.*, 45 (1965), pp. 64–96.

11 The phrase is Girolamo Lando's (*Calendar of State Papers, Venetian, 1621–1623*, p. 430).

12 C. E. Challis, 'The debasement of the coinage, 1542–1551', *Ec.H.R.*, 2nd series, 20 (1967), pp. 441–66; and see also, for a more general view, J. D. Gould's *The Great Debasement. Currency and the Economy in Mid-Tudor England*, 1970.

13 Edwin Welch, 'Some Suffolk Lollards', *Proc. Suffolk Inst. Arch.*, 29 (1961–3), pp. 154–65.

14 David Knowles, *The Religious Orders in England*, 1955, ii:175–84.

15 *King's Works*, iii:195–6.

16 A. Cameron, 'Sir Henry Willoughby of Wollaton', *Trans. Thoroton Soc.*, 74 (1970), p. 19.

17 J. A. F. Thomson, *Clergy and laity in London, 1376–1531*, Oxford D. Phil. thesis, 1960, pp. 198–204, summarized in the same author's 'Piety and charity in late medieval London', *J. Ecclesiastical History*, 16 (1965), pp. 189–90.

18 N. P. Tanner, *Popular religion in Norwich with special reference to the evidence of wills, 1370–1532*, Oxford D. Phil. thesis, 1973, pp. 230–4, 242–4.

19 Ibid., pp. 234–5.

20 G. H. Rooke, 'Dom William Ingram and his account-book, 1504–1533', *J. Eccles-iastical History*, 7 (1956), pp. 31–2.

21 Quoted by Aubrey Gwynn, *The English Austin Friars in the Time of Wyclif*, 1940, p. 74.

22 David Knowles and W. F. Grimes, *Charterhouse. The Medieval Foundation in the Light of Recent Discoveries*, 1954, pp. 5–6.

23 H. M. Colvin, 'The building of St. Bernard's College', *Oxoniensia*, 24 (1959), pp. 40–1.

24 Owen Ashmore, 'The Whalley Abbey bursars' account for 1520', *Trans. Hist. Soc. Lancashire and Cheshire*, 114 (1962), p. 61.

25 Gwynn, op. cit., p. 75.

26 J. H. E. Bennett, 'The Black Friars of Chester', *J. Chester and North Wales Archit., Arch. and Hist. Soc.*, 39 (1952), pp. 48–9.

27 For examples of hostility to individual friaries, see Colin Platt, *Medieval Southampton*, 1973, p. 66; Jennifer Barber, 'New light on the Plymouth friaries', *Report and Trans. Devonshire Assoc.*, 105 (1973), pp. 61–3.

28 *Med. Arch.*, 2 (1958), pp. 191–2, 3 (1959), p. 305; Knowles and Grimes, op. cit., pp. 74–82.

29 K. B. McFarlane, *Lancastrian Kings and Lollard Knights*, 1972, p. 225 and passim.

30 Tanner, op. cit., pp. 254–7.

31 A. G. Dickens, *Lollards and Protestants in the Diocese of York 1509–1558*, 1959, pp. 24–7.

32 G. W. O. Woodward, 'The exemption from suppression of certain Yorkshire priories', *E.H.R.*, 76 (1961), pp. 385–401.

33 Thomas Fuller, *The Church History of England*, 1655, vi:358, quoted by David Knowles, *The Religious Orders in England*, 1959, iii:386.

34 J. C. Dickinson, 'The buildings of the English Austin canons after the dissolution of the monasteries', *J. Brit. Arch. Assoc.*, 31 (1968), p. 72.

35 Michael Sherbrook, *The Fall of Religious Houses*, in A. G. Dickens (ed.), *Tudor Treatises*, Yorkshire Arch. Soc. Record Series, 125 (1959), p. 123.

36 Philip Rahtz and Susan Hirst, *Bordesley Abbey*, British Arch. Reports 23, 1976, pp. 22, 74.

37 G. C. Dunning, 'A lead ingot at Rievaulx Abbey', *Antiq. J.*, 32 (1952), pp. 199–202.

38 *Med. Arch.*, 6–7 (1962–3), pp. 313–5 (Durham); ibid., 17 (1973), p. 155 (Northampton); Dunning, op. cit., p. 202 (Fountains and Muchelney); *Med. Arch.*, 10 (1966), pp. 177–8 (Sopwell); ibid., 16 (1972), p. 176 (Pontefract).

39 Dunning, op. cit., p. 202.

40 C. Vincent Bellamy, *Pontefract Priory Excavations 1957–1961*, Thoresby Society Publications, 49 (1962–4), pp. 48, 58, 122–3.

41 *Med. Arch.*, 8 (1964), p. 242, 9 (1965), p. 179, and 10 (1966), pp. 177–80.

42 Sir Henry Spelman, *The History and Fate of Sacrilege*, 1632 (published posthumously in 1698), chapter VI.

43 David Knowles and J. K. St Joseph, *Monastic Sites from the Air*, 1952, pp. 144–5, 265–6. For another example of former abbot's lodgings converted to form the elements of a new mansion, see the recent excavations at Norton Priory, Cheshire (*Post-Med. Arch.*, 10 (1976), p. 168).

44 Knowles and St Joseph, op. cit., pp. 136–7, 180–1, and the H.M.S.O. guides of 1953 (Netley) and 1969 (Titchfield), amended respectively in 1973 and 1974.

45 Knowles and St Joseph, op. cit., pp. 146–7.

46 Dickinson, op. cit., p. 68.

47 A. D. Saunders, 'Blackfriars (Gloucester)', *Arch. J.*, 122 (1965), pp. 217–19.

48 The words are John Leland's, quoted by Knowles, op. cit., iii:387.

49 Sherbrook, op. cit., p. 125.

50 A. G. Dickens, *The English Reformation*, 1967 (revised edn), p. 300.

51 Peter Heath, *Medieval Clerical Accounts*, St Anthony's Hall Publications 26, 1964; J. F. Fuggles, 'The parish clergy in the archdeaconry of Leicester 1520–1540', *Trans. Leicestershire Arch. and Hist. Soc.*, 46 (1970–1), pp. 25–44; Margaret Bowker, *The Secular Clergy in the Diocese of Lincoln 1495–1520*, 1968, and Peter Heath, *The English Parish Clergy on the Eve of the Reformation*, 1969.

52 Margaret Bowker, 'Non-residence in the Lincoln diocese in the early sixteenth century', *J. Ecclesiastical History*, 15 (1964), pp. 40–50.

53 R. L. Storey, *Diocesan Administration in Fifteenth-Century England*, Borthwick Papers 16, 1972, p. 32.

54 D. M. Palliser, 'The unions of parishes at York, 1547–1586', *Yorkshire Arch. J.*, 46 (1974), pp. 87–102.

55 J. W. F. Hill, *Tudor and Stuart Lincoln*, 1956, pp. 20–1, 56–8.

56 Alan Rogers, 'Parish boundaries and urban history. Two case studies', *J. Brit. Arch. Assoc.*, 3rd series, 35 (1972), p. 56.

57 Jennifer Barber, 'New light on the Plymouth friaries', *Report and Trans. Devonshire Assoc.*, 105 (1973), p. 64.

58 Colin Platt, *Medieval Southampton*, 1973, pp. 211–12.

59 A. L. Rowse, *Tudor Cornwall*, 1969, ch. XI.

60 Christopher Haigh, *Reformation and Resistance in Tudor Lancashire*, 1975, ch. 12.

61 Quoted, in a very useful general discussion of Edwardian and Elizabethan church reforms, by G. W. O. Addleshaw and Frederick Etchells, *The Architectural Setting of Anglican Worship*, 1948, p. 25.

62 Jack Simmons, 'Brooke Church, Rutland, with notes on Elizabethan church-building', *Trans. Leicestershire Arch. and Hist. Soc.*, 35 (1959), p. 43; Addleshaw and Etchells, op. cit., pp. 35–6.

63 William Addison, 'Parish church dedications in Essex', *Trans. Essex Arch. Soc.*, 2 (1966–70), p. 44.

64 J. R. Beresford, 'The churchwardens' accounts of Holy Trinity, Chester, 1532 to 1633', *J. Chester and North Wales Archit., Arch. and Hist. Soc.*, 38 (1951), pp. 95–172.

65 T. H. Swales, 'Opposition to the suppression of the Norfolk monasteries; expressions of discontent; the Walsingham conspiracy', *Norfolk Archaeology*, 33 (1962–5), pp. 254–65.

66 Joyce Youings, 'The Monasteries', in Joan Thirsk (ed.), *The Agrarian History of England and Wales, 1500–1640*, 1967, p. 317.

67 G. Elliott, 'The system of cultivation and evidence of enclosure in the Cumberland open fields in the 16th century', *Trans. Cumberland and Westmorland Antiq. and Arch. Soc.*, 59 (1959), p. 100.

68 John Kew, 'The disposal of crown lands and the Devon land market, 1536–58', *Agric. Hist. Rev.*, 18 (1970), pp. 93–105.

69 Lawrence Stone, 'Social mobility in England, 1500–1700', *Past and Present*, 33

(1966), pp. 29–36.

70 J. R. Ravensdale, 'Landbeach in 1549: Ket's Rebellion in miniature', in Lionel M. Munby (ed.), *East Anglian Studies*, 1968, pp. 94–116.

71 Barbara Harris, 'Landlords and tenants in England in the later Middle Ages: the Buckingham estates', *Past and Present*, 43 (1969), pp. 146–50; for the fifteenth-century material, see Christopher Dyer, 'A redistribution of incomes in fifteenth-century England?', ibid., 39 (1968), pp. 11–33.

72 For a recent powerful restatement of this argument, see Eric Kerridge, *Agrarian Problems in the Sixteenth Century and After*, 1969, passim.

73 William Rollinson, 'The lost villages and hamlets of Low Furness', *Trans. Cumberland and Westmorland Antiq. and Arch. Soc.*, 63 (1963), pp. 160–9.

74 Youings, op. cit., p. 317.

75 Mervyn James, *Family, Lineage, and Civil Society. A Study of Society, Politics, and Mentality in the Durham Region, 1500–1640*, 1974, p. 81; David Marcombe, 'The Durham dean and chapter: old abbey writ large?', in Rosemary O'Day and Felicity Heal (eds), *Continuity and Change. Personnel and Administration of the Church in England 1500–1642*, 1976, pp. 125–44.

76 James, op. cit., p. 77.

77 H. Thorpe, 'The lord and the landscape, illustrated through the changing fortunes of a Warwickshire parish, Wormleighton', *Trans. and Proc. Birmingham Arch. Soc.*, 80 (1962), pp. 38–77.

78 J. T. Cliffe, *The Yorkshire Gentry from the Reformation to the Civil War*, 1969, p. 37.

79 Kerridge, op. cit., pp. 99–102; Julian Cornwall, 'Agricultural improvement, 1560–1640', *Sussex Arch. Coll.*, 98 (1960), pp. 126–7.

80 Cornwall, op. cit., pp. 119–26.

81 For a characteristically powerful revisionary view on the subject of agricultural improvements in this century, see A. R. Bridbury, 'Sixteenth-century farming', *Ec.H.R.*, 2nd series, 27 (1974), pp. 538–56.

82 Julian Cornwall, 'The squire of Conisholme', in C. W. Chalklin and M. A. Havinden (eds), *Rural Change and Urban Growth 1500–1800*, 1974, pp. 32–53.

83 A. C. Chibnall (ed.), *The Certificate of Musters for Buckinghamshire in 1522*, 1973, p. 25.

84 Margaret Spufford, *Contrasting Communities. English Villagers in the Sixteenth and Seventeenth Centuries*, 1974, pp. 46–57.

85 J. P. Cooper, 'The social distribution of land and men in England, 1436–1700', in Roderick Floud (ed.), *Essays in Quantitative Economic History*, 1974, p. 116.

86 Julian Cornwall, 'The people of Rutland in 1522', *Trans. Leicestershire Arch. and Hist. Soc.*, 37 (1961–2), pp. 7–28.

87 John Sheail, 'The distribution of taxable population and wealth in England during the early sixteenth century', *Trans. Inst. British Geographers*, 55 (1972), pp. 111–26, developed more fully in the fine series of regional maps included with Dr Sheail's unpublished *The regional distribution of wealth in England as indicated by the 1524/5 lay subsidy returns*, London Ph.D. thesis, 1968.

88 W. G. Hoskins, *Essays in Leicestershire History*, 1950, p. 130; Spufford, op. cit., p. 36.

89 Georges Edelen (ed.), *The Description of England by William Harrison*, Folger Documents of Tudor and Stuart Civilization, 1968, pp. 200–3.

90 W. G. Hoskins, *Provincial England*, 1965, pp. 131–48.

91 Derek Portman, 'Vernacular building in the Oxford region in the sixteenth and seventeenth centuries', in C. W. Chalklin and M. A. Havinden (eds), *Rural Change and Urban Growth 1500–1800*, 1974, p. 150.

92 Mary Dewar (ed.), *A Discourse of the Commonweal of this Realm of England, attributed to Sir Thomas Smith*, Folger Documents of Tudor and Stuart Civilization, 1969, pp. 83–4.

93 Gwyn I. Meirion-Jones, 'The domestic buildings of Selborne', *Proc. Hampshire Field Club and Arch. Soc.*, 29 (1972), pp. 25–6.

94 R. W. Brunskill, 'Three medieval manor-houses of North Westmorland', *Trans. Cumberland and Westmorland Antiq. and Arch. Soc.*, 56 (1956), pp. 83–6.

95 Peter Smith, *Houses of the Welsh Countryside*, 1975, pp. 147–9, 264–81.

96 M. W. Barley, 'Farmhouses and cottages,

1550–1725', *Ec.H.R.*, 2nd series, 7 (1954–5), p. 300; also C. A. Hewett's handsomely illustrated 'The development of the post-medieval house', *Post-Med. Arch.*, 7 (1973), pp. 60–78.

97 For one of the most recent of these, see Philip Crummy's useful 'Portreeve's House, Colchester, and a method of modernizing Essex houses in the sixteenth and seventeenth centuries', *Post-Med. Arch.*, 10 (1976), pp. 89–103.

98 Denys Spittle, 'Giffords Hall, Stoke by Nayland', *Proc. Suffolk Inst. Arch.*, 30 (1964–6), pp. 183–7; Ernest R. Sandeen, 'The building of Redgrave Hall, 1545–1554', ibid., 29 (1961–3), pp. 1–33.

99 P. S. Spokes and E. M. Jope, 'The "Priory", Marcham, Berkshire: a small 16th century house', *Berkshire Arch. J.*, 57 (1959), pp. 86–97.

100 *Med. Arch.*, 18 (1974), pp. 216–17.

101 John Fletcher, 'Three medieval farmhouses in Harwell', *Berkshire Arch. J.*, 62 (1965–6), pp. 45–69; Guy Beresford, 'Northend Farm House, Long Crendon', *Records of Buckinghamshire*, 18 (1966–70), pp. 125–35.

102 Barley, op. cit., pp. 294–8; but see also J. T. Smith, 'The evolution of the English peasant house to the late seventeenth century: the evidence of buildings', *J. Brit. Arch. Assoc.*, 33 (1970), pp. 136–9, and Portman, op. cit., pp. 152–3.

103 M. A. Havinden (ed.), *Household and Farm Inventories in Oxfordshire, 1550–1590*, Oxfordshire Record Society, 1965, pp. 27–34; W. G. Hoskins, *Essays in Leicestershire History*, 1950, pp. 154–9; David G. Hey, *An English Rural Community. Myddle under the Tudors and Stuarts*, 1974, pp. 124–5.

104 Havinden, op. cit., pp. 33–4.

105 Lawrence Stone, 'The inflation of honours 1558–1641', *Past and Present*, 14 (1958), pp. 45–70.

106 James, op. cit., p. 16; Peter Smith, op. cit., p. 243 and plate 72.

107 Edelen, op. cit., pp. 277, 279.

108 Malcolm Airs, *The Making of the English Country House 1500–1640*, 1975, pp. 3, 5–6.

109 Ibid., pp. 4, 7.

110 Norman Summers, 'Old Hall Farm, Kneesall', *Trans. Thoroton Soc.*, 76 (1972), pp. 17–25. For a useful general discussion of terracotta as a building material in sixteenth-century England, see Jane A. Wight, *Brick Building in England from the Middle Ages to 1550*, 1972, pp. 178–97. More terracotta moulded fragments have recently been found at excavations at Priory Manor, Great Cressingham, Norfolk (*Post-Med. Arch.*, 3 (1969), pp. 196–7).

111 Martin Biddle, 'Nonsuch Palace 1959–60: an interim report', *Surrey Arch. Coll.*, 58 (1961), pp. 1–20.

112 Colin Platt, *The Monastic Grange in Medieval England*, 1969, pp. 168–9, 182.

113 Hugh Tait, 'Two Renaissance tiles from Lacock Abbey, Wilts', *Antiq. J.*, 50 (1970), p. 347 and plate LX. For one of the last of these late-medieval tile-making concerns, see D. C. Mynard, 'The Little Brickhill tile kilns and their products', *J. Brit. Arch. Assoc.*, 3rd series, 38 (1975), pp. 55–80.

114 For a particularly useful account of the building of Hatfield House, strictly a Stuart mansion, see Lawrence Stone, *Family and Fortune. Studies in Aristocratic Finance in the Sixteenth and Seventeenth Centuries*, 1973, chapter 2; Helen Miller, 'Subsidy assessments of the peerage in the sixteenth century', *Bul. Inst. Hist. Research*, 28 (1955), pp. 15–34.

115 For the Willoughbys, see A. Cameron, 'Sir Henry Willoughby of Wollaton', *Trans. Thoroton Soc.*, 74 (1970), pp. 10–21, and the two papers by R. S. Smith in the same journal: 'A woad growing project at Wollaton in the 1580s', ibid., 65 (1961), pp. 27–46, and 'Glass-making at Wollaton in the early seventeenth century', ibid., 66 (1962), pp. 24–34. For the Eyres, see Rosamond Meredith, 'The Eyres of Hassop, 1470–1640', *Derbyshire Arch. J.*, 84 (1964), pp. 1–51, and 85 (1965), pp. 44–91.

116 Spufford, op. cit., pp. 21, 25.

117 Hey, op. cit., pp. 32–6.

118 V. H. T. Skipp, 'Economic and social change in the Forest of Arden, 1530–1649', *Agric. Hist. Rev.*, 18 (1970) supplement, pp. 107–8.

119 *Post-Med. Arch.*, 10 (1976), p. 165, and Alan Carter, personal communication; also M. W. Atkin and A. Carter, 'Excavations in Norwich – 1975/6. The Norwich Survey – fifth interim report', *Norfolk Archaeology*, 36 (1976), pp. 198–200.

120 W. G. Hoskins, *Provincial England*, 1965, p. 188 (Wigston Magna); Margaret Spufford, *A Cambridgeshire Community. Chippenham from Settlement to Enclosure*, 1965, pp. 44–5.

121 This appears to have been the case, for example, in the Forest of Arden (Skipp, op. cit., p. 107).

122 For these, see R. S. Smith's papers in *Trans. Thoroton Soc.*, 65 (1961) and 66 (1962).

123 David Crossley, 'Glassmaking in Bagot's Park, Staffordshire, in the sixteenth century', *Post-Med. Arch.*, 1 (1967), pp. 44–83. For recent surveys of the industry as a whole, see the same author's 'The performance of the glass industry in sixteenth-century England', *Ec.H.R.*, 2nd series, 25 (1972), pp. 421–33, and Eleanor S. Godfrey's comprehensive *The Development of English Glassmaking 1560–1640*, 1975.

124 *Post-Med. Arch.*, 2 (1968), p. 191; 3 (1969), pp. 204–5; 4 (1970), p. 186; 8 (1974), pp. 132–4.

125 N. P. Bridgewater, 'Glasshouse Farm, St Weonards: a small glassworking site', *Trans. Woolhope Naturalists' Field Club*, 37 (1961–3), pp. 300–15.

126 *Post-Med. Arch.*, 4 (1970), pp. 185–6; 5 (1971), p. 217.

127 D. W. Crossley and A. Aberg, 'Sixteenth-century glass-making in Yorkshire: excavations at furnaces at Hutton and Rosedale, North Riding, 1968–1971', *Post-Med. Arch.*, 6 (1972), pp. 107–59.

128 *Post-Med. Arch.*, 6 (1972), p. 221. For the New Draperies, see D. C. Coleman, 'An innovation and its diffusion: the "New Draperies"', *Ec.H.R.*, 2nd series, 22 (1969), pp. 417–29. The industrial innovations of the period are usefully summarized in the same author's *Industry in Tudor and Stuart England*, 1975.

129 J. M. W. Bean, *The Estates of the Percy Family 1416–1537*, 1958, pp. 49–51; T. B. Pugh (ed.), *The Marcher Lordships of South Wales 1415–1536*, 1963, p. 180.

130 D. W. Crossley, 'The management of a sixteenth-century ironworks', *Ec.H.R.*, 2nd series, 19 (1966), pp. 273–88, and the same author's excavation report 'A sixteenth-century Wealden blast furnace: a report on excavations at Panningridge,

Sussex, 1964–1970', *Post-Med. Arch.*, 6 (1972), pp. 42–68. See also David Crossley's edition of the *Sidney Ironworks Accounts 1541–1573*, Camden Fourth Series, 15 (1975).

131 David Crossley, *The Bewl Valley Ironworks c. 1300–1730*, Royal Archaeological Institute Monographs, 1975.

132 G. Hammersley, 'The charcoal iron industry and its fuel, 1540–1750', *Ec.H.R.*, 2nd series, 26 (1973), pp. 593–613.

133 Crossley, op. cit. (1966), p. 285.

134 David Crossley and Denis Ashurst, 'Excavations at Rockley Smithies, a water-powered bloomery of the sixteenth and seventeenth centuries', *Post-Med. Arch.*, 2 (1968), pp. 10–54; for the Eskdale bloomery, see ibid., p. 192, and 3 (1969), pp. 207–8.

135 Ibid., 7 (1973), pp. 115–16.

136 Mary Dewar (ed.), *A Discourse of the Commonweal of this Realm of England, attributed to Sir Thomas Smith*, 1969, pp. 63–4.

137 Ibid., p. 123.

138 For a useful brief account of this late-medieval industry, with a bibliography of the works of major scholars in this field, most notably Dr W. L. Hildburgh, see Francis Cheetham's *Medieval English Alabaster Carvings in the Castle Museum, Nottingham*, 1973 (revised edn).

139 John Hatcher and T. C. Barker, *A History of British Pewter*, 1974, ch. 3. The inventories of three early-modern Norwich pewterers, the first dated 1590, have recently been published by Alayne Fenner, 'Three Norwich pewterers', *Post-Med. Arch.*, 8 (1974), pp. 113–19.

140 For the occurrence of these wares at a representative seaport, see Colin Platt and Richard Coleman-Smith, *Excavations in Medieval Southampton 1953–1969*, 1975, ii (The Finds); and for an unpublished but very similar collection from Hull, see the interim note in *Med. Arch.*, 9 (1965), p. 197.

141 Adrian Henstock, 'The monopoly in Rhenish stoneware imports in Late Elizabethan England', *Post-Med. Arch.*, 9 (1975), pp. 219–24.

142 L. G. Matthews and H. J. M. Green, 'Post-medieval pottery of the Inns of Court', *Post-Med. Arch.*, 3 (1969), pp. 1–17.

143 Platt and Coleman-Smith, op. et loc. cit., in particular catalogue items 700, 705–8, 711.
144 The point is well made by Coleman, op. cit. (1975), pp. 16–17.
145 Transcribed by D. M. Palliser and published as an appendix to his 'The boroughs of medieval Staffordshire', *North Staffordshire J. Field Studies*, 12 (1972), p. 71. The literature on famine and disease in Tudor England is extensive. It includes now papers by Dr Palliser on 'Epidemics in Tudor York', *Northern History*, 8 (1973), pp. 45–63, and 'Dearth and disease in Staffordshire, 1540–1670', in C. W. Chalklin and M. A. Havinden (eds), *Rural Change and Urban Growth 1500–1800*, 1974, pp. 54–75, with the works from which he drew his inspiration, especially W. G. Hoskins, 'Harvest fluctuations and English economic history, 1480–1619', *Agric. Hist. Rev.*, 12 (1964), pp. 28–46, and F. J. Fisher, 'Influenza and inflation in Tudor England', *Ec.H.R.*, 2nd series, 18 (1965), pp. 120–29. For a critical comment on Professor Hoskins's figures, see C. J. Harrison, 'Grain price analysis and harvest qualities, 1465–1634', *Agric. Hist. Rev.*, 19 (1971), pp. 135–55.

Index

Scotland, Abbot, 19
Scredington (Lincs.), 134
Seacourt (Oxf.), 39–40, 41, 42
Secular church, *see* Parish churches
Selborne Priory, 155, 160
Sellergarth (Lancs.), 225
Shareshill (Staffs.), 114
Sharington, Sir William, 218, 236, 239
Sheen Palace, 179
Shrewsbury: Castle, 5; land reclamation, 34–5
Sidney family, 244, 245, 246
Sidney, Sir William, 244
Silver, 46, 100, 102
Simon de Montfort, 88–9
Sims, John, 232–3
Slate, 235, 237
Smith, Sir Thomas, 246
Social change, 131–7, 223–7, 249–50
Social class, 111, 118, 119, 132–4, 225, 227
Social unrest, 108–11, 114, 115, 136–7
Sopwell Priory (Herts.), 215, 216–17
Southampton: imports, 33, 122–4, 125;
    religion, 221; St Denys Priory, 155; urban
    development, 33; wealth, 104, 187, 190,
    194–6
South Mimms, 12–13
Southwick, Richard of, *see* Richard of
    Southwick
South Wingfield (Derbys.), 179
South Witham, 60, 61
Souvenirs, 117, 144–6
Spalding Priory, 43, 92, 115
Spelman, Sir Henry, 217
Spencer family, 225
Spurs, tin-plating, 17
Stafford Castle, 4
Staffordshire: parishes, 25; urban
    development, 31, 249
Stamford, 151, 152, 160, 161, 220
Standards of living, *see* Living standards
Stanford on Avon (Northants.), 147
Stavordale Priory (Som.), 219
Stephen, King, 7, 12, 23, 88
Steventon Priory (Berks.), 155–6, 157–8
Steynforth, Robert, 178
Stoke Orchard (Gloucs.), 79, 80
Stokesay Castle (Shrops.), 113
Stoket family, 132
Stone: building, 33–4, 40–1, 50, 52, 84, 192;
    carving, 74
Street paving, 191–2, 195
Strood, 151
Stucco, 235

Studley (Oxf.), 156–7
Styward family, 139
Sulgrave (Northants.), 2
Supremacy, Act of (1559), 223
Sussex Weald, 42, 43
Sutton Place, 235, 236
Swaffham (Norf.), 138–40
Swinfield, Richard de, *see* Richard de
    Swinfield

Tailboys affair, 177
Talbot family, 184–5
Tattershall Castle (Lincs.), 150, 152–4, 176,
    177, 178–9
Taverner, John, 150
Tavistock Abbey, 161–2
Taxation, 38, 99, 102, 103, 104, 136, 227
Tenant farmers, 46, 105, 126, 130, 133, 224
Taylor family, 139
Temperature, *see* Climate
Templar estates, 60, 188
Tenure: conventionary, 96; gavelkind, 105
Terracing, 45
Terracotta, 235, 236, 237
Tewkesbury Abbey, 163–4
Textile industry, 116, 194, 242–4
Thame hoard, 183
Therfield (Herts.), 11–12
Thetford, 20, 28
Thokey, Abbot, 66
Thomas, abbot of Horton, 65
Three Living and Three Dead, 146, 147
Thurleigh Church (Beds.), 28, 76
Tiles: floor, 80–2, 235–6, 239; industry, 118,
    120–1, 236; roof, 56
Tin, 161
Titchfield estates, 96, 217
Tithes, 1
Tivetshall Church (Norf.), 222
Torbock, Cicely, *see* Cicely de Torbock
Townhalls, *see* Guildhalls
Towns: buildings, 192–5; defences, 35–6;
    development, 30–8; services, 192–6; walls,
    see defences
Trades, 115–25
Trading, 31, 125, 185–6
Traditions, old and new, 17–19
Trailbaston commissions, 109, 110
Tresco Fort (Scillies), 208
Tresham, Sir Thomas, 234–5
Triangular Lodge, Rushton, 234–5

Uniformity, Acts of, 221, 223